ISBN: 9781290631990

Published by:
HardPress Publishing
8345 NW 66TH ST #2561
MIAMI FL 33166-2626

Email: info@hardpress.net
Web: http://www.hardpress.net

THE EMPRESS FREDERICK

THE EMPRESS FREDERICK

A MEMOIR

WITH SIX ILLUSTRATIONS
IN PHOTOGRAVURE

London
JAMES NISBET & CO., LIMITED
22 BERNERS STREET, W.
1913

Printed by BALLANTYNE, HANSON & CO.
at the Ballantyne Press, Edinburgh

TABLE OF CONTENTS

PAGE

LIST OF ILLUSTRATIONS vii

PEDIGREE SHOWING THE FAMILY CONNECTIONS OF THE
EMPEROR AND EMPRESS FREDERICK ix

PREFACE xi

CHAP.

I. CHILDHOOD AND GIRLHOOD 1

II. BETROTHAL 24

III. OPINION IN BOTH COUNTRIES 37

IV. MARRIAGE 59

V. EARLY MARRIED LIFE 72

VI. BIRTH OF ELDEST SON 101

VII. ADVICE FROM ENGLAND 116

VIII. DEATH OF THE KING OF PRUSSIA . . . 134

IX. FIRST RELATIONS WITH BISMARCK . . . 163

X. THE WAR OF THE DUCHIES 179

XI. HOME LIFE AND RELIGION 201

XII. THE AUSTRIAN WAR: WORK IN THE HOSPITALS 213

XIII. THE FRANCO-GERMAN WAR 230

XIV. PUBLIC AND PRIVATE ACTIVITIES . . . 249

XV. THE REGENCY 267

XVI. SILVER WEDDING: THE CROWN PRINCE'S ILLNESS 284

XVII. THE HUNDRED DAYS' REIGN . . . 304

XVIII. EARLY WIDOWHOOD: FALL OF BISMARCK . 320

XIX. PLANNING OF FRIEDRICHSHOF: VISIT TO PARIS . 334

XX. LIFE AT FRIEDRICHSHOF 345

XXI. LAST YEARS 359

INDEX 379

v

LIST OF ILLUSTRATIONS

THE EMPRESS FREDERICK . . . . . *Frontispiece*

QUEEN VICTORIA AND THE PRINCESS ROYAL *Facing page* 8

THE PRINCESS ROYAL AND THE INFANT
   PRINCE OF WALES . . . . ,, ,, 32

THE PRINCESS ROYAL AT THE TIME OF HER
   MARRIAGE . . . . . . ,, ,, 64

THE CROWN PRINCESS AND HER FIRST
   CHILD . . . . ,, ,, 136

THE CROWN PRINCESS AT THE TIME OF HER
   SILVER WEDDING . . . . ,, ,, 284

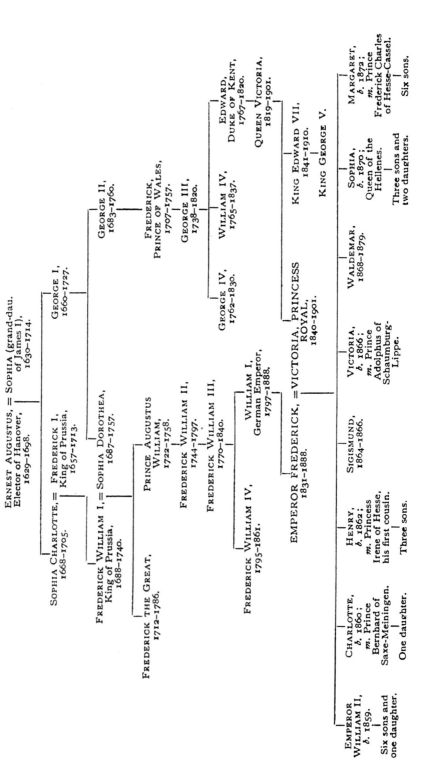

PREFACE

MEMOIRS of Royal personages form not the least interesting part of the whole vast field of biography, in spite of the fact that such memoirs differ from the lives of most persons in a private station because of the reticence and discretion which are necessary, especially in regard to affairs of State and political characters. It is often not until a whole generation has passed that it is possible to publish a full biography of a member of a Royal House, and in the meantime the exalted rank of the subject operates both to enhance and to diminish the interest of the memoir.

This is also true in a modified degree of statesmen, of whom full and frank biographies are seldom possible until their political associates and rivals have alike disappeared from the scene. This necessary delay is a test of the subject's greatness, for it has sometimes happened that by the time a full memoir can be published the public interest in the individual has waned.

By heredity, by training, by all the circumstances of their lives, Royal personages form a caste apart; and though their lot may seem to some persons enviable, it is often not realised how great are the sacrifices of happiness and contentment which they are called upon to make as the inevitable consequence of their exalted position.

The Empress Frederick presents an extraordinary example of what this exalted position may bring in the way of both happiness and suffering. Her life has the added interest that, quite apart from her rank, she possessed an intensely vivid and human personality. History furnishes many examples of Royal personages who have been, so to speak, crushed and stunted in their intellectual and spiritual growth by the restraints of their position.

Not so the subject of this memoir. The Empress was a woman of remarkable moral and intellectual qualities—indeed, it is not difficult to see that, had she been born in a private station, she would have attained certainly distinction, and very possibly eminence, in some branch of art, letters, or science. Her rank, far from crushing and stunting her powers, had the effect of diffusing her intellectual interests over many fields, and perhaps laid her open to the charge of dilettanteism. But such a charge cannot really be maintained in view of the solid constructive work which she achieved, both in the field of philanthropy and in that of the application of art to industry. The exacting mental discipline which she underwent at the hands of her father, though it was in some respects ill-advised as her life turned

out, at any rate supplied her with the habit of
mental concentration which enabled her to carry
out those practical and lasting enterprises with
which her name in Germany should ever be associated. Her early training disciplined her eager,
natural enthusiasm for all that was good and
serviceable to humanity, and directed it especially
to the welfare of soldiers and of women and children. She was " a doer of the Word and not a
hearer only."

All through her life one is perhaps most profoundly impressed by her inexhaustible energy;
her sense of the tremendous importance and interest of life, of the wonders of knowledge, of
the delights of art and literature, and of all that
there is to do and to feel and to think in the
short years that are given us on earth.

One of the greatest dangers to which Royal
personages are exposed by the circumstances of
their position is that of falling into an attitude
of gentle cynicism. Naturally they are often
brought into contact with the seamy side of human
nature, while at the same time they are not perhaps
so well acquainted with its better side as are persons
of less exalted rank. That the cleverer among
them should take up an attitude of humorous
toleration of the whole human comedy is consequently very natural.

It is no small testimony to the Empress
Frederick's moral greatness that, though she had

experiences in plenty of the bad side of human nature, she was never tempted to relapse into such an attitude. No one was ever less of a cynic. She was full of intense passionate enthusiasms, and of a profound sympathy for the unfortunate and the disinherited of the earth. In her warm heart there was no room for hatred or for contempt of others, and she was equally incapable of shrugging her shoulders at the foibles and follies of poor humanity.

This eagerness to be up and doing was, however, combined, as has been often seen in the history of mankind, with a touching faith in the power of logic and reason. It was not exactly that the Empress held too high an opinion of human nature, but she undoubtedly showed too little appreciation of human stupidity, and, we must add, of human malice. She had been brought up with kindly, honourable, well-bred, and, on the whole, very intelligent people, and when she came into rough collision with less agreeable qualities of human nature, she suffered intensely. But she was not soured as a less noble nature might have been ; on the contrary, she continued to the end of her life always to believe the best of people, always to assume that they are actuated by good motives, as well as by reason and common-sense. She seems to have missed the key to the oddities and the vagaries, as well as to the baser qualities of human nature, and therein lies, perhaps, the secret of the tragedy of her life.

That tragedy, as we know, was greatly enhanced by the singular blows of fate. Her rank had, strangely enough, given her a marriage of love and affection more real and more lasting than often falls to the lot of private persons. But the husband whom she adored, as well as two idolized children, were taken from her.

It was her fate also to be constantly misunderstood; to see the purity of her motives doubted and her most innocent actions misconstrued. Owing partly to the circumstances of her time, partly to her own generous and warm-hearted but imprudent impulsiveness, she failed to win the affection of her adopted country as a whole, though she certainly earned its respect and esteem. This was not the least bitter trial of her life, for she was one of those natures who have a craving for affection and understanding sympathy; and the criticism and even the hostility with which she was regarded in Germany were all the more painful to her in that she could not in the least understand on what they were based.

Perhaps she was too deeply convinced of the superiority of England and of English institutions, and made too little allowance for the sensitiveness of a people who were then slowly emerging into a national in place of a particularist consciousness. At the same time it is certain that, however she had comported herself, she could not have escaped criticism of which she was no more than the ostensible object, and the real purpose of which is to be found in the political cross-currents of the period.

In this memoir the attempt is made to draw a true picture of this singularly engaging and generous personality, who played her part in great affairs, and who suffered all reversals of fortune, the anguish of bereavement, and the pain of cruel disease, alike with unflinching courage and dignity.

The materials have been found, not only in many works of history, biography, memoir and reminiscence, both German and English, some of which are little known, especially to English readers, but also in the recollection of persons who were honoured with the Empress's friendship. The aim of the writer has been, while avoiding such indiscriminate laudation as really degrades the subject of it, to draw a full-length portrait of one of the noblest and most attractive characters in the long history of the Royal Houses of Europe.

THE EMPRESS FREDERICK

CHAPTER I

CHILDHOOD AND GIRLHOOD

BEFORE the birth of the Princess Royal in November 1840, no direct heir had been born to a reigning British Sovereign for nearly eighty years. The Prince Regent, afterwards George IV, was born in 1762, two years after his father's accession, and the death in childbirth of the Prince Regent's daughter, Princess Charlotte, when she was only twenty, was still vividly remembered.

Queen Victoria was now but little older than Princess Charlotte, and the birth of her first child was regarded with a certain anxiety by the nation. It might prove to be the only child, and in that event much would hang on the preservation of its life. Those members of the "Old Royal Family" who were next in succession were not popular, and the little Princess Royal may truly be described as having been the child of many prayers.

It was natural that Queen Victoria should have recourse to Prince Albert's confidential adviser,

A

Baron Stockmar, the more so that he was a skilled physician. Stockmar therefore came to London early in November. Those were not the days of trained nurses, but rather of the types immortalised by Dickens, and it is interesting to find the shrewd old German, characteristically in advance of his time, urging the Prince to be most careful in the choice of a nurse, "for a man's education begins the first day of his life, and a lucky choice I regard as the greatest and finest gift we can bestow on the expected stranger."

On November 13 the Court arrived at Buckingham Palace, where on the 21st the Princess was born. "For a moment only," the Queen says, "was the Prince disappointed at its being a daughter and not a son."

The character of the monarchy in England has changed so much, both absolutely and also relatively to the people, that it is difficult for us to realise the measure of prejudice and even contempt which still subsisted before Queen Victoria had had time to win the full confidence of her subjects. It is not therefore really surprising that the little Princess Royal should have been greeted on her first appearance with a shower of caricatures, some of them not remarkable for their refinement.

Still, a good deal of the rough humour lavished on the Princess was kindly in its intention, though sometimes there was a sting in the tail. For instance, Melbourne, the Prime Minister, was shown as nurse, proudly presenting the Princess Royal to John Bull: " I hope the caudle is to your liking, Mr. Bull. It must be quite a treat, for you have not had any for a long time." John Bull replies: " Well, to tell you the truth, Mother Melbourne, I think the caudle the best of it, for I had hoped for a boy."

Melbourne's fatherly devotion to the Queen was indeed a piece of luck for the caricaturists of the day. A cartoon entitled " Old Servants in New Characters " shows him dressed as a nurse with the infant Princess in his care ; she is sitting in a tiny carriage, with Lord John Russell as outrider.

It was arranged that the christening should take place in London on February 10, the anniversary of the Queen's marriage, the infant receiving the names of Victoria Adelaide Mary Louise. Even the christening of the Princess Royal inspired a long satirical poem. One verse ran:

" This is the Bishop, so bold and intrepid,
   A-making the water so nice and so tepid,
   To christen the Baby, who's stated, no doubt,
   Her objection to taking it ' cold without.' "

The sponsors were Prince Albert's brother, the Duke of Saxe-Coburg and Gotha (represented in his absence by the Duke of Wellington), the King of the Belgians, the Queen Dowager (Adelaide), the Duchess of Gloucester, the Duchess of Kent, and the Duke of Sussex. Lord Melbourne remarked of the Princess to the Queen next day: "How she looked about her, quite conscious that the stir was all about herself! This is the time the character is formed!" The Prime Minister would have agreed with Stockmar's view that a man's education (and presumably also a woman's) begins with the first day of life.

Prince Albert sent a vivid account of the ceremony to the venerable Dowager Duchess of Gotha:

"The christening went off very well. Your little great-grandchild behaved with great propriety, and like a Christian. She was awake, but did not cry at all, and seemed to crow with immense satisfaction at the lights and brilliant uniforms, for she is very intelligent and observing. The ceremony took place at half-past six P.M., and after it there was a dinner, and then we had some instrumental music. The health of the little one was drunk with great enthusiasm. The little girl bears the Saxon Arms in the middle of the English, which looks very pretty."

The Princess Royal, like her brothers and sisters, led an ideal childhood. All through her later life she often referred to the unclouded happiness of these early years, and it comes out equally clearly in the published correspondence of her sister, Princess Alice. In this matter both Prince Albert and Queen Victoria were in advance of their time, and the Prince, especially, perceived, what was not then at all generally believed, that children could be made happy without being spoiled.

Perhaps the most sensible decision of the parents was that the Royal children should come in contact as little as possible with the actual life of the Court. Not that the tone of the Court was bad; on the contrary, it was singularly high, but the Queen and Prince Albert knew the subtle danger of even innocent petting and flattery on young and impressionable minds.

So it was that the Royal children had very little to do with the Queen's ladies-in-waiting— indeed they were only seen by them for a few moments after dinner at dessert, or when driving out with their parents. The Queen and the Prince entrusted the care of their sons and daughters exclusively to persons who possessed their whole confidence, and with whom they could be in constant direct communication. Both were kept regularly informed of the minutest details of what was being done for their children, and as the princesses grew older they had an English, a French, and a German governess, who were, in their turn, responsible to a lady superintendent.

It has been the custom of late to speak as if the children of Queen Victoria had been over-educated and over-stimulated. This was at least partly true of their infancy, but if they had been really over-educated, they would not have turned out as well as they did later, nor would they have all delighted in looking back with fond reminiscence to their earliest years.

The Princess Royal was soon recognised by all those about her as intellectually the flower of the happy little flock. She was clever, self-willed, and high-spirited; learning everything that was put before her with marvellous intelligence and rapidity. Her dearest friend and companion was her sister, the sweet-natured, pensive Princess Alice, who was next in age, after the Prince of Wales, to herself. The two lived for some years a life which was exactly alike. They shared the same lessons, the same amusements, the same interests; both had a strong love of art and of drawing; both were, if anything, over-sensitively alive to the claims of duty and of patriotism.

Naturally the most detailed and accurate impression of the Princess Royal's childhood is to be derived from the correspondence of Sarah Lady Lyttelton, who was appointed Governess to the Royal children in April 1842.

This lady, who was then approaching her fifty-fifth birthday, was the daughter of the second Earl Spencer, and sister of that Lord Althorp who was a member of Lord Grey's Reform Ministry, and who played a notable part in politics rather by his strength of character than by any commanding ability. Lady Sarah married the third Lord

Lyttelton in 1813.   It is interesting to recall that her son, afterwards the fourth Lord Lyttelton, married Mrs. Gladstone's sister, Miss Glynne. Sarah Lady Lyttelton was widowed in 1837 after a singularly happy married life, and soon afterwards Queen Victoria appointed her a lady-in-waiting.

When, some four years later, she was given the responsible post of Governess to the Royal children, she was already very well known to the Queen and the Prince Consort, as well as to their closest advisers.   Lord Melbourne, for instance, heartily approved the appointment, declaring that no other person so well qualified could have been selected.

The picture of the Princess Royal which her guardian draws in these letters is one of an extraordinarily winning though precocious child, and if it seems to modern judgment that the precocity was rather too much stimulated, it must be remembered that we are back in the 'forties, when a scientific study of the psychology of infants was not dreamed of.   Moreover, it is abundantly evident that the little Princess had such a way with her, "so innocent arch, so cunning simple," that it must have required no ordinary resolution to avoid spoiling her, while even the most scientific modern expert would probably have found it very hard to draw the line between over-stimulation and proper encouragement of her remarkable intelligence.

Lady Lyttelton had her first glimpse of the

Princess Royal in July 1841. She describes her as a fine, fat, firm, fair, Royal-looking baby, "too absurdly like the Queen." Her look was grave, calm, and penetrating, and she surveyed the whole company most composedly. She was shown at her carriage window to the populace; and Lady Lyttelton, noting the universal grin in all faces, declares that the baby will soon have seen every set of teeth in the kingdom !

Some months later she records that "the dear Babekin is really going to be quite beautiful. Such large smiling soft blue eyes, and quite a handsome nose, and the prettiest mouth." The child early acquired the appropriate pet name of "Pussy," while she herself, finding Lady Lyttelton's name too large a mouthful, simplified it to "Laddle."

It may be here recorded that an absurd rumour had been circulated that the Princess Royal had been born blind, and it was this and other foolish gossip which first induced the Queen, at the suggestion of Prince Albert, to issue an official Court Circular, which has been continued ever since.

The Queen had the baby constantly with her, and thought incessantly about her, with the result that the child was perhaps rather over-watched and over-doctored. She was fed on asses' milk, arrowroot. and chicken broth, which were measured out so carefully that Lady Lyttelton fancied she left off hungry. Lady Lyttelton, indeed, had

QUEEN VICTORIA AND THE PRINCESS ROYAL

some experience of this dieting craze, for her brother, Lord Althorp, at one time, when he had a terror of getting fat, used to weigh out his own breakfast every morning, and when he had consumed the tiny allowance used to hasten out of the room lest he should be led into temptation !

The little Princess was over-sensitive and affectionate, and rather irritable in temper, and with a prophetic eye Lady Lyttelton says that "it looks like a pretty mind, only very unfit for roughing it through a hard life, which her's may be."

After the birth of the Prince of Wales, Lady Lyttelton gives us a passing, but sufficiently terrible, glimpse of the anxieties which Royal parents must all suffer, more or less. She mentions that threatening letters aimed directly at the children were received, and though they were probably written by mad people, nevertheless no protection in the way of locks, guard-rooms, and intricate passages was omitted for the defence of the Royal nurseries ; while the master key was never out of Prince Albert's own keeping

The Princess Royal spent her second birthday at Walmer Castle, and she is described as being "most funny all day," joining in the cheers and asking to be lifted up to look at "the people," to whom she bowed very actively whether they could see her or not.

Perhaps one reason why she became, and remained, so fond of France was that from infancy she was placed in the charge of a French lady, Madame Charlier. She was very advanced through all her childhood, especially in music and painting, yet she remained quite natural and simple in all her ways.

She was only three years old when Prince Albert wrote to Stockmar: "The children in whose welfare you take so kindly an interest are making most favourable progress. The eldest, 'Pussy,' is now quite a little personage. She speaks English and French with great fluency and choice of phrase." But to her parents she generally talked German.

"Our *Pussette*," the Queen writes a few weeks afterwards, "learns a verse of Lamartine by heart, which ends with 'Le tableau se déroule à mes pieds.' To show how well she understood this difficult line, I must tell you the following *bon-mot*. When she was riding on her pony, and looking at the cows and sheep, she turned to Madame Charlier, and said : ' Voilà le tableau qui se déroule à mes pieds !' Is not this extraordinary for a child of three years ?"

It is evident that the oral teaching of languages had very sensibly preceded that of books, for when the Princess is four years and three months old we hear that she is getting on very well with her lessons, "but much is still to be done before she can read."

In spite of her accomplishments, she was a very natural human child, and could be naughty on occasion. Lady Lyttelton records about this time that the Princess, after an hour's naughtiness, said she wished to speak to her; but instead of the expected penitence, she delivered herself as follows : " I am very sorry, Laddle, but I mean to be just as naughty next time "—a threat which was followed by a long imprisonment.

Perhaps the Princess Royal's happiest days were spent at Osborne, where she began going at the age of five. There the Royal children had a cottage, built on the Swiss model, to themselves. It comprised a dining-room, a kitchen, a store-room, and a museum; and in it the princesses were encouraged to learn how to do household work, and to direct the management of a small establishment. When in their Swiss cottage, each princess was allowed to choose her own occupation and to enjoy a certain liberty; their parents used to be invited there as guests at meals which the Princess Royal and Princess Alice had themselves prepared.

Years later, when they had both married, there were certain tunes which neither the Princess Royal nor Princess Alice could hear without tears rising to their eyes, so powerfully did the recollection of the happy birthdays and holidays they spent at Osborne remain with them. Not long before her death Princess

Alice wrote to her mother: "What a joyous childhood we had, and how greatly it was enhanced by dear sweet Papa, and by all your kindness to us!"

Many happy days were also spent by the Princesses at Balmoral. In the Highlands the restraints of Court life were entirely thrown off, and the Queen encouraged her daughters to come into close contact with the poorer classes of their neighbours, indeed everything in reason was done to arouse their sympathies for the needy and the suffering.

The Princess Royal showed even in her early childhood an astonishing power of vivid expression. For example, when she was about five and a half, she found mentioned in a history book the name of an ancient poet called Wace. Lady Lyttelton thereupon observed that she had never heard of that poet till then, but the Princess insisted: "Oh, yes, I daresay you did, only you have forgotten it. Réfléchissez! Go back to your *youngness* and you will soon remember."

That the child had a natural and instinctive religious feeling is shown by another incident. She had narrowly escaped serious injury from treading on a large nail, and Lady Lyttelton explained to her that it had pleased God to save her from great pain. Instantly the child said: "Shall we kneel down?"

In October 1847 the Princess Royal had

an accident which might have been very serious.

The children were riding with their ponies when the Princess was quietly thrown after a few yards of cantering. She was not hurt, but the Prince of Wales's pony ran away with him. Fortunately he was strapped into the saddle, and, after one loud cry for help, he showed no signs of fear, but cleverly kept as tight hold of the reins as he could pull. The Princess Royal was not at all frightened herself until she saw her brother's danger, and then she screamed out: "Oh, can't they stop him? Dear Bertie!" and burst into tears. Fortunately all ended well, and the children went on riding as fearlessly as ever.

In October 1848 the Royal children, crossing in the yacht *Fairy* from Osborne on their way to Windsor, witnessed a terrible accident—the sinking of a boatload of people in a sudden squall. It made a deep impression on all the children, and the Princess Royal kept thinking of it all that night.

It is about this time that Lady Lyttelton observes: "The Princess Royal might pass, if not seen but only overheard, for a young lady of seventeen in whichever of her three languages she chose to entertain the company."

Nearly a year afterwards, Lady Lyttelton notes that "dear Princessey" had been now perfectly good ever since they came to Osborne, and she says that she continues to reflect and observe and reason like a very superior person, and is as affectionate as ever.

Again, in April 1849, she notes every moment more and more "the blessed improvement of the Princess Royal." "She is becoming capable of self-control and principle and patience, and her wonderful powers of head and heart continue. She may turn out a most distinguished character." And a few months later she notes that "the Princess Royal is so enormously improved in manner, in temper, and conduct—altogether as really to give a bright promise of all good. Her talent and brilliancy have naturally lost no ground : she may turn out something remarkable." All the children showed real kindness to the poor, visiting them and beginning to understand what poverty is.

The Princess accompanied her parents and the Prince of Wales on a visit to Ireland in August 1849, and afterwards went to Cherbourg, that being her first visit to France. It was during that stay at Cherbourg that the curé of a neighbouring village gave the young English Princess a charming sketch done by one of his parishioners, a then unknown artist named Jean François Millet.

The Princess Royal and the Prince of Wales made their first official appearance in London on October 30, 1849, when they represented their mother, who was suffering from chicken-pox, at the opening of the new Coal Exchange. The scene has been often described, notably by Miss Alcott, the author of *Little Women*, who was, however, naturally more interested in the Prince than in his sister.

Much to their delight, the children went from Westminster to the City in the State barge rowed by twenty-six watermen, and all London turned out to greet them. They were very wisely not allowed to attend the big public luncheon, but were given their lunch in a private room. Lady Lyttelton mentions that the gentleman who made the arrangements was so overcome by his loyal feelings at the sight of the children that he melted into tears and had to retire !

In the summer before the Princess's tenth birthday, Lady Lyttelton records : " Princess Royal standing by me to-day, as I was trying a few chords on the pianoforte, was pleased and pensive like her old self. ' I like chords, one can *read* them. They make one sometimes gay, sometimes sad. It used to be too much for me to like formerly.' "

The year 1851 was memorable in the Princess Royal's life, for it was then that she first met her future husband.

It has been said that Prince Frederick William of Prussia, who was twenty at the time, became attracted to his future wife during this first visit of his to the English Court, when he accompanied his parents and his only sister to see the Great Exhibition. But that is surely absurd, for the Princess, charming and clever as she was, was then only a child.

Still, the English Court was probably never seen to greater advantage than during that year of miracles, and it is clear that the young Prussian Prince saw for the first time a Royal family leading a happy, natural life, full of affection and kindness. Queen Victoria's children were healthy, well-mannered, and devoted to their parents, and the leader and head of the little band was the Princess Royal, full of eager interest in everything she was allowed to see and know, blessed with high spirits and a keen sense of humour even then already well developed. She was adored by her father, and encouraged in every way to "produce herself," to use an expressive French phrase.

Prince Frederick William could not but note the contrast between the young people whose friendship he was making at Windsor, and the shy, etiquette-ridden Royal children of the minor German Courts. Nor could he help contrasting this delightful domestic scene with what he knew at home. At Berlin he was in constant contact with a Royal family profoundly disunited and unhappy. Only three years before his first visit to England he had stood at the palace window and seen the first shot fired in the Revolution of 1848.

.

Although the Prince had a tenderly-loved sister, he had spent a lonely, austere youth, for his parents, though outwardly on good terms, were in no sense united as Queen Victoria and Prince Albert were united—indeed, it was an open secret that the Prince of Prussia had only had one love in his life—Elise Radziwill.

Prince Frederick William's sister was only a very little older than the Princess Royal. The two princesses formed on this visit a friendship destined never to be broken, and henceforth the Royal children called the Prince and Princess of Prussia " Uncle Prussia " and " Aunt Prussia."

The Great Exhibition itself undoubtedly helped to strengthen Prince Frederick William's attraction to England. The palace of glass in Hyde Park absorbed the minds and thoughts of the whole Royal family, if only because all those who were old enough to understand anything of public affairs were aware that the success or failure of the enterprise would seriously affect the position of Prince Albert in England.

The feeling among the Royal family is shown by a passage in a letter of Queen Victoria to Lady Lyttelton. Writing on May 1, the opening day of the Exhibition, Her Majesty said :

" The proudest and happiest day of—as you truly call it—my happy life. To see this great conception of my beloved husband's mind—to see this great thought and work, crowned with

triumphant success in spite of difficulties and opposition of every imaginable kind, and of every
effort to which jealousy and calumny could resort
to cause its failure, has been an immense happiness
to us both."

Prince Frederick William, thoughtful beyond
his years, and already under the spell of Prince
Albert's kindly and affectionate interest, began
to regard England as the model State, and took
most significant pains to make himself better
acquainted with her national life and polity.
Even on this comparatively short visit he found
time to make an excursion to the industrial
North.

On his return to Bonn University his admiration for England by no means waned, and his
English tutor, Mr. Perry, gives us an interesting
glimpse of the thoroughness with which he set to
work to increase his knowledge :

" At the request of the Prince, I visited him
three times a week, and had the honour of superintending his studies in English history and literature, in both of which he took special interest.
His love for England and his great veneration of
the Queen were most remarkable, and our intercourse became very agreeable and confidential.
He manifested the keenest interest for all that I
was able to tell him of England's political and
social life, and when our more serious studies were
over, we amused ourselves by writing imaginary

letters to Ministers and leading members of English society."

It was in truth with England that Prince Frederick William fell in love on this memorable visit, not with the little Princess Royal, though he was undoubtedly attracted, as all the people round her were, by her winning charm and quick intelligence.

The idea of a marriage between the two had, however, occurred to other people, as is shown by the fact that in the following year the Princess of Prussia desired to visit England with a view to suggesting it. But the Prince's uncle, King Frederick William IV, influenced by his pro-Russian consort, did not look on the proposal with favour, and it remained in abeyance, partly on account of the Princess Royal's youth, partly owing to the outbreak of the Crimean War.

The Crimean War made an immense impression on the Princess Royal. For months the Queen, the Prince, and the elder Royal children thought and talked of nothing else. The children contributed drawings to be sold for the benefit of the war funds, and we know that the Princess's emotions were deeply stirred by the thought of the sufferings of the wounded and by the work of Florence Nightingale, which was followed with intense interest in the Royal circle. The Princess in fact was able at a most impressionable age to realise something of the horrors of war, and this was destined, as we shall see, to bear rich fruit.

The war also led directly to the Princess's first real sight of France. In August 1855 the Princess Royal and the Prince of Wales accompanied their parents on a State visit to the Emperor Napoleon III and the Empress Eugénie.

Of this visit a story was told at the time which greatly delighted all the Royal families of the Continent. Much as Queen Victoria and Prince Albert were respected for their solid virtues, their artistic taste in matters of dress was considered to be not always infallible. It was feared at the French Court that the Princess Royal would be dressed, not exactly unbecomingly, but in a style which would by no means harmonise with Parisian taste and Parisian surroundings. The question was how to beguile her parents into dressing the child in a suitable manner.

In this difficulty someone suggested a really brilliant stratagem. The height and other measurements of the Princess Royal were obtained, and a doll of exactly corresponding size was procured, provided with a large and exquisitely finished wardrobe, and despatched to Buckingham Palace as an Imperial gift to the Princess. The expected then happened. Queen Victoria transferred most of the doll's wardrobe to her daughter, with the result that the Princess appeared at her best and everyone was pleased.

The children stayed at the delightful country palace of Saint Cloud, whence they drove in every day to see the sights of Paris. They were not, of course, present at evening entertainments, but an exception was made on the occasion of the great ball held in the Galeries des Glaces at Versailles, when they supped with the Emperor and Empress. They both became sincerely attached to the Emperor, who was himself very fond of children. Indeed, his young guests enjoyed themselves so much that, according to an oft-quoted story, the Prince of Wales asked that his sister and himself might stay on after their parents had gone home, "for there are six more of us at home and they don't want *us!* "

As to their conduct, Prince Albert wrote to the Duchess of Kent: "I am bound to praise the children greatly. They behaved extremely well, and pleased everybody. The task was no easy one for them, but they discharged it without embarrassment and with natural simplicity."

This visit laid the foundation of that strong affection and admiration for France and the French which thenceforward characterised the Princess Royal. It was on this visit, too, that she conceived her enthusiastic adoration of the Empress Eugénie. Her character was now beginning to be formed, and it is the key to the tragedy of her life, for a cruel fate so ordered her future that, while she was made to pay the full penalty for her failings, her many lovable and generous qualities seemed often to find none but the most grudging recognition.

During the whole of her life, the Princess Royal had a peculiarity which only belongs to the generous-hearted and impulsive. She was apt to be violently attracted, sometimes for very little reason, to those she met, and then she would be proportionately cast down if these new friends and acquaintances did not turn out on fuller knowledge all that she had expected them to be. Those who knew her well are agreed in saying that she was not a good judge of character. She was apt to see in human beings what she expected to see, not what was there. She not only liked some people at first sight, but she had an equally instinctive dislike of others, and this was an even greater misfortune, for sometimes the prejudices she thus formed were hard to eradicate. In this she was quite unlike Queen Victoria, who, having once formed a wrong impression, was capable of altering it entirely if she was given good reason to change her mind.

As she grew up to womanhood, the Princess Royal was very wisely allowed to make the acquaintance of some of the brilliant men and women of the day who were admitted to her parents' friendship. One of these was the second Lord Granville, the " Pussy " Granville who was afterwards Foreign Minister in Mr. Gladstone's

Cabinets, and we may conclude this chapter with a quotation which shows how he could count on the young Princess's appreciation of a funny story.

Lord Granville, who went to St. Petersburg as the head of the special British Mission at the coronation of the Tsar Alexander, wrote a long letter to Queen Victoria, in which he requested the Queen to convey his respectful remembrances to the Princess Royal; and he went on to advise the Princess, when residing abroad, not to engage a Russian maid: "Lady Wodehouse found her's eating the contents of a pot on her dressing-table, which happened to be castor-oil pomatum for the hair!"

CHAPTER II

BETROTHAL

EVEN in the days of her extreme youth, Queen Victoria, owing to the fact that she was the reigning Sovereign, had to know much that is generally concealed from the young concerning the private lives and careers of their relatives. This is made abundantly clear in the extracts from her Majesty's private diary which have already been published.

In these intimate records, written by the girl Queen herself, we see that Lord Melbourne early decided never to treat his Royal mistress as a child. When she asked him a question he evidently answered her truthfully; and she must have asked him many questions concerning that group of princes and princesses who, even then, were already known as the "Old Royal Family." They were Queen Victoria's own aunts and uncles; and over those who were still living when she came to the throne she possessed, as Sovereign, very peculiar and extended powers. It was inevitable that they should play a considerable part, if not in her life, certainly in her imagination; and yet we hardly ever find them mentioned in

the work she directly supervised and inspired—
the life of the Prince Consort. Her fear, her
contempt, her horror, of the way they had conducted their lives, her dread lest even their
innocent follies, and their sad tragedies of the
heart, should be repeated in the lives of her own
sons and daughters, were perhaps only revealed
to trusted friends in her old age.

It may even be doubted if Queen Victoria
ever communicated to Prince Albert certain of
the facts which had necessarily to be made known
to her. Whether she did so or not, the course
she very early set herself to pursue—a course, be
it remembered, in which she persisted at a time
when she seemed to lack courage and energy to
go on even with life itself, that is during the
years that immediately succeeded the Prince
Consort's death—proved how determined she was
to secure that the lives of her children should be
entirely different from those of their great-uncles
and great-aunts.

That her daughters, and later her grand-
daughters, should marry early, and make marriages
of inclination ; that her sons' wives should be
chosen among princesses young, charming, sympathetic, and personally attractive to each prince
concerned — this was one of Queen Victoria's
chief and most anxious preoccupations. She may
have tried to guide inclination, she undoubtedly
tried to arrange suitable alliances, but in no single

case did she ever seriously oppose a marriage based on strong attraction.   *)*

In that matter Queen Victoria was a typical Englishwoman. To her mind, a union between a young man and a young woman based on any other foundation save strong mutual love and confidence, was vile ; and all through her life she wished ardently to ensure that those marital blessings which fall comparatively often on ordinary people, but comparatively seldom on members of the Royal caste, should be the lot of her immediate descendants.

It was natural that the Queen, with that eager enthusiasm which was so much a part of her character, especially in this still radiantly happy period of her life, should have welcomed the thought of a marriage between her eldest daughter and the future King of Prussia. She had formed the most favourable opinion of Prince Frederick William during his brief sojourn in England in 1851. He was a man of high and honourable character at a time when such virtues were rare among the marriageable princes of reigning families, and his parents were regarded by the Queen and Prince Albert as among their dearest and most intimate friends.

The Prince of Prussia had spent some time in England after the Berlin Revolution of 1848, and on parting from Madame Bunsen, the wife of the Prussian Minister, he had exclaimed : " In

no other State or country could I have passed so
well the period of distress and anxiety through
which I have gone." During his stay he had
become intimate with the Queen and Prince
Albert—indeed, the Queen, as was her way when
she trusted and admired, had grown to be warmly
attached to him. She regarded him as noble-
minded, honest, and cruelly wronged; and, what
naturally endeared him to her still more, he
showed great confidence in Prince Albert, apparently always accepting the advice constantly
tendered him by the Prince.

All through his life Prince Albert had seen
a vision of a Germany united under the leadership
of Prussia, and it was delightful to him to learn
that it was now open to him to enter into a close
relationship with one whom he naturally believed
destined to play a supreme part in the regeneration
of his beloved fatherland. It is not generally
known that Prince Albert had written a pamphlet
entitled " The German Question Explained," in
which he propounded a scheme for a federated
German Empire with an Emperor at the head.
This pamphlet must have been either privately
printed or withdrawn from circulation, for not
even Sir Theodore Martin, when writing the
Prince's life, could procure a copy.

This suggested marriage of the Princess Royal
opened out to her father the fair prospect of being
able to bring about by his counsel and assistance

the realisation of his disinterested ambitions for the future welfare of Germany. The then King of Prussia was already sick unto 'death ; the Prince of Prussia had now passed middle age ; everything pointed to the probability that within a reasonable time Prince Frederick · William would become ruler of Prussia and, incidentally, overlord of the German peoples.

There is good authority for the truth of the now famous story of " La Belle Alliance."

In 1852 the Princess of Prussia came to England on a short visit to her aunt, Queen Adelaide. The then Prussian Envoy, Baron von Bunsen, while waiting to be received by the Princess, turned over in her sitting-room some engravings which had been sent by a print-seller ; among them was that of a painting of the farm-house at Waterloo named by the Belgians, "La Belle Alliance." In the same room was a portrait of the Princess Royal and one of Prince Frederick William. The Baron placed the two portraits side by side over the engraving, and when the Princess entered the room, he silently pointed out to her what he had done, and she saw the two young faces above the words " La Belle Alliance." " A rapid glance was exchanged, but not a word was spoken," wrote Baron von Bunsen's son many years after.

As for the young Prince himself, when the question of his marriage had to be discussed, it was natural that his first thought, as also, it is clear, that of his mother, turned to England—to that affectionately united Royal family who were the envied model of all European Courts. The feeling of that day is indicated by a curious caricature, which was largely reproduced on the Continent. It shows a huge pair of scales. In one scale, high in the air, stand huddled together the then reigning sovereigns of Europe; in the other, touching the ground, proudly alone, stands the slight figure of Queen Victoria. Under the cartoon runs the significant words, "Light Sovereigns."

England alone among the nations had had no trouble worth speaking of in '48, and among the Princesses and Queens of her day it was believed that Queen Victoria alone possessed the faithful love of her husband.

The greatest obstacle to the marriage, though neither Queen Victoria nor Prince Albert suspected it, was the King of Prussia himself. It is plain that at no time did he favour the suggestion, and that at last he yielded was in response to a strong appeal made to him in person by the young Prince. But, even so, the King desired the matter to be kept secret as long as possible. He did not even tell his Queen, and his own immediate circle and Household only heard of the betrothal when it was being widely rumoured in the German newspapers.

General von Gerlach came to the King one day with a sheet of the *Cologne Gazette* and indig-

nantly complained of the "absurd reports that
were being spread about." It was said that the
young Prince was going on to England from
Ostend for the purpose of proposing for the hand
of an English Princess. The King laughed aloud,
and observed: "Well, yes, and it is really the
case," to the amazement and consternation of
von Gerlach.

While the matter was being thus discussed
at Berlin, the Princess Royal was kept in
absolute ignorance. But the Crimean War and
the subsequent visit to France had quickened
her sensibilities, turned her from a child into a
woman, and made her in a measure ready for the
event which was about to occur. It should, however, be plainly said—the more so because later
historians have blamed Queen Victoria and Prince
Albert in the matter—that neither of her parents
was willing even to consider the idea of any immediate betrothal. On the contrary, they wished
that the two young people should meet in an
easy friendly fashion, and thus have a real opportunity of becoming well acquainted the one with
the other.

Prince Frederick William of Prussia arrived
at Balmoral on September 14, 1855. He allowed
some days to elapse, and then, on the morning of
the 20th, he sought out Queen Victoria and laid
before her and Prince Albert his proposal of
marriage. That proposal the parents of the

Princess Royal accepted in principle, but they requested him to say nothing to their daughter till after she had been confirmed. It was their wish that, for some months at any rate, the young Princess should continue the simple yet full life of unconstrained girlhood. It was therefore suggested that the Prince should return in the following spring. The Queen also stipulated that the marriage should not take place till after the Princess Royal's seventeenth birthday.

After this interview with Prince Frederick William, Prince Albert wrote to Stockmar:

" I have been much pleased with him. His prominent qualities are great thought, straightforwardness, frankness, and honesty. He appears to be free from prejudices, and pre-eminently well-intentioned; he speaks of himself as personally greatly attracted by Vicky. That she will have no objection to make I regard as probable."

Prince Albert wrote the following day to Lord Clarendon, who was then Foreign Minister, informing him that he might communicate the news to the Prime Minister, Lord Palmerston, and to no one else. " Pam " was pleased to approve, declaring that the marriage would be in the interest, not only of the two countries, but of Europe in general.

Queen Victoria did not fail to communicate the important secret to her beloved uncle, King Leopold, observing that her wishes on the subject of the future marriage of her daughter had been realised in the most gratifying and satisfactory manner.   Indeed, she spoke of the joy with which she and Prince Albert for their part had accepted the suitor, while she reiterated that "the child herself is to know nothing till after her confirmation, which is to take place next winter."

The days went on, and a sincere effort was made to keep what had taken place from the knowledge of the young Princess.   Letters of warm congratulation arrived from Coblentz, as well as a very cordial message from the King of Prussia.   Prince Frederick William's relations were quite at one with the Queen and Prince Albert as to the propriety of postponing the betrothal till after the Princess Royal's confirmation.

But the plan so carefully made was not destined to be carried out.   The Prince was very much in love, and, as the Emperor of the French truly observed in a letter to Prince Albert: "On devine ceux qui aiment."   It was impossible to keep such a secret, and one which so closely concerned herself, from a girl as clever and mentally alive as the Princess Royal.   What happened is best told in Queen Victoria's entry in her diary on September 29:

"Our dear Victoria was this day engaged to Prince Frederick William of Prussia, who had been on a visit to us since the 14th.   He had

THE PRINCESS ROYAL
AND THE INFANT PRINCE OF WALES

already spoken to us, on the 20th, of his wishes;
but we were uncertain, on account of her extreme
youth, whether he should speak to her himself, or
wait till he came back again. However, we felt
it was better he should do so, and during our ride
up Craig-na-Ban this afternoon, he picked a piece of
white heather (the emblem of 'good luck,') which
he gave to her; and this enabled him to make an
allusion to his hopes and wishes as they rode down
Glen Girnoch, which led to this happy conclusion."

A few days later her father wrote to Stockmar:
" She manifested towards Fritz and ourselves
the most childlike simplicity and candour. The
young people are ardently in love with one another, and the purity, innocence, and unselfishness
of the young man have been on his part touching."
To Mr. Perry, his English tutor at Bonn, the
Prince declared that his engagement was not
politics, nor ambition, " It was my heart."

At the time of her engagement the Princess
Royal was not yet fifteen, and it was arranged
that the marriage should take place in two years
and three months.

In one respect the Princess was singularly
fortunate. In the majority of Royal marriages,
the bride has not only to make her home in a
country where everything will be foreign to her,
but she is sometimes even ignorant of the
language, manners, and customs which she will
have henceforth to adopt as her own.

C

The Princess Royal, however, had to undergo no such sudden initiation. To her Germany was in truth a second fatherland, if only as the birthplace of her beloved father. She had been as familiar with the German as with the English language from her birth, constantly writing long letters to German relations and friends, and keeping up—to give but one instance—a close correspondence with her parents' trusted friend, Baron Stockmar, who had for her the greatest affection and admiration.

In a letter quoted in his memoirs Stockmar says: " From her youth upwards I have been fond of her, have always expected great things of her, and taken all pains to be of service to her. I think her to be exceptionally gifted in some things, even to the point of genius."

This familiarity with the German language was very well as a foundation, but Prince Albert considered that there was much to build on it. The whole of the Princess's education was now arranged solely with a view to the life she was to lead as wife of the Prussian heir-presumptive. In addition to giving her, for an hour every day, special instruction in German political and legal institutions and sociology, Prince Albert made her henceforth his intellectual companion, preparing her as if she was destined to be a reigning sovereign rather than a queen consort. Not only did he discuss with her all current international questions, but he read her the long political letters he received daily from abroad, and discussed with her what he should write in reply.

It was indeed a mental training which, particularly in those 'fifties which now seem so remote from us, would have been deemed only appropriate for the cleverest of boys in a private station. But Prince Albert had long known that his daughter was a good deal cleverer than most boys, and he was really running no risks in subjecting her to this intelligent preparation for her high destiny. As much as he could, he taught her himself, and such teaching as was entrusted to others he supervised with conscientious care.

In one of his letters to his future son-in-law, the Prince wrote: "Vicky is learning many and various things. She comes to me every evening from six to seven, when I put her through a kind of general catechising. In order to make her ideas clear, I let her work out subjects for herself, which she then brings to me for correction. She is at present writing a short compendium of Roman history."

In order to give the Princess a clear picture of German policy—or rather of German policy as Prince Albert then hoped it would become, that is, broad and liberal in conception and aim—he set her to translate a German pamphlet published at Weimar. This essay by J. G. Droysen, entitled "Karl August und die Deutsche Politik," would be counted rather stiff reading even by experts. But the Princess seems to have done her task admirably, and the proud father sent the manuscript to Lord Clarendon, who was genuinely impressed by the way it had been translated.   He wrote back to the Prince :

" In reading Droysen I felt that the motto of Prussia should be *semper eadem,* and in thinking of his translator I felt that she is destined to change that motto into the *vigilando ascendimus* of Weimar."

. The statesman added the further tribute to the young translator : " The Princess's manner would not be what it is if it were not the reflection of a highly cultivated intellect, which, with a well-trained imagination, leads to the saying and doing of right things in right places."

CHAPTER III

OPINION IN BOTH COUNTRIES

THE Queen and Prince Albert, as we know, much wished to keep the fact of the Princess's engagement a secret from the public. But rumour was naturally busy with the visit of the Prussian Prince to Balmoral, and on the day after his departure, that is on October 3, there appeared in the *Times* a leading article, in which the proposed alliance of the Princess Royal was alluded to with anything but approval—indeed, in Germany the article was considered grossly insulting both to the King of Prussia and to Germany. Prince Albert was very much angered at the terms in which it was written, which he described as "foolish and degrading to this country."

But the article was really inspired by a consciousness of the violent dislike of England entertained by the Court of Prussia, and especially by the camarilla surrounding the then sovereign and his consort, and this was better realised by publicists than by Royal circles in England.

Amazing as it may seem to us now, it is nevertheless abundantly clear that neither Queen

Victoria nor Prince Albert, well served as they were in some respects by the faithful Stockmar, had any idea of the real situation at the Prussian Court. The extreme youth of their daughter made them wish to postpone the marriage for a while, but there is no hint in any of the many letters and documents which have now come to light of the slightest fear that she would lack a good reception in that new country which she already loved as part of Prince Albert's fatherland. On the contrary, the Prince had evidently persuaded himself that his daughter's marriage would be very popular in Germany—more popular than it happened to be just then in England. Like most men of high, strong, narrow character, Prince Albert never allowed himself to perceive what at the moment he did not wish to see.

This view is entirely borne out by the letters which Prince Albert wrote then and later to the Prince of Prussia. Even when addressing one who was far older than himself, and already in the position of a ruler, he always assumed the attitude of mentor rather than of adviser; and as one glances over the immensely long epistles, dealing with a state of things of which the writer could know but very little, one wonders if the future Emperor William had the patience always to read them to the very end. Even were there no other evidence existing, these letters remain to show how curiously lacking Prince Albert was in that knowledge of elementary human nature which belongs to so many commoner types of mind.

The Prince Consort's misapprehension is the more extraordinary when we consider that his brother, Duke Ernest of Saxe-Coburg-Gotha, judged the situation with accuracy. In a letter published in his memoirs the Duke says:

"The family events at Balmoral and Stolzenfels [King Frederick William IV was staying at Stolzenfels when he received the news of the engagement of his nephew to the Princess Royal and of his niece, Princess Louise, to the Prince Regent of Baden] gave rise to all kinds of dissatisfaction in many reactionary circles of the Prussian capital. The more the Liberal papers of Germany applauded, the more disagreeably was the other side affected by the unpopularity of the circumstances which threatened to strengthen, at the Court of Berlin, the influence of the Royal relations whose sentiments were not regarded with favour. One of the peculiarities of Frederick William IV was that, with reference to his personal sympathies, he would not submit to any coercion from those who were familiar with politics and affairs of State, so that the secret opponents had to beware of expressing their displeasure at the new family connections."

As we have seen, the King of Prussia had kept his own counsel in the affair of his nephew's engagement, which he had only sanctioned in consequence of Prince Frederick William's strong personal appeal. His Queen was intensely pro-Russian, and as a result of the Crimean War had conceived a positive hatred for England and the English.

As for the Princess of Prussia, afterwards the Empress Augusta, she was a woman of the highest cultivation, the old cultivation of Weimar and of the French eighteenth century, but she had not much influence in Berlin, where even then she was said to be strongly inclined to Roman Catholicism. The Prince of Prussia was himself not really popular. It was inevitable therefore, in all the circumstances, that the prospect of an English alliance should become a fresh cause of contention and division, in which the voices of disapproval decidedly prevailed.

Even after the engagement had been actually announced, Prince Frederick William told Lady Bloomfield, the wife of the British Minister in Berlin, that, though he was very much disappointed that the Queen and Prince Albert wished the marriage to be postponed as the Princess Royal was so young, it was perhaps a good thing, for by that time party spirit in Prussia would run less high. The strength of that party spirit was ominously shown on the occasion of the marriage of the Prince's sister, Princess Louise, when the great nobility of Prussia ostentatiously absented themselves from the festivities.

General von Gerlach, who as we have seen extracted from the King of Prussia that dry admission that the rumours of the English engagement were well-founded, drew also a more interesting comment on the news from a very different personage. Bismarck, who was already regarded as a man with a future, and at the time held an important diplomatic post at the Diet at Frankfort, wrote to the General on April 8, 1856, a commentary which was in some ways extraordinarily prophetic :·

"You ask me in your letter what I think of the English marriage. I must separate the two words to give you my opinion. The 'English' in it does not please me, the 'marriage' may be quite good, for the Princess has the reputation of a lady of brain and heart. If the Princess can leave the Englishwoman at home and become a Prussian, then she may be a blessing to the country. If our future Queen on the Prussian throne remains the least bit English, then I see our Court surrounded by English influence, and yet us, and the many other future sons-in-law of her gracious Majesty, receiving no notice in England save when the Opposition in Parliament runs down our Royal family and country. On the other hand, with us, British influence will find a fruitful soil in the noted admiration of the German 'Michael' for lords and guineas, in the Anglomania of papers, sportsmen, country gentlemen, &c. Every Berliner feels exalted when a real

English jockey from Hart or Lichtwald speaks to him and gives him an opportunity of breaking the Queen's English on a wheel. What will it be like when the first lady in the land is an English-woman?"

Not less interesting in their way are the comments which Prince Albert's brother, Duke Ernest, made on his niece's betrothal:

"The Royal House of Prussia has long afforded in its genealogical history a singular spectacle of waverings between the West and East of Europe. While family alliances between Orthodox Russia and Catholic Austria were almost wholly excluded, the Protestant faith did not at all prevent the Hohenzollerns from having a strong leaning towards the family of the Tsars, and the connections which were thus made undoubtedly exerted their influence upon Germany. The Crimean War may be regarded as a political lesson on this concatenation of circumstances. Was it not most extraordinary that, even before peace had been concluded with Russia, the Royal House of Prussia was, in its matrimonial aims, on the point of exhibiting a marked tendency towards the West of Europe? The union of a Prussian heir-apparent with a Princess of my House, with its numerous branches, was an event which at the time unquestionably seemed opposed to the Russian tradition.

"If we remember how at the end of the war

everyone looked upon my brother as the active force against Russia, though at the beginning this was by no means clear, the marriage of a Prussian Prince who was destined to the succession with a daughter of the Queen of England necessarily possessed a decided political character. My brother, however, loved his eldest daughter too well to be influenced entirely by political considerations in respect of her marriage ; and I often had an opportunity of observing that the chief wish of his heart for many years had been to see his favourite child occupy some exalted position. With paternal ambition, he was wont to picture to himself his promising daughter, whose abilities had been early developed, upon a lofty throne, but, more than all, I know that he was anxious to make her also truly happy. The Prince of Prussia, above all other scions of reigning Houses, afforded the greatest hopes for the future."

There was another Court at which the news of the engagement was regarded with mixed feelings. The Emperor Napoleon at first received the Anglo-Prussian alliance almost with dismay. He feared that, by strengthening Prussian influence, it would have the effect of weakening, and possibly destroying, the French understanding with England. But he allowed himself to be reassured by Lord Clarendon, who declared that Queen Victoria's affection for the House of Prussia was private and personal, and had nothing to do with politics. Prince Frederick William, rèturning by way of Paris as a successful suitor, had brought the Emperor a letter from the Queen, and to it Napoleon replied, rather coldly :

" We like the Prince very much, and I do not doubt that he will make the Princess happy, for he seems to me to possess every characteristic quality belonging to his age and rank. We endeavoured to make his stay here as pleasant as possible, but I found his thoughts were always either at Osborne or at Windsor."

It was on this visit of the Prince's that the Empress Eugénie made the following comments in a letter to an intimate friend, which, in view of those later events in which Moltke played so great a part, possess a pathetic significance :

" The Prince is a tall, handsome man, almost a head taller than the Emperor ; he is slim and fair, with a light yellow moustache—in fact, a Teuton such as Tacitus described, chivalrously polite, and not without a resemblance to Hamlet. His companion, Herr von Moltke (or some such name), is a man of few words, but nothing less than a dreamer, always on the alert, and surprising one by the most telling remarks. The Germans are an imposing race. Louis says it is the race of the future. Bah ! Nous n'en sommes pas encore là."

There was also a neighbouring sovereign to whose opinion all those who appreciate the complex dynastic relations of that period will be inclined to attach importance.   This was the King of the Belgians.

Though he was in no sense the noble, selfless human being Queen Victoria took him to be, King Leopold was nevertheless a very shrewd judge of human nature, and had evidently seen enough of the Princess Royal to note certain peculiarities in her character which had escaped the loving, partial eyes of her parents.   This is clearly shown in a letter written by Queen Victoria in the December of 1856.   In this letter there is a passage, prefaced by " Now one word about Vicky," in which the Queen protests that she has never seen her daughter take any predilection to a person which was not *motive* by a certain amiability, goodness, or distinction of some kind or other.   She goes on to say : " You need be under no apprehension whatever on this subject; and she has moreover great tact and esprit de conduite."

This surely makes it clear that King Leopold was aware of the sudden fancies which the Princess Royal, even at that early age, often showed to those who attracted her, and that for no sufficient reason.   Probably in this case he was thinking of the Princess Royal's passionate attachment to the Empress Eugénie—an attachment which lasted all through her youth, and which perhaps had more justification for it than some other of her enthusiasms for individuals.

In England, at any rate at first, the news of the
engagement was received rather coldly, almost as
if it was a *mésalliance*, though the knowledge that
it was really a love-match did much to reconcile
public opinion. The following passage from a
letter written by Mr. Cobden, at this time the
triumphant protagonist of the Anti-Corn Law
League, reflects as well as anything the general
feeling that the bridegroom was indeed "a lucky
fellow":

"It is generally thought that the young Prince
Frederick William of Prussia is to be married to
our Princess Royal. I was dining *tête-à-tête* with
Mr. Buchanan, the American Minister, a few days
ago, who had dined the day before at the Queen's
table, and sat next to the Princess Royal. He
was in raptures about her, and said she was the
most charming girl he had ever met: 'All life
and spirit, full of frolic and fun, with an excellent
head, and a *heart as big as a mountain*'—those
were his words. Another friend of mine, Colonel
Fitzmayer, dined with the Queen last week, and,
in writing to me a description of the company, he
says that when the Princess Royal smiles, 'it
makes one feel as if additional light were thrown
upon the scene.' So I should judge that this
said Prince is a lucky fellow, and I trust he will
make a good husband. If not, although a man
of peace, I shall consider it a *casus belli!*"

To the bride's parents, if not to herself and her

betrothed, the fact that the marriage negotiations were not quite pleasantly conducted must have been not only painful but astonishing. It was actually suggested that the ceremony should take place in Berlin, but Queen Victoria very properly scouted the proposal, which was really in the circumstances disagreeably like an insult. She wrote in her emphatic, italicising way to Lord Clarendon, the Foreign Secretary :

"The Queen *never* could consent to it, both for public and private reasons, and the assumption of its being *too much* for a Prince Royal of Prussia to *come* over to marry *the Princess Royal of Great Britain* IN England is too *absurd*, to say the least. The Queen must say that there never was even the *shadow* of a *doubt* on *Prince Frederick William's* part as to *where* the marriage should take place, and she suspects this to be the mere gossip of the Berliners. Whatever may be the usual practice of Prussian Princes, it is not *every* day that one marries the eldest daughter of the Queen of England. The question therefore must be considered as settled and closed."

In view of all this and of what was to befall the Princess Royal in the land for which she even then cherished so fond an affection, and of which she had already formed so high an ideal, there is something intensely pathetic in the blindness of her parents to the real conditions of her future life. This blindness is shown with amazing clearness in the sentence, certainly inspired and very likely written by Queen Victoria herself, which concludes the chapter, in Sir Theodore Martin's *Life of the Prince Consort*, dealing with the betrothal of the Princess Royal:

" No consideration, public or private, would have induced the Queen or himself [*i.e.* Prince Albert] to imperil the happiness of their child by a marriage in which she could not have found scope to practise the constitutional principles in which she had been reared."

The idea that the Prussia of that day, or indeed of any day, would have amiably afforded a foreign princess scope to practise constitutional principles of any sort seems extraordinary, and yet, as we shall see, there was some little justification for it at the time, though it was quickly swept away by the course of events.

The confirmation of the Princess Royal took place on March 20, 1856, in the private chapel at Windsor Castle. The Princess was led in by her father, followed by her godfather, the King of the Belgians, who had come to England on purpose, and the Royal children and most of the members of the Royal family were present, as were also the Ministers, the great officers of State, and many of those whom Disraeli was wont to describe as the " high nobility."

In fact, everything was done to make the rite a State ceremony—a striking contrast to the more recent practice by which the princes and princesses of England have all been confirmed privately, in the presence of their near relatives only.

The second Lord Granville, the statesman who shared with the Princess Royal the flattering nickname of "Pussy," wrote to Lord Canning this lively account of the confirmation. The inaudible Archbishop was J. B. Sumner; his Lordship of Oxford was the Samuel Wilberforce, called by his enemies "Soapy Sam," who played a conspicuous part in the Court and social life of the period:

"Had a slight spasm in bed; sent for Meryon. It was well before he came. He desired me not to go to Windsor for the confirmation of the Princess Royal. I went, and am none the worse; my complexion beautiful. It was an interesting sight. As Pam observed, 'Ah, ah! a touching ceremony; ah, ah!' The King of the Belgians the same as I remember him when I was a boy, and he used to live for weeks at the Embassy, using my father's horses, and boring my mother to death. The Princess Royal went through her part well. The Princess Alice cried violently. The Archbishop read what seemed a dull address; luckily it was inaudible. The Bishop of Oxford rolled out a short prayer with conscious superiority. Pam reminded Lord Aberdeen of their being confirmed at Cambridge, as if it was yesterday. I must go to bed, so excuse haste and bad pens,

D

as the sheep said to the farmer when it jumped out of the fold."

There was certainly too much pomp about the Princess Royal's confirmation for the taste of another spectator, Princess Mary of Cambridge, afterwards Duchess of Teck. She succeeds in drawing in a few words a remarkably vivid picture of what happened :

" The ceremony was very short (the service for the day being omitted) and not solemn enough for my feeling, although the anthems were fine and well-chosen. It was followed by a great deal of standing in the Green Drawing-room, where the Queen held a kind of tournée in honour of the Ministers, who had come down for the confirmation ; after which dear Victoria, who looked particularly nice, and was very much impressed with the solemnity of the rite, received our presents on the occasion, and about half-past one we sat down to lunch *en famille* as usual."

It was on April 29, 1856, that the betrothal was publicly announced on the conclusion of the Crimean War, and in the following month the Princess appeared as a débutante at a Court ball at Buckingham Palace.

This spring " Fritz of Prussia," as his future father-in-law called him, came to pay a long visit to his fiancée. It is curious that Queen Victoria, in spite of her strong belief in love as the only right foundation for an engagement, had by no means the English notion of discreetly leaving the young people a good deal alone together.   On the contrary, she seems to have entirely adopted the Continental practice of chaperonage; a passage in a letter written by her to King Leopold shows that she was always with them, and that she naturally found it very boring, but she endured it because she thought it was her duty.

Prince Frederick William was still in England when in June the Princess Royal met with rather a terrifying accident, which is worthy of mention because it showed how strong was her character and how high her physical courage.

The Princess was sealing a letter at her writing-table, when suddenly the sealing-wax flamed out and the flames caught her muslin sleeve.   Her English governess, Miss Hildyard, was fortunately seated close to her, and her music mistress, Mrs. Anderson, was also in the room, giving Princess Alice a lesson.   They sprang at once to the Princess's assistance and beat out the flames with a hearthrug; but not before her right arm had been severely burned from below the elbow to the shoulder.   She showed the greatest self-possession and presence of mind, her first words being: "Send for Papa, and do not tell Mamma till he has been told."

The Princess Royal had a long engagement, probably the longest that any lady of her rank has had, at least in modern times, but the months as they went by were fully occupied with her father's sedulous preparation of her intellect, as well as with the more frivolous preparations of her trousseau.

In May 1857 Parliament voted for the Princess a dowry of £40,000 and an annuity of £4000—a provision which does not now seem to have erred on the side of generosity. But it must be remembered that what economists call "the purchasing power of the sovereign" was considerably greater then than now, and to find the modern equivalent of these sums one would have to add probably as much as 25 per cent.

Prince Frederick William, attended by Count Moltke, paid another visit to England in June, and made his first public appearance with the Princess at the Manchester Art Exhibition. The young couple seem to have corresponded on quite the old-fashioned voluminous scale. After the Prince had gone home again in August, Moltke writes to his wife that the Princess had written a letter of forty pages to the Prince, and he adds the sarcastic comment: "How the news must have accumulated!"

Whatever the aide-de-camp may have thought, the Prince himself was certainly a happy lover in his own characteristically serious way. We find him a few months later writing to his French tutor, the Swiss Pastor Godet, a long and moving letter, in which he alludes very frankly to the

difficulties which even then surrounded his position
Then, going on to speak of his coming marriage,
he says:

"Yes, if you knew my betrothed you would,
I am sure, thoroughly understand my choice, and
you would realise that I am truly happy. I can
but bless and thank God to have given me the
happiness of finding in her everything which
ensures the true union of hearts, and repose and
calm in home life, for I do not care, as you know,
for the world, which I find empty and with very
little happiness in it."

The seventeenth birthday of the Princess
Royal, the last she was to spend with her family
before her marriage, was saddened by the death of
Queen Victoria's half-brother, Prince Leiningen.
The Royal family were all extremely fond of him,
especially the Princess Royal, to whom he had
ever shown himself a most affectionate and kindly
uncle. This was the first time the Princess had
come in close contact with death, and it made
the more impression on her owing to the passionate grief which her grandmother, the Duchess of
Kent, showed at the loss of her only son.

The wedding had now been fixed for January
25, 1858, and already in October the bride had
taken leave of those places in Balmoral which
were dear to her. Of this Prince Albert writes
to the widowed Duchess of Gotha:

"Vicky suffers from the feeling that all those

places she visits she must look upon for the last time as her home. The Maid of Orleans with her 'Joan says to you an everlasting farewell,' often comes into my mind." And in another letter: "The departure from here will be heavy for all of us, particularly for Vicky who is going away for good, and the good Highland people who love her so much say: 'I suppose we shall never see you again,' which naturally upsets her."

These rather sentimental farewells had been going on for a long time. Queen Victoria, in a letter a fortnight before the wedding, says that her daughter had had ever since January 1857 a succession of emotions and leave-takings which would be most trying to anyone, but particularly so to so young a girl with such powerful feelings. The loving mother goes on to say that she is much improved in self-control, and is so clever and sensible that her parents can talk to her of anything.

Her other parent, in a letter to his grandmother, spoke of the frightful gap which the separation for ever of this dear daughter would make in the family circle, and then, with his characteristic optimism, he adds that in Germany people seem ready to welcome her with the greatest friendliness.

Here perhaps is the place to consider what sort of a country was the "Germany" whither

Prince Albert was sending his cherished daughter as future Queen.

To begin with, it was not yet "Germany" at all; it was Prussia. We are well accustomed in the twentieth century to regard Germany as one of the Great Powers of Europe, with her enormous army and her expanding navy and mercantile marine, with all else for which the Fatherland stands in science, letters, and industry. It is necessary, however, to realise that the Princess Royal's marriage was to bring her to what was then a very different country. Prussia was in fact not to be compared in power, wealth, or security with the Princess's native land. Including Silesia, Brandenburg, and Westphalia, the country only had a population of some seventeen millions in 1858, or about that of England alone. The revenue was comparatively insignificant, but the army numbered 160,000 officers and men; the navy had 55 ships, 3500 officers and men, and 265 guns; while the mercantile marine is given as 826 ships of 268,000 tons.

The Germanic Confederation had superseded the Confederation of the Rhine formed by Napoleon. It included Austria, as well as Prussia and the various German States, and by the nature of its constitution it was weak where it should have been strong. The jealousy felt by Austria for the hegemony of Prussia among the smaller German States, and the internal jealousies of those States

among themselves, almost doomed the Confederation to impotence. Indeed, the primary object of
the Confederation, namely, the maintenance of the
external security of the States, was in constant
danger, owing partly to the complicated regulations
for voting in the Diet, partly to a military system
which was full of compromises and certain to produce, on the outbreak of war, a maximum of
confusion and a minimum of efficiency.

The constitutional liberties of the individual
States had been gravely menaced by a series of
feudal decrees passed between 1830 and 1840;
while in 1850 the Confederation had actually
suppressed the constitution of Hesse-Cassel. In
Prussia itself the Manteuffel Ministry had been
working, beneath the cloak of the constitutional
reforms granted in 1850, to establish a centralised
police State on the model of the French préfet
system combined with typical Prussian mediæ-
valism.

It was in 1847 that King Frederick William
IV uttered the famous words that he would never
allow a piece of written parchment to be placed,
like a second Providence, between God in heaven
and his country. Now the constitution of only
two years later did seem to be such a piece of
written parchment, but this was only in appearance, because it did not settle by organic laws the
crucial questions of political liberty, but left them
in practice to the Chambers which it called into

existence. The task of Baron Manteuffel's Ministry, therefore, resolved itself into obtaining a sufficiently reactionary Parliament which could be trusted to remove the foundations of political liberty laid by the great constitutional lawgiver, Stein, and his follower, Hardenburg.

It was not till 1855, three years before the Princess Royal's marriage, that a thoroughly servile Chamber was obtained. The two principal reforms effected by Stein, namely, the localising of the administration and the independence of officials, were abolished, and the administration was carefully centralised on the French model, and the whole official class was made dependent upon the Government. This latter object was effected by an ingenious theory—that any opposition to a constitutional Ministry which enjoyed the confidence of the sovereign became constructively an offence against the Crown, and therefore punishable.

It is significant that it took five years before a really servile Chamber was obtained, even by these methods. The Prussian mediævalists did not altogether like the police supremacy established by the Manteuffel Ministry; but, on the other hand, by their alliance with the Ministry they had the satisfaction of staving off certain reforms which they especially dreaded, notably the equalisation of the land tax, the removal of the rural police from the control of the lord of the manor, and the liberal organisation of the rural communes. Moreover, they were given practical freedom to do what they liked in ecclesiastical and educational administration.

It must be remembered that, while England has had from time to time her mediævalists, they have, on the whole, failed to make any real impression on politics, and have exerted their influence only in the province of religious belief and in that of art. It was different in Prussia, where feudalism as a practical system had a much longer life.

Numerous small States within the kingdom of Prussia, with their feudal powers and rights, had to be broken up by the Great Elector as a first step towards a Prussian nationality. It was really by continuing the Great Elector's work in this respect that Stein had aroused that national movement which eventually threw off the French yoke. But Frederick William III had set-himself to reorganise the provincial States on the basis of a strict observance of their historical rights. This reorganisation did not satisfy the mediævalists because it failed to provide any real check upon the bureaucratic character of the remaining part of the King's administration.

At the time of the Princess Royal's marriage there still survived an extraordinary number of little States, each with its ruling family, and for the most part as poor as they were proud.

CHAPTER IV

MARRIAGE

IT is the universal testimony that at the time of her wedding the Princess Royal was at the height of her youthful beauty and charm. This is not the mere flattery of courtiers, to whom all Royal ladies are beautiful as a matter of course ; it is the opinion expressed by a multitude of observers in contemporary private letters, diaries, and reminiscences. And of all the descriptions of her at this time in existence the most lifelike we owe to a German lady of rank, one of the Princess's future ladies-in-waiting, Countess Walpurga de Hohenthal, who afterwards married Sir Augustus Berkeley Paget, British Ambassador in Rome and Vienna. This lady gives in her book of reminiscences, *Scenes and Memories*, this vivid vignette of her Royal mistress as she looked just before her marriage :

" The Princess appeared extraordinarily young. All the childish roundness still clung to her and made her look shorter than she really was. She was dressed in a fashion long disused on the Continent, in a plum-coloured silk dress fastened at the back. Her hair was drawn off her forehead.

Her eyes were what struck me most; the iris was green like the sea on a sunny day, and the white had a peculiar shimmer which gave them the fascination that, together with a smile showing her small and beautiful teeth, bewitched those who approached her. The nose was unusually small and turned up slightly, and the complexion was ruddy, perhaps too much so for one thing, but it gave the idea of perfect health and strength. The fault of the face lay in the squareness of the lower features, and there was even a look of determination about the chin, but the very gentle and almost timid manner prevented one realising this at first. The voice was very delightful, never going up to high tones, but lending a peculiar charm to the slight foreign accent with which the Princess spoke both English and German."

As we have already seen, Queen Victoria felt strongly that it was not every day that even a future King married the daughter of a Queen of England, and she was resolved to surround the ceremony with all possible pomp and circumstance. The reader may for the most part be spared the details of these functions. What is interesting to us, looking back on that age which seems so remote from our own, is the curious note of tearful sentiment, which some would now call by a harsher name, yet mingled with high hopes and pathetic confidence in the future.

The Court spent the early part of January

1858 at Windsor Castle, and on the 15th, the day
of the departure for London, the Queen wrote in
her diary :

"Went to look at the rooms prepared for
Vicky's 'Honeymoon.' Very pretty. It quite
agitated me to look at them. Poor, poor child !
We took a short walk with Vicky, who was dread-
fully upset at this real break in her life ; the real
separation from her childhood ! She slept for the
last time in the same room with Alice. Now all
this is cut off."

And we may quote, too, a characteristic passage
from a letter written to the Queen by her sister,
the Princess of Hohenlohe-Langenburg, with
reference to another young Royal bride :

"Poor little wife now ! I have quite the same
feeling as you have on these dear young creatures
entering the new life of duties, privations, and
trials, on their marrying so young. Alas ! the
sweet blossoms coming in contact with rude life
and all its realities so soon, are changed into mature
and less lovely persons, so painful to a mother's
eye and feeling ; and yet we must be happy to see
them fulfil their *Bestimmung* (destiny) ; but it is
a happiness not unmixed with many a bitter drop
of anguish and pain."

By the 19th all the Royal guests had arrived
in London, among them the King of the Belgians
with his sons, the Prince and Princess of Prussia,
and Princes and Princesses in such numbers that

the accommodation of Buckingham Palace was taxed to the uttermost. "Such a house-full," says the Queen in her diary. "Such bustle and excitement!" Between eighty and ninety sat down to dinner at the Royal table daily. "After dinner," says the same record, "a party, and a very gay and pretty dance. It was very animated, all the Princes dancing."

The first of the public festivities was a performance at Her Majesty's Theatre of *Macbeth*, by Helen Faucit and Phelps, while Mr. and Mrs. Keeley appeared in a farce. This was the first of four representations, organised at the Queen's command in honour of the marriage, and each was made the occasion of an extraordinary popular demonstration. A great ball, at which over a thousand guests were present, was given at the Palace, and there was also a State performance of Balfe's opera, *The Rose of Castille.*

Prince Frederick William arrived on January 23, and on the next day Queen Victoria writes:

"Poor dear Vicky's last unmarried day. An eventful one, reminding me so much of mine. After breakfast we arranged in the large drawing-room the gifts (splendid ones) for Vicky in two tables. Fritz's pearls are the largest I ever saw, one row. On a third table were three fine candelabra, our gift to Fritz. Vicky was in ecstasies, quite startled, and Fritz delighted."

More magnificent presents kept on arriving, and the Queen goes on:

"Very busy—interrupted and disturbed every instant! Dear Vicky gave me a brooch (a very pretty one) before Church with her hair; and, clasping me in her arms, said: 'I hope to be worthy to be your child!'" At the end of the day the Queen and the Prince "accompanied Vicky to her room, kissed her and gave her our blessing, and she was much overcome. I pressed her in my arms, and she clung to her truly adored papa with much tenderness."

Of the wedding itself Queen Victoria made herself the historian for all time, and we cannot do better than quote her vividly emotional account of the scene:

"Monday, January 25. — The second most eventful day in my life as regards feelings. I felt as if I were being married over again myself, only much more nervous, for I had not that blessed feeling which I had then, which raises and supports one, of giving myself up for life to him whom I loved and worshipped—then and ever! Got up, and, while dressing, dearest Vicky came to see me, looking well and composed, and in a fine quiet frame of mind. She had slept more soundly and better than before. This relieved me greatly. Gave her a pretty book called *The Bridal Offering.*"

Before the procession started for the Chapel

Royal at St. James's Palace, the Queen and the Princess were daguerreotyped together with Prince Albert, but, says the Queen, " I trembled so, my likeness has come out indistinct." Her Majesty continues:

· "Then came the time to go. The sun was shining brightly ; thousands had been out since very early, shouting, bells ringing, &c. Albert and Uncle, in Field Marshal's uniform, with bâtons, and the two eldest boys went first. Then the three girls in pink satin trimmed with Newport lace, Alice with a wreath, and the two others with only *bouquets* in their hair of cornflowers [the favourite flower of Queen Louise of Prussia and of all her children and descendants], and marguerites ; next the four boys in Highland dress. The flourish of trumpets and cheering of thousands made my heart sink within me. Vicky was in the carriage with me, sitting opposite. At St. James's took her into a dressing-room prettily arranged, where were Uncle, Albert, and the eight bridesmaids, who looked charming in white tulle, with wreaths and bouquets of pink roses and white heather.

" Then the procession was formed, just as at my marriage, only how small the *old* Royal family has become ! Mama last before me—then Lord Palmerston with the Sword of State—then Bertie and Alfred. I with the two little boys on either side (which they say had a most touching effect)

THE PRINCESS ROYAL
AT THE TIME OF HER MARRIAGE

and the three girls behind. The effect was very solemn and impressive as we passed through the rooms, down the staircase, and across a covered-in court.

" The Chapel, though too small, looked extremely imposing and well,—full as it was of so many elegantly-dressed ladies, uniforms, &c. The Archbishop, &c., at the altar, and on either side of it the Royal personages. Behind me Mama and the Cambridges, the girls and little boys near me, and opposite me the dear Princess of Prussia, and the foreign Princes behind her. Bertie and Affie, not far from the Princess, a little before the others.

" The drums and trumpets played marches, and the organ played others as the procession approached and entered. There was a pause between each, but not a very long one, and the effect was thrilling and striking as you heard the music gradually coming nearer and nearer. Fritz looked pale and much agitated, but behaved with the greatest self-possession, bowing to us, and then kneeling down in a most devotional manner. Then came the bride's procession and our darling Flower looked very touching and lovely, with such an innocent, confident, and serious expression, her veil hanging back over her shoulders, walking between her beloved father and dearest Uncle Leopold, who had been at her christening and confirmation.

"My last fear of being overcome vanished on seeing Vicky's quiet, calm, and composed manner. It was beautiful to see her kneeling with Fritz, their hands joined, and the train borne by eight young ladies, who looked like a cloud of maidens hovering round her, as they knelt near her. Dearest Albert took her by the hand to give her away. The music was very fine, the Archbishop very nervous; Fritz spoke very plainly, Vicky too. The Archbishop omitted some of the passages."

Sarah Lady Lyttelton, too, noted the calm and rather serious, though happy and loving, expression of the Princess's look and manner—"not a bit of bridal missiness and flutter."

Another eye-witness of the scene supplies a moving touch: "The light of happiness in the eyes of the bride appealed to the most reserved among the spectators, and an audible 'God bless you!' passed from mouth to mouth along the line."

The Queen's description proceeds:

"When the ceremony was over, we both embraced Vicky tenderly, but she shed not one tear, and then she kissed her grandmama, and I Fritz. She then went up to her new parents, and we crossed over to the dear Prince and Princess [of Prussia], who were both much moved, Albert shaking hands with them, and I kissing both and pressing their hands with a most happy feeling. My heart was so full. Then the bride and bridegroom left hand in hand, followed by the supporters, the 'Wedding March' by Mendelssohn being played, and we all went up to the Throne Room to sign the register. Here general congratulations, shaking hands with all the relations. I felt so moved, so overjoyed and relieved, that I could have embraced everybody."

The young couple drove off to Windsor for a honeymoon of only two days, as was then the custom with Royal personages.

"We dined," says Queen Victoria, "*en famille*, but I felt so lost without Vicky." In the evening, however, there came a messenger from Windsor with a letter from the bride, containing the news that the Eton boys had dragged the carriage of the Prince and Princess from the railway station to the Castle, and that they had been welcomed by immense crowds and with the greatest enthusiasm. All London, too, was illuminated, and there were great rejoicings in the streets. The Duke of Buccleuch made it his business to mingle with the humblest people in the crowds, and he afterwards greatly pleased the Queen with his account of their simple, hearty enthusiasm.

Of those two days at Windsor, the bride, thirty-six years later, when she was already a widow, spoke to her old friend, Bishop Boyd Carpenter. She received the Bishop in the red brocade drawing-room which overlooks the Long

Walk, a room which awakened memories: "We spent," she said, "our honeymoon at Windsor. This room was one of those we occupied. It was our private sitting-room. I remember how we sat here—two young innocent things—almost too shy to talk to one another."

The Court moved to Windsor on the 27th, and on the following day the bridegroom was invested with the Order of the Garter. On the 29th the Court returned to town, and in the evening the Queen and Prince Albert, and the bridal pair, went in state to Her Majesty's Theatre. The audience demanded the National Anthem twice before and once after the play, two additional verses appropriate to the occasion being added. Prince Frederick William led his bride to the front of the Royal box, and they stood to receive the acclamations of the house.

On January 30 the Queen held a Drawing-room, at which there were no presentations, "only congratulations," and the Princess wore her wedding dress and train. In the evening the eight bridesmaids, with their respective parents, came, but though there were no young men, they all danced till midnight.

The dreaded separation was fast approaching. Those were days in which people of all classes seemed to give freer play to their natural emotions than they do now, and the actual parting at Buckingham Palace may almost be described as agonising. " I think it will kill me to take leave of dear Papa ! " were the words of the Princess to her mother. " A dreadful moment, and a dreadful day," wrote the Queen. " Such sickness came over me, real heartache, when I thought of our dearest child being gone, and for so long—all, all being over ! It began to snow before Vicky went, and continued to do so without intermission all day. At times I could be quite cheerful, but my tears began to flow afresh frequently, and I could not go near Vicky's corridor."

Even the less emotional but not less warm-hearted Princess Mary of Cambridge writes in her diary of February 2 :

" A very gloomy, tearful day ! At eleven-thirty we drove to the palace to see poor dear Vicky off. It was our intention to wait downstairs ; but we were sent for, and found dear Victoria [the Queen] surrounded by a number of crying relations in the Queen's Closet. It was a sad, a trying scene. We all accompanied her to the carriage, and, after bidding her adieu, Mamma and I hurried to one of the front rooms to see her drive up the Mall."

There exists a private photograph, or rather a daguerreotype, taken of the Princess Royal that morning, her face unrecognisable, swollen with tears.

It may be imagined how delighted the populace were when they saw that, though it was snowing

hard, their Princess had chosen an open carriage
for her drive through the London she even then
loved so well, and went on loving to the very end.
The route taken was through the Mall, Fleet
Street, Cheapside, and over London Bridge, and
in spite of the terrible weather enormous crowds
gathered to see the last of the bride.   The stalwart
draymen of Barclay and Perkins's brewery shouted
out to the bridegroom in menacing tones, " Be
kind to her—or we'll have her back ! "

The Princess was accompanied by her father
and her two elder brothers ; and at Gravesend,
where the Royal yacht, the *Victoria and Albert*,
was waiting to take her and her bridegroom across
the Channel, the scene was again most affecting.
The Prince Consort was deeply moved, but he
was determined to appear composed, and he kept
his look of serenity.   Not so the Prince of Wales
and Prince Alfred ; they wept openly, and their
example was followed by many, for there was
something profoundly moving in this departure
of the Daughter of England—as Cobden had called
her—for a country of which the great majority of
Englishmen and Englishwomen at that time knew
little or nothing.

Perhaps the general feeling among the educated
classes of the England of that day is best reflected
in a leading article in the *Times*, which said :

" We only trust and pray that the policy of
England and of Prussia may never present any

painful alternatives to the Princess now about to leave our shores ; that she will never be called on to forget the land of her birth, education, and religion ; and that, should the occasion ever occur, she may have the wisdom to render what is due both to her new and her old country. There is no European State but what changes and is still susceptible of change, nor is this change wholly by any internal law of development. We influence one another. England, indeed, has ever been jealous of foreign influence, and she would be the last to repudiate the honour of influencing her neighbours. For our part, we are confident enough of our country to think an English Princess a gain to a Prussian Court, but not so confident to deny that we may be mutually benefited, and Europe through us, by a greater cordiality and better acquaintance than has hitherto been between the two countries."

CHAPTER V

EARLY MARRIED LIFE

THE bridal journey to Berlin was in the nature of a triumphal progress, and it was well that the Prince and Princess were both young and full of healthy vitality. At Brussels they were present at a great Court ball given in their honour, but early the next morning they were again on their route, and all the way there were receptions, addresses of congratulations, &c., to be received and answered.

It was probably at Brussels that the Princess received a touching letter from her father, written on the day after her departure from England :—

" My heart was very full when yesterday you leaned your forehead on my breast to give free vent to your tears. I am not of a demonstrative nature, and therefore you can hardly know how dear you have always been to me, and what a void you have left behind in my heart : yet not in my heart, for there assuredly you will abide henceforth, as till now you have done, but in my daily life, which is evermore reminding my heart of your absence."

Three days later Prince Albert again wrote to her:

"Thank God, everything apparently goes on to a wish, and you seem to gain 'golden opinions' in your favour; which naturally gives us extreme pleasure, both because we love you, and because this touches our parental pride. But what has given us most pleasure of all was the letter, so overflowing with affection, which you wrote while yet on board the yacht. Poor child! well did I feel the bitterness of your sorrow, and would so fain have soothed it. But, excepting my own sorrow, I had nothing to give; and that would only have had the effect of augmenting yours."

To Stockmar, whose son, Baron Ernest Stockmar, was appointed Treasurer to the Princess Royal on her marriage, he wrote:

"Throughout all this agitated, serious and very trying time, the good child has behaved quite admirably, and to the mingled admiration and surprise of every one. She was so natural, so childlike, so dignified and firm in her whole bearing and demeanour, that one might well believe in a higher inspiration. I shall not forget that your son has proved himself in all ways extremely useful, and takes and holds his ground, which, among the Berliners, is no easy matter."

The progress to Berlin was, at any rate, by no means dull; it was marked by plenty of incident, sometimes not of a pleasant nature. For instance, when the bridal pair were entertained at a great Court banquet at Hanover, whether by malice, or more probably by sheer stupidity, the feast was spread on the very gold dinner-service which had been a subject of dispute between Queen Victoria and King Ernest, a dispute which had been decided by the English law officers of the Crown in favour of Hanover. The Princess Royal, who knew all about the affair, felt deeply hurt, but she did not allow this to be noticed except by her intimate entourage.

In Magdeburg Cathedral the crowd became so obstreperous in their eager desire to see the Princess that shreds of her gown, a dress of tartan velvet, were actually torn off her back.

Just before Potsdam was reached, the famous Field-Marshal Wrangel, who had played so great a part in the Revolution of 1848, jumped into the train. After he had complimented the Royal bride, he sat down on a seat on which had been placed an enormous apple-tart which had just been presented to the Princess at Wittenberg, a town noted for its pastry. Fortunately the old soldier took the accident in good part, and joined in the hearty laughter which accompanied the efforts of the Princess and her ladies to clean his uniform.

The whole of the Prussian Royal family assembled at Potsdam to greet the bride and bridegroom, who made their State entry into Berlin on February 8. It was a fine day, but the cold was of an intensity never before experienced by the Princess. Nevertheless, she and her ladies were all in low Court dresses, and, by her express wish, the windows of the State carriages were kept down, so that the eager populace might be the better able to see inside.

The drive lasted two hours and ended at the Old Schloss, where the Prince and Princess found once more the whole of the Prussian Royal family assembled, headed by the then King and his Queen. As the Queen embraced the bride, she observed coldly: "Are you not frozen?" The Princess replied with a smile: "I have only one warm place, and that is my heart!"

It is a curious fact that on that night of the State entry into Berlin, when every house, and especially every palace and embassy, was brilliantly illuminated, the English Legation alone remained in darkness. This was simply because the gas company had undertaken to do more than it could accomplish, for gas had never been used in Berlin before that night for public illumination. Still, the circumstance was long remembered by the more superstitious of the Berliners.

The youthful bride made a very favourable impression on those who saw her on that first day in Berlin. Her manner was singularly quiet and self-possessed, and she found a kind and suitable word to say to everyone. Yet, even so, feeling ran so high in Prussian society, and especially at the Court, that Lord and Lady Bloomfield, the then English Minister and his wife, made a point of avoiding the Princess Royal, so desirous were they of giving no cause of offence to the King and Queen.

Meanwhile, the loving parents in London were kept busy in reading the accounts, which poured in on them from every quarter, of their daughter's reception in her new home. Thus, Queen Victoria's sister, the Princess of Hohenlohe-Langenburg, writes from Berlin on February 17 :

" You know of everything that is going on, and how much she [the Princess Royal] is admired, and deserves so to be. The enthusiasm and interest shown are beyond everything. Never was a Princess in this country received as she is. That shows where the sympathies turn to, certainly not towards the North Pole."

This was perhaps a little too *couleur de rose*, and when Prince Frederick William telegraphed to his parents-in-law, " 'The whole Royal family is enchanted with my wife," Prince Albert's dry comment, in writing to his daughter, was that the telegraph must have been amazed at the message. Nor did the anxious father fail to seize the opportunity for a little sermon. In this same letter, dated February 11, he writes to the Princess :

" You have now entered upon your new home, and been received and welcomed on all sides with the greatest friendship and cordiality. This kindly and trustful advance of a whole nation towards an entire stranger must have kindled and confirmed within you the determination to show yourself in every way worthy of such feelings, and to reciprocate and requite them by the steadfast resolution to dedicate the whole energies of your life to this people of your new home. And you have received from Heaven the happy task of effecting this object by making your husband truly happy, and of doing him at the same time the best service, by aiding him to maintain and to increase the love of his countrymen.

"That you have everywhere made so favourable an impression has given intense happiness to me as a father. Let me express my fullest admiration of the way in which, possessed exclusively by the duty which you had to fulfil, you have kept down and overcome your own little personal troubles, perhaps also many feelings of sorrow not yet healed. This is the way to success, and the *only* way. If you have succeeded in winning people's hearts by friendliness, simplicity, and courtesy, the secret lay in this, that you were not thinking of yourself. Hold fast this mystic power ; it is a spark from Heaven."

Admirable advice in a sense, but unfortunately too general to be of much service to the warm-hearted, impulsive Princess, before whom lay so many unsuspected pitfalls. Prince Albert believed, as he had said to his son-in-law, that his daughter possessed "a man's head and a child's heart," an allusion to the poet's words, "In wit a man, simplicity a child." But Prussia was not Coburg, and even from Coburg Prince Albert had now been away for nearly twenty years. He does not appear at all to have appreciated either the situation which now confronted the Princess Royal, or how little adapted she was by her temperament and her training to meet it.

In the Princess of Prussia (afterwards the Empress Augusta) her English daughter-in-law ever had a true friend and ally, and during the forty years which followed, the two ladies were on far better terms than anyone could have expected, considering how entirely different had been their upbringing and outlook on life.

For example, Princess Augusta had been taught as a child to *tenir cercle* in the gardens of the Palace at Weimar—that is to say, she had to make the round of the bushes and trees, each of which represented for the moment a lady or gentleman of the Court, and say something pleasant and suitable to each! In this curious but extremely practical fashion was inculcated one of the most fundamentally important duties of Royal personages, and it may be suggested with all respect that the future Empress Frederick would have benefited if she had had some similar training.

The Princess who was to become Queen of

Prussia and the first German Empress had been brought up at Goethe's knee. She belonged, in an intellectual sense, to the eighteenth rather than the nineteenth century. She knew French as well as she knew German—indeed, it is said that she often thought in French, and perhaps her chief friend, at the time of her son's marriage to the Princess Royal, was Monsieur de Bacourt, the French diplomatist to whom the Duchesse de Dino's diary-letters were for the most part addressed. Among her intimates were many Catholics, and for many years it was believed in Berlin that she had been secretly received into the Roman Church. As a young woman she was full of heart and warmth of feeling, but she soon learnt, what her daughter-in-law never succeeded in mastering, the wisdom of circumspection and the painful necessity for prudence. She early made up her mind to remain on the whole in shadow. While never concealing her point of view from those about her, she yet never took any public part in the affairs of State.

During the Crimean War, when the whole of the Prussian Court was pro-Russian, the Princess of Prussia had been pro-English—a fact which naturally endeared her to Queen Victoria, but which had made her Prussian relatives very sore and angry. When the Princess Royal arrived in Berlin as the bride of the King of Prussia's heir-presumptive, the Crimean War was already being forgotten. Among the Liberals there was what may be called a pro-English party, and the joyous simplicity and youthful charm of the Princess silenced criticism, at any rate for a time.

It must be remembered that the Princess Royal had left a young Court. At the time of her marriage her parents were still young people —she made them grandparents when they were only thirty-eight. But the Court in which she now became an important personage was composed of middle-aged men and women, with some very old people. There was still living in the Court circle a lady who was said to remember Frederick the Great. This was the Countess Pauline Neale, who had been one of Queen Louise's ladies-in-waiting. She could recollect with vivid intensity every detail and episode associated with Napoleon's treatment of the King and Queen.

Of great age, too, was the gigantic Field-Marshal Wrangel, who had actually carried the colours of his regiment at the battle of Leipzig.

Another interesting personality in the Princess Royal's new family circle was her husband's aunt, Princess Charles, sister of the Princess of Prussia, who afterwards became the grandmother of the Duchess of Connaught. She still bore traces of the wonderful beauty for which she had been famed in the 'twenties, but was, of course, no longer a young woman.

Not long after the Princess Royal's arrival in

Berlin, a German observer wrote to the Prince Consort: "She sees more clearly and more correctly than many a man of commanding intellect, because, while possessing an acute mind and the purest heart, she does not know the word 'prejudice.'"

Less than a month after her marriage, on February 17, the Prince Consort sent his daughter a letter full of wise warning:

"Your festival time, if not your honeymoon, comes to an end to-day; and on this I take leave to congratulate you, unfeeling though it may sound, for I wish for you the necessary time and tranquillity to digest the many impressions you have received, and which otherwise, like a wild revel, first inflame, and then stupefy, leaving a dull nerveless lassitude behind. Your exertions, and the demands which have been made upon you, have been quite immense; you have done your best, and have won the hearts, or what is called the hearts, of all. In the nature of things we may now expect a little reaction. The public, just because it was rapturous and enthusiastic, will now become minutely critical and take you to pieces anatomically. This is to be kept in view, although it need cause you no uneasiness, for you have only followed your natural bent, and have made no external demonstration which did not answer to the truth of your inner nature. It is only the man who presents an

F

artificial demeanour to the world, who has to dread being unmasked.

" Your place is that of your husband's wife, and of your mother's daughter. You will desire nothing else, but you will also forego nothing of that which you owe to your husband and to your mother. Ultimately your mind will, from the over-excitement, fall back to a little lassitude and sadness. But this will make you feel a craving for activity, and you have much to do, in studying your new country, its tendencies and its people, and in overlooking your household as a good housewife, with punctuality, method, and vigilant care. To success in the affairs of life, apportionment of time is essential, and I hope you will make this your *first* care, so that you may always have some time over for the fulfilment of every duty."

Baron Stockmar had also been watching the details of the Princess's reception in her new country with anxious interest. He, too, saw the danger of a reaction, and he wrote a letter to the Prince Consort, in reply to which the father, after commending the Princess's tact, said :

" The enthusiasm with which she seems to have been everywhere received exceeds our utmost calculations and hopes, and proves that the people approved the idea of this alliance, and have found Vicky in herself answer to their expectations. It is only now, indeed, the difficulties of her life

will begin, and after the excitement of the festivities a certain melancholy will come over the poor
child, however happy she may feel with her husband. With marriage, a new life has opened for
her, and you would have marvelled at the sudden
change and development which even here became
at once apparent.

" We, that is she and I, have, I think, remained,
and I believe will remain, the same to one another.
She continues to set great store by my advice
and my confidence ; I do not thrust them upon
her, but I am always ready to give them. During
this time of troubles she has written less to me,
and communicated the details of her life, and
what she is doing, more to her mother. I had
arranged this with her, but I hold her promise to
impart to me faithfully the progress of her inner
life, and on the other hand have given her mine,
to take a constantly active part in fostering it.
You may be sure I will not fail in this, as I see
in it merely the fulfilment of a sacred duty.

" What you say about an early visit had already
been running in my head, and I will frankly explain what we think on this subject. Victoria
and I are both desirous to have a meeting with
the young couple, somewhere or other in the
course of the year, having moreover given them
a promise that we would. This could only be in
the autumn. A *rendezvous* on the Rhine—for
example at Coblentz—would probably be the right

thing. This does not exclude a flying visit by myself alone, which, if it is to be of any use, must be paid earlier in the year. How and where we could see each other I have naturally weighed, and am myself doubtful whether Berlin is the appropriate place for me. I have therefore come to the conclusion that I might go to Coburg, and give the young people a *rendezvous* there."

The Princess Royal spent her first winter in Berlin in the Old Schlöss. The castle had not been lived in for a considerable time, and to one accustomed to the even then high standard of English living and hygiene, it must have seemed almost mediæval in its lack of comfort, and of what the Princess had been brought up to regard as the bare necessities of life—light, warmth, and plenty of hot water.

The young couple were allotted a suite of splendidly decorated but very dark and gloomy rooms ; and none of the passages or staircases were heated. The Princess, who had always been encouraged to turn her quick mind to practical matters, and who delighted in creating and in making, found her way blocked at every turn owing to the fact that nothing could be done in the Old Schloss without the direct permission of the King. Not only was Frederick William IV in a very bad and mentally peculiar state of health, but to him and to his Queen any attempt to change or modify anything in the ancient pile of buildings where his predecessor had lived savoured of sacrilege. To give one instance, King Frederick William III had died in the very suite of rooms allotted to the Prince and Princess, and his children had piously preserved the "death-chamber," as it was still called, in exactly the same state as it was on the day of his death. This room was situated next to the Princess's boudoir, and every time she went to her bedroom or dressing-room she was obliged to pass through it.

The Old Schloss was widely believed to be haunted, not only by the "White Lady" but by other ghosts, and the door between the Princess Royal's boudoir and the "death-chamber" would sometimes open by itself. One winter evening, the Princess and one of her ladies were sitting together in the boudoir. The lady, who was reading aloud, raised her eyes and suddenly saw the door of the death-chamber, which was covered, like the walls, with blue silk, open noiselessly, as if pushed by an invisible hand. She stopped reading abruptly. The Princess asked nervously, "What's happened? Do you see anything?" The lady answered, "Nothing, ma'am," and, getting up, shut the door.

But it would be absurd to suppose that the Princess allowed the ungraciousness of the King and the material discomforts which surrounded her at this time to cloud the beginning of a singularly happy married life. She threw herself with eager zest into her husband's interests, and for the time she seemed completely merged in him. Having regard to the mental equipment and demands of the Princess, it is obvious that she found in her husband great intellectual gifts. The theory that the Prince was wholly influenced by his wife, who took the lead in all, cannot be maintained. He was nine years older than the Princess, who was little more than a child when they married, and his character and outlook were formed long before. His uncle, Duke Ernest, testifies, on the contrary, to the influence which the Prince exerted over his wife.

It must, however, be acknowledged that Prince Frederick William, especially in these early days, agreed with the Princess in regarding England as a perfect country with a perfect constitution. He was deeply grateful to her for having left an ideally happy home to become his wife, and his entire devotion was shown in many ways. Indeed, the only thing in which the Prince Frederick William of these days seems to have ever withstood the Princess Royal was in his refusal to give up his solitary evening walk in the streets of Berlin. The Princess used to go to bed quite early, and then the Prince would go out and walk about quite unattended.

Years later, in reference to her domestic happiness, the Empress wrote feelingly to a friend: " The peace and blessed calm that I ever found in my home, by the side of my beloved husband, when powerful influences from outside were first distressing me, are blessings which I cannot describe."

Some of the conditions of the Princess Royal's new life were undoubtedly very irksome to her. The tone of the Prussian Court in matters, not only of religion and politics, but also of etiquette, was very much narrower than that of the English Court. She seems to have found it impossible to guard her tongue, to conceal her convictions, or to hold aloof from political discussion. At "home," as she soon very unwisely began to call England, she had been used to say everything she thought from childhood upwards, sure of not being misunderstood, and reticence would have seemed to her mean, if not absolutely dishonest.

It is difficult to say when the Prussian reactionary party first became aware that in the bride of Prince Frederick William they had a determined and a brilliant opponent. It must, however, have been fairly early, for it is on record that during that first winter in Berlin "the very approach of a Tory or a reactionary seemed to freeze her up."

Nor is it easy to see how much her father, watching anxiously from England, knew of this. She continued with unabated enthusiasm those historical and literary studies to which the Prince Consort had accustomed her, and she wrote him a weekly letter, asking his advice on political

questions. She wrote to her mother daily, sometimes twice a day, but it was her father's influence
which really counted with her, and that remained
quite unimpaired. It is reasonable to suppose
that he attributed whatever seemed to annoy and
distress her in Prussian public life to the still
paramount influence of the dying King. But he
evidently did not at any time realise that, though
factious persons might be ready enough to use her
in their own interests, no one in Prussia really
wanted to see a Princess dabbling in politics at
all. Thus, we find the Prince writing to Stockmar
in March 1858 :

" From Berlin the tenor of the news continues
excellent. Vicky appears to go on pleasing, and
being pleased. She is an extremely fortunate,
animating, and tranquillising element in that
region of conflict and indecision."

And again :

" Brunnow had reckoned upon Moustier from
Berlin, whom he would have had in his pocket,
and through him Walewski. Now he gets the
Duke of Malakoff! He has not yet been able to
realise the position, and is by way of being
extremely confidential ; it is he alone who has
made Vicky's marriage popular in Berlin, where
it was at first very unpopular, and he weeps tears
of emotion when he speaks of her ! "

To the Princess herself he wrote also in
March :

"You seem to have taken up your position with much tact. The bandage has been torn from your eyes all at once as regards all the greatest mysteries of life, and you stand not only of a sudden before them, but are called upon to deal with them, and that too on the spur of the moment. 'Oh! It is indeed most hard to be a man,' was the constant cry of the old Würtemberg Minister, von Wangenheim, and he was right!"

The Prince was generally philosophising, but even so the following, written a few days later, seems an extraordinary letter for any father to write to a girl not much over seventeen:

"That you should sometimes be oppressed by home-sickness is most natural. This feeling, which I know right well, will be sure to increase with the sadness which the reviving spring, and the quickening of all nature that comes with it, always develop in the heart. It is a painful yearning, which may exist quite independently of, and simultaneously with, complete contentment and complete happiness. I explain this hard-to-be-comprehended mental phenomenon thus. The identity of the individual is, so to speak, interrupted; and a kind of Dualism springs up by reason of this, that the *I which has been*, with all its impressions, remembrances, experiences, feelings, which were also those of youth, is attached to a particular spot, with its local and personal associations, and appears to what may be called *the new I* like a vestment of the soul which has been lost, from which nevertheless *the new I* cannot disconnect itself, because its identity is in fact continuous. Hence the painful struggle, I might almost say the spasm, of the soul."

To the faithful Stockmar the Prince confided his belief:

"As to Vicky, unquestionably she will turn out a very distinguished character, whom Prussia will have cause to bless."

The Prince's cherished scheme of a visit to Coburg began to take shape, and he writes:

"My whole stay in Coburg can only be for six days. To see you and Fritz together in a quiet homely way without visits of ceremony, &c.—I dare not picture it to myself too strongly. Talk it over with Fritz, and let me know if I can count on you, but do not let the plan get wind, otherwise people will be paying us visits, and our meeting will lose its pleasant private character."

Another letter, dated April 28, is interesting as showing that the Prince was beginning to perceive some of the difficulties in his daughter's path:

"What you are now living through, observing, and doing, are the most important experiences, impressions and acts of your life, for they are the first of a life independent and responsible to itself. That outside of and in close proximity to your true and tranquillising happiness with dear Fritz your path of life is not wholly smooth, I regard as a most fortunate circumstance for you, inasmuch as it forces you to exercise and strengthen the powers of your mind."

Nothing that concerned her but was of moment to her father:

"I am delighted to see by your letter that you deliberate gravely upon your budget, and I shall be most happy to look through it, if you send it to me; this is the only way to have a clear idea to one's self of what one has, spends, and ought to spend. As this is a business of which I have had long and frequent experience, I will give you one rule for your guidance in it, namely, to set apart a considerable balance *pour l'imprévu*. This gentleman is the costliest of guests in life, and we shall look very blank if we have nothing to set before him."

During the first summer of their married life, the Prince and Princess set up quite a modest establishment at the Castle of Babelsberg, and this made the Princess very happy.

Seated on a declivity of a richly-wooded hill, about three miles from Potsdam, and looking down upon a fine expanse of water, the little Castle of Babelsberg commands a charming view of the surrounding country. "Everything there," wrote Queen Victoria on her first visit, "is very small, a Gothic *bijou*, full of furniture, and flowers (creepers), which they arrange very prettily

round screens, and lamps, and pictures.   There
are many irregular turrets and towers and steps."

It was at Babelsberg that the Princess Royal
began to try and see something of the intellectual
and artistic world of Berlin.   Neither the husband
nor the wife was under the dominion of the class
and caste prejudices which even now are so
astonishing a feature of German social life, and
which were then even more powerful and far-
reaching.   That the Prince and Princess should
appear actually to enjoy the society of mere painters
and writers and scientists, whether they occupied
any official positions or not, seemed extraordinary
and highly improper to the whole bureaucratic
element of Berlin, and must, we can well imagine,
have seriously offended the Prince's father.

It is easy to be wise after the event.   No one
now can help seeing that it would have been the
truest wisdom for the young Princess to have
rigidly suppressed her natural tastes and intellectual interests, and to have led a life of the narrowly
conventional character which Prussian princesses
were expected to lead.   But she was incapable of
such self-suppression, which would have seemed
to her deceitful, and the mild cautions and hints
at prudence in her father's letters were pathetically
inadequate to the needs of her critical position.
She was herself still quite unaware of how closely
she was being watched and criticised.   "I am
very happy," she told a guest at one of the Court

receptions, "and I am intensely proud of belonging to this country."

The more the Princess's social preferences aroused the suspicion and indignation of the Court world, the more popular she became with the "intellectuals," unfortunately not a profitable exchange for her as she was then situated. We become aware of this by a passage in the *Reminiscences* of Professor Schellbach, who had been mathematical tutor to Prince Frederick William. He writes:

"The first words which the Princess addressed to me with the greatest kindness were, 'I love mathematics, physics, and chemistry.' I was much pleased, for I saw that the Prince must have given her a pleasant account of me. Under the direction of her highly cultivated father, who had himself studied it, Princess Victoria had become acquainted with natural science, and had even received her first teaching from such famous men as Faraday and Hoffman. Our beloved Princess soon revealed her love for art and science, as well as her pleasure in setting problems of her own. Her Royal Highness at first tried to go on with her studies in physics and mathematics under my direction, but soon her artistic work took up the remainder of time which the requirements of Court life left to her."

Early in June Prince Albert carried out his plan of visiting his daughter and son-in-law, but it was at Babelsberg, not at Coburg, as he had hoped. He was able to report to Queen Victoria: "The relation between the young people is all that can be desired. I have had long talks with them both, singly and together, which gave me the greatest satisfaction."

Prince Albert was, however, shocked to find the King of Prussia in a terrible state:

"The King looks frightfully ill; he was very cordial and friendly, and for the half hour he stayed with us, did not once get confused, but complained greatly about his state of health. He is thin and fallen away over his whole body, with a large stomach, his face grown quite small. He made many attempts at joking in the old way, but with a voice quite broken, and features full of pain. *'Wenn ich einmal fort bin, wieder fort bin,'* he said, grasping his forehead and striking it, 'then the Queen must pay us a visit here, it will make me so happy.' What he meant was, *'Wenn ich wieder wohl bin.'* 'It is so tedious,' he murmured; thus it is plainly to be seen that he has not quite given up all thought of getting better. The Prince's whole aim is to be serviceable to his brother. He still walks very lame, but looks well. I kept quietly in the house all day with Vicky, who is very sensible and good."

The Princess had special reasons for being "sensible" at this time, for, to the great joy of the Prussian Royal family, she was enceinte.

In August, Queen Victoria and the Prince Consort paid a visit of some length to their daughter. The Queen herself describes the visit as " quite private and unofficial," although - she carried in her train not only Lord Malmesbury, the Foreign Secretary in Lord Derby's Government (which had been formed in February), but also Lord Clarendon, his predecessor, and Lord Granville, who had been Lord President of the Council in Palmerston's Government.

Prince Albert, at any rate, did not neglect the opportunity of studying the political situation. He wrote to Stockmar a letter highly approving the Prince of Prussia's political views, while his son-in-law he described as firm in his constitutional principles and despising the Manteuffel Ministry, the members of which he met with obvious coolness.

The Berliners gave a hearty reception to Queen Victoria and Prince Albert, and the Queen declared to the Burgomaster of Berlin that she felt exceedingly happy there, because she had realised with what love and devotion everyone was attached to the Royal house and to her daughter.

She was delighted with old Wrangel, whom she calls a great character. " He was full of Vicky and the marriage, and said she was an angel." There was a great deal of sight-seeing, mitigated by charming little *gemuthlich* family dinners, and a grand review at Potsdam.

Prince Albert's birthday occurred during the visit, and one of the Queen's presents to him was "a paper-weight of Balmoral granite and deer's teeth designed by Vicky." "Vicky gave her portrait, a small oil one by Hartmann, very like though not flattered, and a drawing by herself. There were two birthday-cakes. Vicky had ordered one with as many lights as Albert numbered years, which is the Prussian custom."

Her Majesty notes with pleasure the arrival of "our dear, excellent old friend Stockmar," whose presence, however, by no means gave universal satisfaction. Indeed, Sir Theodore Martin says frankly that, although his visit was due solely to his desire to meet the Queen and Prince Consort, it was viewed with rancorous suspicion by the aristocratic party, who held in abhorrence the man whom they knew to be the great advocate for the establishment of constitutional government in Germany. He was even accused of actively intriguing for the downfall of the Manteuffel Administration, having, it was said, "brought in his pocket, all cut and dry from England, the Ministry of the new era."

Stockmar's views of what was needful to raise Germany to her proper place among the nations were unchanged, but age and infirmity had for some time made him a mere looker-on. Nevertheless, it is probable that neither the Queen nor Prince Albert in the least realised how inadvisable, in the interests of the Princess Royal, was the old man's visit.

It must not, however, be thought that the Prussians were indifferent to the Princess Royal's singular personal charm. We have a most interesting glimpse of this in a long letter written to Queen Victoria by the beautiful and brilliant Duchess of Manchester, herself a Hanoverian by birth, who afterwards married the Duke of Devonshire and for many years held a remarkable position in English society.

The Duchess relates how well the Princess Royal was looking during the manœuvres on the Rhine, and how much she seemed to be beloved, not only by all those who knew her, but also by those who had only seen and heard of her.

" The English could not help feeling proud of the way the Princess Royal was spoken of, and the high esteem she is held in. For one so young it is a most flattering position, and certainly, as the Princess's charm of manner and her kind unaffected words had in that short time won her the hearts of all the officers and strangers present, one was not astonished at the praise the Prussians themselves bestow on her Royal Highness. The Prussian Royal Family is so large, and their opinions politically and socially sometimes so different, that it must have been very difficult indeed at first for the Princess Royal, and people therefore cannot praise enough the high principles,

G

great discretion, sound judgment, and cleverness her Royal Highness has invariably displayed."

And the Duchess adds, on the authority of Field-Marshal Wrangel, that the soldiers were particularly delighted to see the Princess on horseback and without a veil.

The Royal visit to Babelsberg came to an end all too soon, and the leave-taking was tearful and emotional in the extreme. Queen Victoria wrote with natural feeling, " All would be comparatively easy, were it not for the one thought that I cannot be with her at the very critical moment when every other mother goes to her child ! "

In the October of that first year of the Princess Royal's married life, her father-in-law became permanent Regent, owing to the continued mental incapacity of King Frederick William IV. This filled the young Princess with intense satisfaction, which was increased when the new Prince Regent declared it to be his intention strictly to adhere to the letter and the spirit of the Constitution of 1850. The great bulk of the nation rallied instantly round him, and it seemed as if the gulf between the House of Hohenzollern and the people of Prussia had been suddenly bridged. The Manteuffel Ministry fell in the following month, a general election produced an enormous Liberal majority, and the hopes of the Constitutionalists ran high. The Manteuffel Ministry was succeeded by one of which Prince Charles Anthony of

Hohenzollern was the President.   From this time forward Prince Frederick William regularly at-tended the meetings of the Ministry, and Privy Councillor Brunnemann was assigned to him as a kind of secretary and channel of communication on State affairs.

The Princess Royal imprudently expressed to a gentleman of the Court her satisfaction at the change in the political situation, and her words, being repeated and exaggerated, gave great offence to the Conservative party, which was also the party of the King.   The Princess's satisfaction was of course shared by her father, who wrote to the sympathetic Stockmar a letter showing no prevision of that great rock of Army administration on which these high hopes were destined to be wrecked :

" The Regency seems now to have been secured for the Prince.   We have only news of this at present by telegrams from our children, but are greatly delighted at this first step towards the reduction to order of a miserable chaos.   Will the Prince have the courage to surround himself with honourable and patriotic men ?   That is the question, and what shape will the new Chamber take, and what will its influence on him be ? "

On November 20, 1858, Prince and Princess Frederick William moved into the palace in Unter den Linden which was henceforth to be their residence in Berlin ; and on the following day, the Princess's eighteenth birthday, there was a kind of dedicatory service in the palace chapel, which was attended by all the members of the Royal House.

This palace had been the scene of the happy life of the Prince's grandfather, King Frederick William III, and of Queen Louise. The intimate and beautiful family life that had filled these rooms was the best of omens for the young pair, and the Princess Royal was delighted with her new home. But the palace required to be brought up to modern standards of comfort, and it was very difficult to have the alterations approved by the moody and violent King. What he allowed on one day he took back with hasty blame on the morrow. At last Prince Frederick William obtained the Royal assent to those alterations which were absolutely urgent, together with a grant of 350,000 thalers. Among other improvements was added an eight-cornered " Gedenkhalle " or " Memory-Hall," in which were placed the numerous wedding presents of the young pair, and to these, from time to time, were added other rare and beautiful objects.

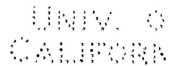

CHAPTER VI

BIRTH OF THE ELDEST SON

ON January 27, 1859, Berlin was on the tip-toe of expectation. The custom is that 101 guns announce the birth of a Prince, and only twenty-one that of a Princess, and as in Prussia the Salic Law still obtains, it may easily be imagined with what anxiety the Berliners counted the successive discharges. There was indeed no need to wait for the whole tale of the 101 guns, for the firing of the twenty-second was enough to spread the glad news.

The story goes that when old Field-Marshal Wrangel, "Papa Wrangel" as the Berliners affectionately called him, left the palace, the populace crowded round him and demanded to know what he could tell them. "Children," he answered, "all is well! It is as fine and sturdy a recruit as one could wish!"

It soon became known, however, that all had not gone well with the young mother and her child. There had been one of those unfortunate mishaps, the exact truth of which it is always so difficult to disentangle, but the following account, we believe, represents what actually happened:

It had been Queen Victoria's wish that the Princess should be attended in her confinement by Dr. Martin, her English doctor, as well as the German Court physicians. About eight o'clock in the morning of January 27, one of the latter wrote to his English colleague, asking him to come at once to the Palace. But the servant to whom the letter was entrusted, instead of taking it to Dr. Martin's house, put it in the post, and it never reached him till the afternoon. To that fact the Princess Royal's friends always attributed the circumstances which resulted in the weakness of the infant's left arm. Be that as it may, both mother and baby were for a time in imminent danger. No anæsthetic was administered, and the Princess with characteristic courage looked up to her husband, who held her in his arms the whole time, and asked him to forgive her for being impatient. None of those about her thought her strength would hold out, and one of the German doctors actually said in her presence that he thought she would die, and her baby too. But at last her ordeal came to an end, and to her intense joy she was told that she had given birth to a fine healthy boy.

The news of the birth of their first grandchild was quickly flashed to the anxious parents at Windsor. " A boy " ran the telegram, and Queen Victoria characteristically replied, " Is it a fine boy?" But it was not till the following day, so Prince

Albert told Stockmar, that the courier brought "our first information of the severe suffering which poor Vicky had undergone, and of the great danger in which the child's life had hovered for a time." To King Leopold the Prince wrote, " The danger for the child and the sufferings for the mother were serious.   Poor Fritz and the Prince and Princess must have undergone terrible anxiety, as they had no hope of the birth of a living child, and their joy over a strong, healthy boy is therefore all the greater."

On the evening of the baby's birth, the Prince Regent, also a grandfather for the first time, held a reception of which we have a vivid description from the pen of the dramatist, Gustav zu Putlitz, then a member of the Prussian Landtag, and afterwards chamberlain to Princess Frederick William.   He says: /

" It was like a great family festival.   Everyone hurried there with congratulations, and when the young father, beaming with happiness, appeared, the rejoicings increased.   This delight is shared by all classes of society, and is a testimony to the extent of the popularity of the Prince and Princess."

Prince Frederick William received on January 29 the congratulations of the Prussian Chambers, to which he made the following reply :

" I thank you very heartily for the interest you have shown in the joyful event, which is of such consequence to my family and to the country. If God should preserve my son's life, it shall be my chief endeavour to bring him up in the opinions and sentiments which bind me to the Fatherland. It is nearly a year ago to-day since I told you how deeply moved I was by the universal sympathy which was exhibited towards me, as a young married man, by the country as a whole. This sympathy it was which made the Princess, my wife, who had left her home to come to a new Fatherland, realise those ties of affection which have now, owing to the birth of this son, become unbreakable. May God therefore bless our efforts to bring up our son to be worthy of the love which has been thus early manifested towards him. The Princess, to whom I was able to communicate your intention, desires me to express her most sincere thanks."

The christening was fixed for March 5, but neither of the parents of the Princess could be present. "I don't think I ever felt so bitterly disappointed," wrote the Queen to Uncle Leopold. "It almost breaks my heart. And then it is an occasion so gratifying to both nations and brings them so much together that it is peculiarly mortifying." However, the Queen consoled herself by doing all she could to mark the importance of the occasion. She sent a formal mission to represent her and the Prince Consort at the christening, consisting of Lord Raglan, the son of the victor of the Alma, Inkerman, and Balaclava, and Captain (afterwards Lord) de Ros, equerry to Prince Albert. They were both old friends of the Princess, to whom her father wrote :

" I was certain that the presence of Lord Raglan and Captain de Ros would give you pleasure. Ours will come when they return, and we can put questions to them. My first will be : Has the Princess gone out ? and does she begin to enjoy the air, to which alone she can look for regaining strength and health ? Or is she in the way to grow weak and watery by being baked like a bit of pastry in hot rooms ? My second : Is she grown ? I will spare you my others.

" Your description of the Prince's kindness and loving sympathy for you makes me very happy. I love him dearly, and respect and value him, and I am glad too, for his sake, that in you and my little grandchild he has found ties of family happiness which cannot fail to give him those domestic tastes, in which alone in the long run life's true contentment is to be found."

The baby Prince was duly christened on March 5, when he received the names of Frederick William Victor Albert, and on the following day his parents issued a touching expression of their gratitude for the sympathy and congratulations they had received from the public. In it they pledged themselves afresh to bring up their son, with the help of God, to the honour and service of the Fatherland.

After the special envoys had returned from Berlin, the Prince writes to his daughter a letter on the duties of motherhood, which was decidedly candid for those rather prudish days :

" Lord Raglan's and Captain de Ros's news of you have given me great pleasure. But I gather from them that you look rather languid and exhausted. Some sea air would be the right thing for you ; it is what does all newly-made mothers the most good when their ' campaign is over.' I am, however, delighted to hear you have begun to get into the air. Now pass on as soon as possible to cold washing, shower baths, &c., so as to brace the system again, and to restore elasticity to the nerves and muscles.

" You are now eighteen years old, and you will hold your own against many a buffet in life ; still, you will encounter many for which you were not prepared and which you would fain have been spared. You must arm yourself against these, like Austria against the chance of war, otherwise you will break down and drop into a sickly state, which would be disastrous to yourself, and inflict a frightful burden upon poor Fritz for life ; besides which, it would unfit you for fulfilling all the duties of your station.

" In reference to having children, the French proverb says : *Le premier pour la santé, le second pour la beauté, le troisième gâte tout.* But England proves that the last part of the saying is not true, and health and beauty, those two great blessings, are only injured where the wife does not make zealous use of the intervals to repair the exhaustion, undoubtedly great, of the body, and to strengthen it both for what it has gone and what it has to go through, and where also the intervals are not sufficiently long to leave the body the necessary time to recruit."

The Princess had a favourable convalescence, during which her active mind was troubled by an article on Freemasonry. Her father, to whom of course she turned for counsel, had never consented to be initiated as a Mason, though his sons, King Edward and the Duke of Connaught, both became enthusiastic members of the craft. The Princess seems to have been troubled by the idea that her husband's connection with the order—he had been appointed patron of the Masonic Lodges of Prussia and head of the Grand Lodge in Berlin—would in some way lessen the confidence between them. Prince Albert endeavours to reassure her with a paradox which she probably found quite unconvincing :

" I will get Alice to read to me the article about Freemasons. It is not likely to contain the whole secret. The circumstance which provokes you only into finding fault with the Order, namely that husbands dare not communicate the secret of it to their wives, is just one of its best features. If *to be able to be silent* is one of the chief virtues of the husband, then the test which puts him in opposition to that being towards whom he constantly shows the greatest weakness, is the hardest of all, and therefore the most compendious of virtues, and the wife should not only rejoice to see him capable of withstanding such a test, but should take occasion out of it to vie with him in virtue by taming the inborn curiosity which she inherits from her mother Eve. If the subject of the secret, moreover, be nothing more important than an apron, then every chance is given to virtue on both sides, without disturbing the confidence of marriage, which ought to be complete."

The baby Prince William thrived, in spite of the defect in his left arm, which was shorter than the other. We have some entertaining glimpses of him, and of his parents' pride in him, in the correspondence of Priscilla Lady Westmorland. A German friend of hers, a lady of high rank, wrote to Lady Westmorland when the Prince was only about a week old :

" I must tell you of my wonderful good fortune —I have actually seen this precious child in his father's arms ! You will ask me what this child of so many prayers and wishes is like. They say all babies are alike : I do not think so : this one has a beautiful complexion, pink and white, and the most lovely little hand ever seen ! The nose rather large ; the eyes were shut, which was as well, as the light was so strong. His happy father was holding him in his arms, and himself showed traces of all he has gone through at the time. The child was believed to be dead, so you may conceive the ecstasy of everyone at his first cry."

Prince Frederick William was indeed, as this lady put it, beside himself with joy. He delighted in showing his baby to his friends and loyal servants, calling him " mein Junge."

In the early summer of 1859 the Princess Royal spent a happy holiday at Osborne, and her English relatives and friends thought her extraordinarily well and happy; it was also considered that she had become much better looking. The Queen describes her as " flourishing, and so well and gay," and as " a most charming companion," while Prince Albert tells Stockmar that " We found Vicky very well, and looking blooming, somewhat grown, and in excellent spirits. The short stay here will certainly be beneficial both to her health and spirits."

While the Princess was in England, she was asked by her parents if she would make private inquiries as to any German princesses who might be suited to become Princess of Wales, but the search does not seem to have been successful. It was then that Sir Augustus Paget, who had been for two years British Minister in Copenhagen, spoke to his fiancée, the Princess Royal's lady-in-waiting, of Princess Alexandra. It was from this lady, now Walpurga Lady Paget, that Queen Victoria and the Prince Consort first heard of the beauty and many endearing graces of the Danish princess. So impressed were they by her account that it was arranged that the Princess Royal should meet Princess Alexandra informally at Strelitz, in the palace of the Grand Duchess of Mecklenburg.

This meeting duly took place, and the Princess Royal wrote most enthusiastically of the result of their informal interview. It was directly owing to this fact that it was settled that the Prince of Wales and Princess Alexandra should meet, as if by chance, in the cathedral of Spiers with a view to making close acquaintance.

The birth of Prince William brought a considerable change in the lives of his parents. Babelsberg had become too small to make a convenient summer home, and so the King granted them the use of the New Palace at Potsdam, which is only about half an hour's journey from Berlin.

This enormous rococo building with its two hundred rooms was erected by Frederick the Great at the end of the Seven Years' War, in order to show his enemies that he had plenty of money still left with which to go to war again if necessary. Prince Frederick William was very fond of the New Palace, where he had himself been born, and which was full of reminders of his great namesake. Apparently the only thing he did not like about it was its name, for it will be remembered that during his brief reign he altered it to Friedrichskron.

Queen Victoria, on her visit to Babelsberg in

August, 1858, had gone to see the Palace, and she describes it in her diary as " a splendid building that reminded me much of Hampton Court—the same colour, same style, same kind of garden, with splendid orange trees which in the cool calm evening sent out a delicious smell. The Garten-Saal, one enormous hall, all in marble with incrustations of stones, opening into a splendid room or gallery, reminded me of the Salle des Glaces at Versailles. There is a theatre in the Palace, and many splendid fêtes have been given there. There are some rooms done in silver, like those at Sans Souci and Potsdam, and all in very rich Renaissance style. The millions it must have cost ! But none of these palaces are *wohnlich* (liveable in). None like dear Babelsberg ! "

The Princess Royal was determined to make at any rate her own rooms in the Palace *wohnlich*. After the fashion of the period, she surrounded herself with portraits of her relations, and with paintings of her various beloved English homes. There were endless souvenirs of her childhood scattered about in her rooms—souvenirs of her Christmases and of birthdays, little gifts presented to her as a child and young girl by her grandmother, by her " Aunt Gloucester," and by all those who had surrounded her during the days of her happy youth.

It is curious to reflect that, twenty years after the Princess Royal first took up her residence there, an English visitor was to write : " Without

Carlyle's *Frederick the Great*, Potsdam would be a collection of mere dead walls enclosing a number of costly objects. Illuminated by the book, each room, each garden wall thrills with human interest." But when the Princess Royal first went there to make the New Palace her home for a part of each year, it might much more truly have been described as an arid and dusty waste, and that though it was surrounded by many waters. The gardens were very stiff, indeed ugly, but the Princess's active, creative mind saw their possibilities, and under her fostering hand and taste they were transformed and made to yield the utmost of beauty and delight.

The New Palace henceforth became associated, in the minds of all those who were truly attached to the Princess, with all that was best and most peaceful in her life. It was there that she was able to set the example of that helpful and happy country life which she had learned to value in England, and it was not long before its simple domestic character became known far and wide, and exercised an influence the extent of which it is impossible to estimate.

The Prince and Princess had a farm at Bornstedt, not far off, and there the Prince delighted to become for the time a simple farmer, managing himself all the details of the crops and the labourers, while the Princess occupied herself with the poultry and her model dairy. It may, indeed, be doubted whether the Prince and Princess found the farm a very good investment financially, but that was of small importance compared with the spiritual refreshment which they derived from this close periodical contact with the simple, natural gifts of mother earth.

Among the neighbouring villagers, too, they found plenty of scope for the exercise of an intelligent philanthropy, in gradually modifying the primitive ideas then prevalent on sanitation, and in caring for the children and the old people. The Prince would himself sometimes teach in the village schools. A pretty story is told that one day, when he was questioning a class, he asked a little girl to what kingdom his watch-chain and a flower in his button-hole respectively belonged, and when she had answered correctly, he went on to ask, "To what kingdom do I belong?" and the child replied, "To the kingdom of Heaven."

In June, 1859, the war between Austria and the allied French and Sardinian armies, culminating in the defeat of the Austrians at Solferino, brought natural anxieties to the Princess. The Prince Regent, while declaring the neutrality of Prussia, nevertheless ordered a mobilisation of the Army for the protection of Germany, and Major-General Prince Frederick William, commanding the First Infantry Brigade of Guards, was appointed to the command of the First Infantry Division of Guards. Though the Princess, thus

H

early in her married life, showed by her quietude that she was a true soldier's wife, it was a great relief to her when the threatened danger was over and the mobilisation rescinded on the conclusion of the Peace of Villafranca in July.   Prince Frederick William's promotion to command a division was then confirmed by his father.

The political situation, however, remained difficult, and Prince Albert and his daughter watched it with anxious concern.   The following passage in a letter of his dated September is no doubt in reply to some comments of hers on the position of Prussia and Germany in view of the rising agitation for unity in Italy :

" I am for Prussia's hegemony ; still *Germany* is for me first in importance, Prussia as Prussia second.   Prussia will become the chief if she stand at the head of Germany : if she merely seek to drag Germany down to herself, she will not herself ascend.   She must, therefore, be magnanimous, act as one with the German nation in a self-sacrificing spirit, prove that she is not bent on aggrandisement, and then she will gain pre-eminence, and keep it," and he goes on to point the moral in the sacrifices which Sardinia had already made for the Italian idea.

In November the Princess Royal paid a visit to England with her husband in time to celebrate the Prince of Wales's birthday on the 9th, and Prince Albert tells Stockmar :

" We find the Princess Royal looking extremely well, and in the highest spirits, infinitely lively, loving, and mentally active. In knowledge of the world, she has made great progress." The visit lasted till December 3, and Prince Albert wrote to the Dowager Duchess of Coburg that Prince Frederick William " has delighted us much. Vicky has developed greatly of late, and yet remains quite a child ; of such indeed is the kingdom of Heaven."

And after his daughter had gone back to Berlin, the loving father wrote to her :

" Your dear visit has left upon us the most delightful impression ; you were well, full of life and freshness, and withal matured. I may therefore yield to the feeling, sweetest of all to my heart as your father, that you will be lastingly happy. In this feeling I wait without apprehension for what fate may bring."

On this visit to England the Princess did not fail to see her old friend and ruler, Sarah Lady Lyttelton, who records :

" The dear Princess came in, habited and hatted and cockfeathered from her ride, looking very well though in a *very* bad cold. She embraced me and received me *most* kindly, and took me into her magnificent sitting-room, where I spent almost an hour with her, till she had to go and change her dress for luncheon. She talked much of her baby and inquired after everybody belonging to me and seemed as happy as ever."

CHAPTER VII

ADVICE FROM ENGLAND

THE year 1860 was on the whole a happy one for the Princess Royal. It brought her a long visit from her parents and the birth of her eldest daughter, but on the other side of the account the relations between her two countries, England and Prussia, became perceptibly worse.

For the New Year her father sent her one of his customary letters of sagacious counsel, in which may be detected a certain note of uneasiness as to the development of his daughter's powers of self-control :

" You enter upon the New Year with hopes, which God will surely graciously suffer to be fulfilled, but you do also with good resolutions, whose fulfilment lies within your own hand and must necessarily contribute to your success, also happiness, in this suffering and difficult world. Hold firmly by these resolutions, and evermore cherish the determination, with which comes also the strength, to exercise unlimited control over yourself, that the moral law may govern and the propensity obey,—the end and aim of all education and culture, as we long ago discovered and reasoned out together."

It is remarkable that early in this year Prince
Frederick William appears to have been for a
time the centre of the hopes of the reactionary
party. The Junkers actually planned to bring
about the resignation of the Prince Regent, and to
induce Prince Frederick William to assume the
supreme power and govern without a constitution,
which formed the great obstacle to their military
ambitions. This scheme argued an extraordinary
misapprehension, not only of Prince Frederick
William's honest, straightforward character, but
also of all his political ideals. He was, especially
at this period of his life, a pure Constitutionalist,
with a profound admiration for the free polity of
England, and it would be difficult to imagine any
form of government which would have seemed
both to him and to his wife more immoral, as well
as more certain to entail a counter-revolution, than
a military dictatorship. It is perhaps not without
significance that in March a British warship was
launched at Portsmouth and was named *Frederick
William* by way of compliment to the husband of
the Princess Royal.

In June there was a parade at the Königsberg
garrison, at which the Prince Regent said to his
son, "Fritz, I appoint you to the First Infantry
Regiment, the oldest Corps in the service," and
about a month afterwards the young commander
was promoted to the rank of Lieutenant-General.

The Princess Royal's eldest daughter was born

on July 24, and was christened Victoria Augusta Charlotte, being known as Princess Charlotte till her marriage in 1878 to the Hereditary Prince of Saxe-Meiningen.   Queen Victoria records the news of the baby's birth in her usual vivid style :

" Soon after we sat down to breakfast came a telegram from Fritz—Vicky had got a daughter at 8.10, and both were well! What joy! Children jumping about—everyone delighted—so thankful and relieved."

Only the day before there had come a letter from the Princess Royal containing the intelligence that Prince Louis of Hesse was ardently desirous of paying his addresses to Princess Alice, the Princess Royal's much-loved sister and companion of her childhood.   To this Prince Albert refers in writing to his daughter :

" Only two words of hearty joy can I offer to the dear newly-made mother, and these come from an overflowing heart.   The little daughter is a kindly gift from heaven, that will (as I trust) procure for you many a happy hour in the days to come.   The telegraph speaks only of your doing well; may this be so in the fullest sense !

" Upon the subject of your last interesting and most important letter, I have replied to Fritz, who will communicate to you as much of my answer as is good for you under present circumstances.   Alice is very grateful for your love and kindness to her, and the young man behaves in a manner truly admirable."

A few days later the anxious father writes to the young mother one of his curious medical homilies :

" I hope you are very quiet, and keep this well in mind, that although you are well, and feel yourself well, the body has to take on a new conformation, and the nervous system a new life. Only rest of brain, heart, and body, along with good nourishment, and its assimilation by regular undisturbed digestion, can restore the animal forces. My physiological treatise should not bore you, for it is always good to keep the GREAT PRINCIPLES in view, in accordance with which we have to regulate our actions."

But it was not all physiological treatise that was despatched from Osborne to Berlin. The Prince has an amusing reference to the busy importance with which the little Princess Beatrice, who was then three and a quarter years old, regarded the arrival of her first niece :

"The little girl must be a darling. Little maidens are much prettier than boys. I advise her to model herself after her Aunt Beatrice. That excellent lady has now not a moment to spare. 'I have no time,' she says, when she is asked for anything, 'I must write letters to my niece.'

" It will make you laugh, if I tell you that I

have christened a black mare Ayah (as black nurse). I lately asked the groom what was the horse's name, which I had forgotten. 'Haya,' was the answer. 'What?' I asked. 'We spell it Hay, Why, Hay.' You should call your West-phalian nurse, 'Hay, Why, Hay!'"

It had been arranged that the Queen and Prince Albert should pay their visit to their daughter and son-in-law at Coburg at the end of September. By a most unfortunate chance there had occurred about the middle of the month one of those "in-cidents" which are sometimes, when mishandled by officialdom and magnified by offended national pride, allowed to exercise an influence ludicrously disproportionate to their real triviality. The Mac-donald affair, as it was called, at one moment threatened to bring about a serious breach between England and Prussia, and as it was unquestion-ably one of the causes of the dislike and suspicion with which the Princess Royal was to be regarded by a section of the Prussians, it is worth while to record it in some detail.

A Scottish gentleman, a certain Captain Mac-donald, had a dispute about a seat in a railway carriage at Bonn. He knew no German, was ignorant of Prussian law, and very likely behaved, or was considered by the authorities to have behaved, in an autocratic manner. However that may be, he was not only ejected from the carriage but was committed to prison, where he remained from September 12 to 18.   On the 18th he was tried and fined twenty thalers and costs.   The English residents at Bonn warmly espoused his cause, and Captain Macdonald seems, apart from the original dispute, to have had reason to complain of violence used to him and also of his treatment while in prison.   It was also particularly unfortunate that at the trial the Staatsprocurator, or public prosecutor, should have denounced the behaviour when abroad of English people generally.   "The English residing and travelling," he said, "are notorious for the rudeness, impudence, and boorish arrogance of their conduct."

This accusation, whether well founded or not, naturally seemed to English lawyers and the English public a piece of gratuitous irrelevance, intended merely to excite prejudice against Captain Macdonald.   It is impossible now to apportion the blame for the way in which the incident was allowed to embitter public opinion in both countries.   The affair dragged on for months—indeed, it was not finally disposed of till the following May.   There were questions in Parliament, Lord Palmerston was extremely angry, and an article in the *Times* served to pour oil on the flame.

In the circumstances the incident inevitably rather dashed the joy of the happy family party at Coburg.   The Queen conferred with Lord John Russell, then Foreign Secretary, whom she had brought with her, and she alludes in her journal to

" the ejection and imprisonment (unfairly, it seems) of a Captain Macdonald, and the subsequent offensive behaviour of the authorities. It has led to ill blood, and much correspondence, but Lord John is very reasonable about it, and not inclined to do anything rash. These foreign governments are very arbitrary and violent, and our people apt to give offence, and to pay no regard to the laws of the country."

The Queen and Prince Albert arrived at Coburg on September 25, and the Princess Royal delighted in visiting with her father the scenes of his boyhood. She went with the guns to a drive of wild boars, and almost every day there was an expedition to some interesting place in all the relief of *incognito*. One day Prince Albert had a narrow escape. He was alone in an open carriage when the horses ran away. With great presence of mind, he jumped out, and happily got off with nothing worse than a few cuts and bruises. Gustav Freytag, the distinguished German novelist and dramatist, was received, and the Queen records that there was much conversation with him after dinner. As we shall see later, Freytag was admitted to the confidence of the Princess Royal and her husband, and he repaid their kindness in strange fashion.

It was on this visit that the Queen saw her eldest grandchild for the first time. Writing on September 25, she says :

" Our darling grandchild was brought.   Such a little love !   He came walking in at Mrs. Hobbs's [his nurse's] hand, in a little white dress with black bows, and was so good.   He is a fine, fat child, with a beautiful white soft skin, very fine shoulders and limbs, and a very dear face, like Vicky and Fritz, and also Louise of Baden.   He has Fritz's eyes and Vicky's mouth, and very fair curly hair. We felt so happy to see him at last ! "

This was the beginning of an enduring friendship between grandmother and grandson, and no one with any historical imagination can help recalling the last scene of that friendship, when this fine little boy, grown to be a mighty Emperor, hastened to share the grief of the English people at the death-bed of their great Queen.

The Queen was evidently much attracted by the already characteristic energy of the little Prince, for there are references to him all through her records of this visit :

" Dear little William came to me as he does every morning.   He is such a darling, so intelligent."   " Dear little Wilhelm as usual with me before dinner—a darling child."   " The dear little boy is so intelligent and pretty, so good and affectionate."   " Had a last visit from dear Stockmar.   Towards the end of his stay, dear little William came in and played about the room." " The darling little boy with us for nearly an hour, running about so dearly and merrily."   " At

Cologne our darling little William was brought into our carriage to bid good-bye. I felt the parting deeply."

Prince Albert wrote to the Duchess of Kent:

" Your great-grandson is a very pretty, clever child—a compound of both parents, just as it should be."

Mrs. Georgina Hobbs, the nurse mentioned above, first went to Germany as a maid in the service of the Princess Royal on her marriage, and was afterwards promoted to be chief nurse to the Royal children. Prince William and his brother and sisters were devotedly attached to " Hobbsy," as they called her, and it was from " Hobbsy " that they learnt English, for their parents always talked German to one another.

The Princess Royal, perhaps naturally, preferred to have her children's nursery arranged and conducted on the English rather than on the German model, but who can doubt that in this, as in other matters of even less importance, she would have done better to have studied the susceptibilities of her adopted country? Indeed, Dr. Hinzpeter, who was afterwards appointed the tutor of her sons, bears witness that her nursery management became a great subject of gossip among the Berliners, and stories were even current of corporal punishment administered before the Court to princes with dirty faces. It is true that Dr. Hinzpeter describes these stories as mythical, but

the fact that they were circulated and believed
helps to account for the Princess's growing unpopularity.

At this period Prince Albert was seriously disturbed by the attacks which the *Times* was constantly making on Prussia and everything Prussian.
In an article in the *Saturday Review*, recommended by him to his daughter, it was said:
" The only reason the *Times* ever gives for its
dislike of Prussia, is that the Prussian and English
Courts are connected by personal ties, and that
British independence demands that everything pro-
ceeding from the Court should be watched with
the most jealous suspicion."

The Prince was honestly indifferent to the in-
sinuations against himself by which these attacks
were frequently pointed, but he was reasonably
anxious about the bad effect they would have in
Germany.   Writing to his daughter on October 24,
after his return to England, he refers to the Macdonald affair, which had already become acute :

" What abominable articles the *Times* has
against Prussia ! That of yesterday upon Warsaw
and Schleinitz is positively too wicked.   It is the
Bonn story which continues to operate, and a
total estrangement between the two countries may
ensue, if a newspaper war be kept up for some
time between the two nations.   Feelings, and not
arguments, constitute the basis for actions.   An
embitterment of feeling between England and

Prussia would be a great misfortune, and yet they are content in Berlin to make no move in the Bonn affair."

It was only too true that the Prussian Government was in no hurry to settle the Macdonald affair. The bitterness which it engendered did not die out till long after its formal termination in May of the following year, and undoubtedly it contributed far more than was suspected at the time to increase the delicacy and difficulty of the Princess Royal's position. It was actually thought in Germany that she inspired the attacks in the British Press. "This attitude of the English newspapers preys upon the Princess Royal's spirits and materially affects her position in Prussia," so wrote Lord Clarendon.

This autumn and winter Prince Albert, in spite of many political and other anxieties and a sharp attack of illness, faithfully continued to instruct his daughter in the art of government.

It does not seem ever to have crossed his mind that such instruction, though admirable in itself, was ill-advised in view of his pupil's position. The ideal woman in Prussia was then, and still is to a large extent, one who, conscious of her intellectual inferiority, contents herself with managing her household and children. If this view obtained with regard to women in private stations, much more was it considered to be the duty of princesses of the Royal House to abstain from any active interest in public affairs. But either Prince Albert did not appreciate this, or it is possible that he thought his daughter to be freed by her exceptional ability from the ordinary restrictions and limitations of her rank. There is yet a third possibility—that he did not altogether trust his son-in-law's political judgment, and was anxious to give him, in the troublous times that seemed impending, an help-meet who could influence him in the right, that is in the Coburg, direction. Whatever may have been the reason, the Prince certainly continued to the end of his life to cultivate his daughter's knowledge and grasp of public affairs.

In December, 1860, the Prince Consort received from Berlin a memorandum upon the advantages of a law of Ministerial responsibility. Its object was to remove the apprehensions entertained in high quarters at the Prussian Court as to the expediency of a measure of this kind. This memorandum was the work of the Princess Royal, and it is easy to imagine what a storm of indignation would have arisen in Prussia if by any accident or indiscretion the knowledge that the Princess had written such a paper had leaked out.

Still, it was undoubtedly an able piece of work. Sir Theodore Martin says that it would have been remarkable as the work of an experienced statesman ; and, as the fruit of the liberal political views in which the Prince had been at pains to train its author, it must have filled his mind with the happiest auguries for her fulfilment of the great career which lay before her. " It would have delighted your heart to read it," were his words in writing to Baron Stockmar.

To his daughter he sent a long and flattering reply beginning : " It is remarkably clear and complete, and does you the greatest credit. I agree with every word of it, and feel sure it must convince everyone who is open to conviction from sound logic, and prepared to follow what sound logic dictates."

This pathetic faith in the potency of logic in political affairs is hard to reconcile with the Prince Consort's earlier and sounder dictum that feelings, not arguments, constitute the basis for actions. It is evident from the rest of the letter that the Princess had laid it down that the responsibility of his advisers does not in fact impair the monarch's dignity and importance, but is really for him the best of safeguards. She had gone on to discuss the proposition that the patriarchal relation in which the monarchs of old were supposed to stand towards their people was preferable to the constitutional system which interposes the Minister between the sovereign and his subjects. Her father's comments on this would have seemed to many Prussians most heretical doctrine to be imparted to their future Queen.

The patriarchal relation, he says, is pretty much

like the idyllic life of the Arcadian shepherds—a figure of speech, and not much more. It was thé fashionable phrase of an historical transition-period. Monarchy in the days of Attila, of Charlemagne, of the Hohenstaufen, of the Austrian Emperors, of Louis XI, XII, XIII, XIV, XV, &c., was as little like a patriarchal relation as anything could be. On the contrary it was sovereignty based upon spoliation, war, murder, oppression, and massacre. That relation was sedulously developed in the small German States, whose rulers were little more than great landed proprietors, during a short period in the eighteenth century, and was cherished out of a sentimental feeling. It then gave way before the Voltairean philosophy during the reigns of Frederick II, Joseph II, Louis XVI, &c., was turned topsy-turvy by the French Revolution, and finally extinguished in the military despotism of Napoleon.

The Prince went on to say that in the great war of liberation the people and their princes stood by one another in struggling for the establishment of civic freedom, first against the foreign oppressor, and then as citizens in their own country ; and the treaties of 1815, as well as the appeal to the people in 1813, decreed constitutional government in every country. The charter was granted in France, and special constitutions were promised in all the States ; even to Poland the promise of one was made, although there, as well as in

I

Prussia and Austria, that promise was not kept. Then came the Holy Alliance and introduced reaction into Germany, France, Spain, and Italy, by dint of sword and Congress (in 1817–1823). Once more the patriarchal relation was fostered with the sentimentalism of the Kotzebue school, and the betrayed peoples were required to become good children, because the Princes styled themselves good fathers! The July Revolution, and all that has taken place since then, sufficiently demonstrate that the peoples neither will nor can play the part of children.

As for the personal government of absolute Sovereigns, Prince Albert declared that to be a pure illusion. Nowhere does history present us with such cases of government by Ministers and favourites as in the most absolute monarchies, because nowhere can the Minister play so safe a game. A Court cabal is the only thing he has to fear, and he is well skilled in the ways by which this is to be strangled. History is full of examples. Recent instances have occurred where the personal discredit into which the Sovereign has fallen makes the maintenance of the monarchy, not as a form of government, but as an effective State machine, all but impossible. When, as in the case of the King of Naples, this result has arisen, all that people are able to say in defence is, " He was surrounded by a bad set, he was badly advised, he did not know the state the country was in."

To what purpose, then, is personal government, if a man in his own person knows nothing and learns nothing?

The Sovereign should give himself no trouble, said the Prince in conclusion, about details, but exercise a broad and general supervision, and see to the settlement of the principles on which action is to be based. This he can, nay, must do, where he has responsible Ministers, who are under the necessity of obtaining his sanction to the system which they pursue and intend to uphold in Parliament. This the personally ruling Sovereign cannot do, because he is smothered in details, does not see the wood for the trees, and has no occasion to come to an agreement with his Ministers about principles and systems, which to both him and them can only appear to be a great burden and superfluous nuisance.

How these doctrines would have been regarded by probably the majority of Prussians appears from another letter which the Prince wrote a fortnight later. His daughter had sent him an article from the Conservative *Kreuz-Zeitung*, and on it he comments:

" The article expresses in plain terms the view that *Monarchy* as an institution has for that party a value only so long as it is based upon arbitrary will; and so these people arrive at precisely the same confession of faith as the Red democrats, by reason of which a Republic is certain to prove neither more nor less than an arbitrary despotism. Freedom and order, which are set up as political antitheses, are, on the contrary, in fact, synonymous, and the necessary consequences of *legality*. ' The majesty of the law ' is an idea which upon the Continent is not yet comprehended, probably because people cannot realise to themselves a dead thing as the supreme power, and seek for *personal* power in government or people. And yet virtue and morality are also dead things, which nevertheless have a prerogative and a vocation to govern living men—*divine laws*, upon which our human laws ought to be moulded."

Christmas brought the customary exchange of loving gifts. Prince Louis of Hesse, now the betrothed of Princess Alice, joined the family circle in England, and Prince Albert writes to his daughter in Berlin :

" Oh ! if you, with Fritz and the children, were only with us ! Louis was an accession. He is a very dear good fellow, who pleases us better and better daily. In my abstraction I call him ' Fritz.' *Your Fritz* must not take it amiss, for it is only the personification of a beloved, newly-bestowed, full-grown son.

" But to return to the dear Christmas festival ! Your gifts which were there have caused the highest delight, and those we have yet to expect will be looked for with impatience. To the latter belong Wilhelm's bust, Fritz's boar's head—for which in the meantime I beg you will give the lucky huntsman my hearty thanks. Wilhelm shall be placed in the light you wish when he issues (I hope unbroken) from his dusty box. The album, which arrived yesterday morning, is very precious to us, as it enables us to live altogether beside you —in imagination.

" Prejudice walking to and fro in flesh and blood is my horror, and, alas, a phenomenon so common ; and people plume themselves so much upon their prejudices, as signs of decision of character and greatness of mind, nay of true patriotism ; and all the while they are simply the product of narrowness of intellect and narrowness of heart."

CHAPTER VIII

On January 2, 1861, died the King of Prussia, Frederick William IV, and his brother, the Prince Regent, succeeded as William I. Prince Frederick William became Crown Prince of Prussia, and henceforth the Princess Royal was called, both in England and in Germany, the Crown Princess.

In the *Letters of Queen Victoria* there is a most impressive account, written by the Princess Royal, and there published for the first time, of the death of the King of Prussia. The event moved her the more deeply because, not only was she present at the death-bed, but it was really her first sight of death.

The King had been ailing so long that those about him had ceased to be specially anxious. On Monday evening, December 31, the Prince and Princess Frederick William were sitting at tea with the Prince Regent and the Princess of Prussia, when there was brought bad news from Sans Souci, but still nothing to make them particularly uneasy. In the middle of the night, or rather early next morning, they were called up with the intelligence that all hope for the King had been abandoned.

Without waiting for any kind of carriage, although, as the Princess notes, there were twelve degrees of cold Réaumur, she and Prince Frederick William hurried on foot to the Prince of Prussia's palace. From thence they went in a special train to Potsdam. There they found the King dying, and the members of the Royal family standing round watching the death struggle. The painful scene went on till five the next afternoon, when Prince Frederick William wisely sent the Princess off to bed. At one o'clock in the morning of January 2 they were again called, with the news that the King had not many minutes more to live.

The letter in which all these facts are recorded is a remarkable composition, especially when it is remembered that the writer was only twenty. We may be sure that any thought of literary effect was far from her, and yet no one, reading it now after the lapse of so many years, can be insensible to the poignancy of this simple, unstudied, almost artless description of the scene in the death-chamber—the dim lamp; the silence broken only by the crackling of the fire and the death-rattle; the Queen, Elizabeth, continually wiping the perspiration from the dying man's forehead.

But the letter also shows how really noble was the new Crown Princess's outlook on life. She speaks with the warmest affection of her parents-in-law: "May God bless and preserve them, and may theirs be a long and happy reign," and she goes on to describe the King as he lay dead, peaceful and quiet like a sleeping child. She could hardly bring herself to believe that this was really death, "that which I had so often shuddered at and felt afraid of"; there was nothing dreadful or appalling, only a heavenly calm and peace.

The Crown Princess also speaks with deep feeling for the Queen Dowager, who had never really liked her, and who, as we know, had been in sympathy so pro-Russian all through the Crimean War. But this grief brought the two together as perhaps nothing else could have done, and the Princess says: "She was so kind to me, kinder than she has ever been yet, and said I was like her own child and a comfort to her."

Prince Albert was evidently greatly moved by his daughter's letter. In his reply he reminds her that in one of the most impressive experiences of life she was now older than himself. "The more frequently you look upon the body, the stronger will be your conviction that yonder casing is not the *man*, yea, that it is scarcely conceivable how it can have been. In seeing and observing the approach of death, as you have been called upon to do, you have become older in experience than myself. I have never seen anyone die." To Stockmar the Prince wrote that "The Princess, now Crown Princess, has in the late trying time at Berlin again behaved quite admirably, and receives on all sides the most entire recognition."

That same eventful January of 1861, the Princess lost two firm and loyal friends in Lord and Lady Bloomfield. She parted with them with great regret, and presented to Lady Bloomfield a bust of little Prince William done by herself.

At that time it must indeed have seemed to the Crown Princess as if all her own and her husband's hopes and aspirations for a full and useful public life were about to be amply fulfilled. The new King had not only always been an affectionate father to his only son and heir, but he had also been marked among the princes of his time for his liberal opinions and English sympathies.

The third anniversary of the Crown Princess's marriage came very soon after the death of the old King, and writing on that day to her mother she said: "Every time our dear wedding day returns I feel so happy and thankful—and live every moment of that blessed and never-to-be-forgotten day over again in thought. I love to dwell on every minute of that day; not a hope has been disappointed, not an expectation that has not been realised, and much more—that few can say—and I *am* thankful as I ought to be."

Soon after the accession of William I, Herr Max Duncker was formally attached to the

Crown Prince as a channel of communication in State matters. Duncker had been Professor of History at the Universities of Halle and Tubingen, and had also obtained some practical experience of politics as a member of the Frankfort and Erfurt Diet, and as a Prussian deputy. He had indeed been chosen by Stockmar for the position of confidential adviser to the Prince, with whom and with the Princess he was already in favour; and he saw in his new post an opportunity of sowing seed which might one day spring up and bear fruit an hundred-fold.

In March the death of the Duchess of Kent deprived the Crown Princess of a grandmother to whom she had been very warmly attached, and with whom was associated all the events of her happy childhood and girlhood.

On ·receiving the unexpected news, for the Duchess of Kent had only been really ill a few hours, the Princess started for England, not entirely with the approval of her father-in-law. The Prince Consort, who in this matter of his daughter's relations to her father-in-law always showed exceptional tact, wrote and thanked the King: "Her stay here has been a great comfort and delight to us in our sorrow and bereavement, and we are truly grateful for it."

The problem of the Schleswig-Holstein duchies and the unfortunate Macdonald affair combined to draw England and Prussia still further apart.

It is true that the latter was formally settled in May, but the bad feeling it created was not appeased. Lord Palmerston said in the House that the conduct of the Prussian Government had been a blunder as well as a crime, while the Prussian Foreign Minister (Baron von Schleinitz), then on the eve of his retirement, retaliated with a stiff rejoinder.

A leading article in the *Times*, backing up Palmerston's view, is described by Prince Albert, in a letter to Berlin, as " studiedly insulting." At the same time the Prince saw clearly that Schleinitz had made a mistake in mixing up the Macdonald affair with *la haute politique*. " In Germany the idea of the State in the abstract is a thing divine ; here it means the freedom of the individual citizen." And he goes on to say that the feeling in England ought to teach Prussia that mere talk will not do.

" Prussia has been always talking of being the only natural and real ally of England, but since 1815 she has taken no part in any European question. Prussia sets up a claim to stand at the head of Germany, but she is not German in her conduct. The Zollverein was the only really German action to which she can point. She leads Germany, not upon the path of liberty and constitutional development, which Germany (Prussia included) requires and desires. I can imagine that with the high military pretensions to which she has laid claim for the last forty-five years, she suffers under an oppressive consciousness that her army is the only one which during this long period has not been called into action. I repeat, however, that a large, liberal, generous policy is the preliminary condition for an alliance with England, for hegemony in Germany, and for her military renown."

These were the views with which the Crown Princess was steadily indoctrinated. It is possible that she found them a little too cool and impartially objective for her patriotism, but if so, there is no trace of such disagreement in Prince Albert's correspondence.

It was fortunate that Prussian opinion was at this time distracted by the thought of the coming coronation of the new King. The ceremony raised certain questions which, though nominally concerned with mere ceremonial, possessed in reality considerable importance from a constitutional point of view. The principal question was whether the oath of allegiance traditionally taken by the estates of the realm was consistent with the new constitutional law desired by the King. Apparently the King wished the oath to be taken, but was dissuaded by his Ministers, and it was decided that his Majesty should simply be crowned at Königsberg in the presence of the Landtag.

In July, 1861, the Crown Prince, who had gone with the Crown Princess to pay a visit to

Queen Victoria, wrote from Osborne a long and remarkable letter to his father, a passage in which shows how constantly he consulted his wife on questions of high politics.

The Crown Prince begs the King not to regard the coronation with repugnance on account of the omission of the oath of allegiance. He describes the act of assuming the crown as a despotic act, and as a solemn proof that the crown is not conferred by any earthly power, in spite of the prerogatives abandoned in 1848. He goes on to argue that the ceremony will compel the Great Powers to show deference to Prussia by sending ambassadors, and that therefore it ought to take place in Berlin. In this way it would exhibit the development of Prussia. Frederick I, by being crowned at Königsberg, marked the beginning of a new era for the State, but now a coronation at Berlin would mark the new future which opened out for Prussia as the defender of the united German territories. The Crown Prince advised that the King and Queen should go to Königsberg before the coronation in Berlin, either to receive the oath of allegiance or to hold a great reception, and then he goes on :

" I have ventured, dear father, to express my opinion quite frankly, though you may perhaps be surprised by my strong inclination for the coronation ceremony. The fact is simply that I have often calmly discussed this with Vicky as the only desirable conclusion, when I saw the increasing difficulties arising in your mind with reference to the oath of allegiance."

These opinions of the Crown Prince's, in which his wife evidently concurred, would hardly have been approved by Prince Albert. They show the future Emperor Frederick in a new light—no longer as the liberal constitutionalist, the firm admirer of England's free polity, but as the champion of the divine right of the Hohenzollerns, with a splendid vision of a united Germany under the military protection of Prussia. At the same time there is that qualifying sentence in which the Crown Prince refers to the plan of a coronation at Berlin almost as if he and his wife had been driven to recommend it as the only solution of the King's difficulties regarding the oath of allegiance.

The whole question becomes the more interesting in the light of a remarkable piece of dynastic history which was revealed for the first time at the jubilee celebrations of the Emperor William II in June, 1913, in an address by Professor Hintze at the Berlin University. It seems that his Imperial Majesty was informed, before his father's death in 1888, that upon that event a sealed document of high importance would be placed in his hands. When he read it, he found that it was the political testament of his great-uncle, King Frederick William IV of Prussia, brother of the Emperor who made united Germany.

As its name implies, the paper contained King Frederick William's advice to his successors on the Throne of Prussia. Part at least of these counsels was deemed to be possibly so seductive to Sovereigns of a certain temperament that the Emperor William II felt it his duty to commit the whole paper to the flames. The Royal testator, who inherited from his mother, Queen Louise, an exceedingly exalted idea of the rights of the Crown, recommended his successors to revoke the written Constitution which he himself had granted his people. But he had a high sense of the obligations of his kingly word and of his Royal oath, and accordingly he advised any of them who might take the step to take it before he had sworn to observe the Constitution at his coronation.

The Emperors William I and Frederick III seem to have been content with ignoring the testament. It was left for their successor, William II, fearful lest it might one day tempt some "young and inexperienced ruler" into dangerous paths, to destroy it. His apprehensions were curiously strong. He felt, he told Professor Hintze, as if he had a barrel of gunpowder in his house, and he knew no peace until he had got rid of the terrible document.

We need not discuss here whether these apprehensions were well founded. What is of the highest interest is the knowledge, thus come to light after so many years, of this extraordinary political testament.   It had unquestionably been read at this time, July, 1861, by the new King William I, and it is equally certain that it had not then been read by the Crown Prince and Crown Princess.   Probably the knowledge of the document would have modified the views expressed in the Crown Prince's letter from Osborne.   In any case, it seems so far to have influenced the new King that he rejected his son's advice and adhered to his decision in favour of a coronation at Königsberg, which duly took place there with all suitable pomp on October 18.

Among the very few published letters of the Crown Princess is one which she wrote to her mother describing the ceremony.   She modestly declares herself " a very bad hand at descriptions," but no one who reads the letter now could possibly agree with that.   On the contrary, she shows the same remarkably vivid and picturesque power of narration of which we had an example in her account of the death-bed of King Frederick William IV.

The fact that the day chosen for the coronation was her husband's birthday gave the Crown Princess great pleasure, as also that an English artist, Mr. George Housman Thomas, was commissioned to paint a picture entitled " Homage of the Princess Royal at the Coronation of the King of Prussia."

Lord Clarendon, who was the British Special Ambassador on the occasion, writing to Queen Victoria on the day after the coronation, observed that " *the* great feature of the ceremony was the manner in which the Princess Royal did homage to the King. Lord Clarendon is at a loss for words to describe to your Majesty the exquisite grace and the intense emotion with which her Royal Highness gave effect to her feelings on the occasion. Many an older as well as younger man than Lord Clarendon, who had not his interest in the Princess Royal, were quite as unable as himself to repress their emotion at that which was so touching, because so unaffected and sincere."

Lord Granville also wrote to Prince Albert, " One of the most graceful and touching sights ever seen was the Princess's salute of the King."

Lord Clarendon added, in his letter to the Queen, the striking words : " If his Majesty had the mind, the judgment. and the foresight of the Princess Royal, there would be nothing to fear, and the example and influence of Prussia would soon be marvellously developed. Lord Clarendon has had the honour to hold a very long conversation with her Royal Highness, and has been more than ever astonished at the *statesmanlike* and comprehensive views which she takes of the policy of Prussia, both internal and foreign, and of the *duties* of a Constitutional King."

Unfortunately, Prussia was far from desiring the

K

wife of the Heir Apparent to entertain any views, statesmanlike or other, on either domestic or foreign policy.

Lord Clarendon also told the Queen that the Princess was appreciated and beloved by all classes. Every member of the Royal Family, he said, had spoken of her to him in terms of admiration, and through various channels he had had opportunities of learning how strong was the feeling of educated and enlightened people towards her.

There is significance in the English statesman's reference to "educated and enlightened" people. He must have been aware that the majority of Prussians of that day were neither educated nor enlightened in his sense of the words, and that the Princess was really only appreciated by the small intellectual group who were flattered by the recognition which she and the Crown Prince bestowed on them. But Lord Clarendon was perhaps disposed to see everything *en beau*. The Crown Princess mentions that the King and Queen showed a marked cordiality to him, contrasting with the stiff etiquette observed in their reception of the other Ambassadors.

To return to the Crown Princess's account of the coronation. She contrives to give in comparatively few words an unforgettable picture of the *coup d'œil* in the chapel—the Knights of the Black Eagle in their red velvet cloaks, the various colours of the uniforms, and the diamonds and

Court dresses of the ladies, all harmonised by the sun pouring in through the high windows. The Princess says that she herself was in gold with ermine and white satin, while one of her ladies wore blue and the other red velvet. " Dearest Fritz was in a great state of emotion and excitement, as we all were." The King looked so handsome and noble with the crown on, and the moment when he put the crown on the Queen's head was so touching that there was hardly a dry eye in the chapel.

The Princess's keen sense of humour was stirred by the large assemblage of princes and other notables. " Half Europe is here, and one sees the funniest combinations in the world. It is like a happy family shut up in a cage ! " and she mentions as an example the Italian Ambassador sitting close to a Cardinal. There is also a young prince of Hesse who nearly dies of fright and shyness among so many people ; he at once excites the sympathy of the warm-hearted Princess, though she herself had no experience of the agonies of shyness.

But the Princess was even more diverted by a compliment which the King paid her :

" The King gave me a charming little locket for his hair, and only think—what will sound most extraordinary, absurd, and incredible to your ears —made me second *Chef* of the 2nd Regiment of Hussars ! I laughed so much, because really I thought it was a joke—it seemed so strange for ladies; but the Regiments like particularly having ladies for their *Chefs!* The Queen and the Queen Dowager have Regiments, but I believe I am the first Princess on whom such an honour is conferred."

Possibly the Princess thought at first that she was being appointed honorary cook to the regiment! In any case it is curious that she should not have known of the custom of conferring such distinctions on Royal ladies, which obtains in the British Army as well as on the Continent.

We have no means of knowing how the Crown Prince and Crown Princess regarded the new King's declaration at Königsberg — that declaration which amounted to an explicit assertion of the divine right of Kings. But in Queen Victoria's Letters there is a curious revelation of the anxiety with which her Majesty regarded the constant attacks of the *Times* on everything German, and particularly everything Prussian. She even wrote to Lord Palmerston about it, suggesting that he might see his way to remonstrate with the conductors of the journal. "Pam" did see his way, and he got an entertaining answer from the great Delane, then at the zenith of his power, which he forwarded to her Majesty. The editor says that he would not have intruded advice on the Prussians during the splendid ceremonies of the coronation "had not the King uttered those surprising anachronisms upon the Divine Right."

We learn from a letter written by Lord Clarendon to Queen Victoria that the Crown Princess was much alarmed at the state of affairs in Berlin at this time. The King saw democracy and revolution in every symptom of opposition to his will. His Ministers were mere clerks, content to register his decrees, and there was no one from whom he sought advice, or indeed who was capable or would have the moral courage to give it. The King would never accept the consequences of representative government or allow it to be a reality, though at the same time he would always religiously keep his word and never overturn the institutions he had sworn to maintain. Such was this experienced statesman's diagnosis of the situation, arrived at after an audience of the Crown Princess.

The Princess celebrated her twenty-first birthday on November 21, 1861. In the letter which she received from her father, almost the last which he was ever to write to her, one detects a pathetic note, as if the Prince, wearied and out of health, actually foresaw his approaching death and wished to give her his parting counsel and blessing:

"May your life, which has begun beautifully, expand still further to the good of others and the contentment of your own mind! True inward happiness is to be sought only in the internal consciousness of effort systematically directed to good and useful ends. Success indeed depends upon the blessing which the Most High sees meet to vouchsafe to our endeavours. May this success not fail you, and may your outward life leave you unhurt by the storms, to which the sad heart so often looks forward with a shrinking dread! Without the basis of health it is impossible to rear anything stable. Therefore see that you spare yourself now, so that at some future time you may be able to do more."

The death of Prince Albert on December 14, 1861, at the age of forty-two, profoundly affected the lives of both his widow, on her now lonely throne, and his idolized daughter in Berlin. It is evident from Queen Victoria's correspondence that she was quite unprepared. Her letters to King Leopold almost up to the last are full of the most pathetic hopefulness, and she certainly wrote in the same vein of cheery optimism to Berlin. The blow fell therefore with all the more stunning effect on both mother and daughter—indeed, it is hard to say which of the two felt more utterly crushed and broken-hearted.

The Crown Princess, as we have seen, was much more her father's child than is usual in family life in any station. The tie between them was something deeper and stronger even than the natural affection of parent and daughter; he had sedulously formed her mind and tastes, and he had become the one counsellor to whom she felt she could ever turn in any perplexity or trouble, sure of his helpful understanding and sympathy. Very soon after her marriage, in a letter to the Prince of Wales, she dwelt on their father as the master and leader ever to be respected: "You don't know," she wrote, "how one longs for a word from him when one is distant."

Nor did the Princess, like many daughters, allow her marriage to weaken this tie; indeed, the thought of the physical distance between them seemed to bring them, if possible, spiritually nearer. For her mother, the Princess felt the tenderest and most filial affection, writing to her every day, sometimes twice a day, about the little details of her personal life. But though she and her father only wrote to one another once a week, it was to him that she poured out her full self, the total of her varied interests in politics, literature, science, art, and philosophy. The citations already made in the preceding pages from the Prince's letters to her show, not only the many fields over which their correspondence ranged, but also the singular charm of their mutual confidence. It would be difficult to find in history a more touching and beautiful example of spiritual and intellectual communion between father and daughter.

And now this great solace and stay of the Princess's life is suddenly withdrawn from her, practically without any warning. If only she had

known, even suspected, that there was danger,
how she would have hurried to him! No one
with any imagination and human sympathy can
think of it without profound pity.

During the first weeks which followed the
receipt of the telegram announcing his death, the
Crown Princess fell into a silent, listless state, only
rousing herself to bursts of grief which were terrible to witness. The simple religious faith to
which her mother turned could not bring her the
same consolation. In her extremity it was on
her husband that she leaned. He was untiringly
patient and tender, though it must have been
most painful for him to be told that she felt as if
her life was over and she could never be happy
again.

It is surely true to say that in these difficult
days the Crown Prince revealed the essential
nobility of his character quite as much as he did
in the great spectacular moments of his life—on the
stricken field and in the glory of conquest. Many
a husband would have shown a certain resentment
at his wife's absorption in her father, but it is clear
that the Crown Prince, far from feeling any such
petty jealousy, brought his wife the truest consolation by understanding and himself sharing in her
sorrow. He knew what a really remarkable man
Prince Albert was, he had felt the charm of his
personality and of his intellectual gifts ; and so we
find him looking back on this bereavement, in a

letter written some months later to his old tutor,
M. Godet:

"Our whole life is, if such a thing be possible,
increasing in happiness daily. All the tribulation,
all the bitterness, of my outside life, and of what
I may call my practical life, I am able to leave
behind me when I reach the door which leads to
my 'home.' We had the great grief of losing
my dear father-in-law, the most intimate and
tender friend of my wife, and to me a true second
father. It came like a clap of thunder on our
peaceful, happy life. We are now deprived of
him whom we thought would help to guide us
during many many years, and now the British
Sovereign is bereft of her only help, while Europe
is deprived of one of her most brilliant and most
distinguished minds."

It may reasonably be doubted whether to the
Crown Princess the prolongation of her father's
life would have been of great service. We cannot
feel at all sure that in her critical relations with
Bismarck, for instance, his counsel would always
have been of the safest kind. He had not brought
her up to be the wife of an autocratic sovereign,
still less that of the wife of an Heir Apparent;
she was brought up as might have been a Prince
of Wales in a constitutional country.

By an unfortunate irony of fate, all those who
warmly and sincerely sympathised with the point
of view of the Prince Consort, and of herself and

the Crown Prince, were not Prussians; they were
—in the phrase then generally used—Coburgers.
This was pre-eminently the case with Stockmar,
and in a less degree with Bunsen and other Liberal
Germans. The mere fact that they were not
Prussians discounted any value their opinions
might otherwise have had, both with the then
King of Prussia and with those who surrounded
him.

Fortunately for the Crown Princess, the course
of public events soon came to rouse her from her
apathy and grief.

Early in that same December which saw the
death of the Prince Consort, the Prussian elections
had resulted in large democratic gains, thus considerably weakening the Ministry. In a memorandum addressed to the Crown Prince just before
he left for England to attend the funeral of his
father-in-law, Duncker prophesied the fall of the
Ministry, and for the first time suggested the plan
of calling Bismarck to office. In his reports during the Ministerial crisis which followed, Duncker
warned both the Crown Prince and the Crown
Princess of the danger of trying to govern at one
time with the Liberals and at another with the
Conservatives. He advocated a Ministry composed
of business rather than party men, who would
know how to govern as Liberals on a Conservative
basis; and he again urged that Bismarck should
be utilised to strengthen the Ministry.

The Crown Princess after her bereavement seemed to cling the more closely to the ties which bound her to the land of her birth and of her father's adoption, and this, as we shall see later, provoked a good deal of criticism in Berlin. She went to England as often as she could, or perhaps it would be truer to say as often as her father-in-law could be induced to give his permission.

Her first visit after the Prince Consort's death was in March, 1862. Princess Mary of Cambridge went to Windsor especially to see her cousin. She says: " We found her well, and better in spirits than we expected." But it must have been a very sad and mournful time, for the Queen was " rigid as stone, the picture of desolate misery " ; and everything reminded the Crown Princess of the father she had lost.

In the following May, the Crown Prince, at the special request of Queen Victoria, represented his father at the Great Exhibition of 1862, but the Crown Princess, much to her regret, could not accompany him. He had served as chairman of the committee appointed to secure an adequate representation of German arts and industries, and had thus greatly promoted the success of the enterprise.

The Crown Princess, however, went to England at the end of June to be present at the quiet wedding of her favourite sister, Princess Alice, to Prince Louis, afterwards Grand Duke of Hesse. It was solemnised at Osborne on July 1.

On August 14, 1862, a second son, Prince Henry, destined to be Germany's Sailor Prince, was born. The choice of his name seems to have troubled his grandmother, Queen Augusta. She wrote to her son from Baden: " My dear Fritz, your first letter moved me deeply, because of your affectionate heart, and because of all the particulars it contained about our beloved Vicky. I certainly anticipated that your son would be called Albert, for that name, no matter whether it is more or less German, really ought to be handed down as a legacy from the never-to-be-forgotten grandfather—and I believe that Queen Victoria expected it too."

As a matter of fact the baby was christened Albert William Henry, but probably what Queen Augusta meant was that he ought to have been generally known as Prince Albert instead of Prince Henry.

It might have been expected that the birth of three healthy children, two of whom were boys, would have, at least in a measure, disarmed the hostility with which the Crown Princess was regarded by a powerful section in Prussia. But these people were dissatisfied because the arrival of the children naturally strengthened the position of the Princess, and they also feared that the Princes in the direct line of succession to the throne would be brought up under English rather than Prussian influence.

There was, it must be admitted, a certain justification for the belief that the Crown Princess had never really ceased to be an Englishwoman.

In 1855 there had been presented to Prince Albert a remarkable young Englishman who was destined to play a considerable part in the life of the Crown Princess. This was Robert Morier, already well and affectionately known to Baron Stockmar, who even styled him his " adopted son." It was natural that Prince Albert should take a warm interest in the young man who came to him with such credentials—indeed, Morier was quickly made to understand that the Prince wished him to prepare himself in every way for diplomatic work in Germany. And in January, 1858, at the time of the Royal marriage, Prince Albert did everything in his power to have Morier appointed an attaché to the British Embassy in Berlin.

Morier had another good friend in the Princess of Prussia, the Princess Royal's mother-in-law. She had known, not only Morier but his distinguished father, for many years, and it was her personal wish, which she expressed to Lord Clarendon, that the young man should be sent to Berlin in order that he might be of use to her son and her daughter-in-law. It need hardly be said that Morier was also on intimate terms with Ernest von Stockmar,

who at the same time was appointed private
secretary to the Princess.

Morier obtained the appointment, and it was
the beginning of a lifelong intimacy with Prince
Frederick William and the Princess Royal. He
became and remained one of their most trusted
friends and advisers, a fact which undoubtedly injured his diplomatic career. When, many years
later, it was proposed that Sir Robert Morier,
as he had then become, should be appointed Ambassador in Berlin, his name was the only one
which was absolutely vetoed by the then all-
powerful Bismarck.

Probably because Morier had a remarkably
strong and original personality, he at once aroused
jealousy, dislike, and suspicion; he was even said
to influence the then dying King, as afterwards he
was supposed to influence King William through
Queen Augusta, and the Crown Prince through
the Crown Princess.

When one now reads the very frank letters
written by Morier to English relations and friends,
one cannot help feeling an uncomfortable suspicion
that the contents of some of them may have gone
back to Germany, perhaps in exaggerated and
distorted versions, in spite of the great precautions
taken to keep their contents secret. One observation in one of his letters certainly leaked out—
namely, that his long experience of German little
statesmen had taught him that " like certain plain

middle-aged women, they delight in nothing so much as to talk with pretended indignation of attacks supposed to have been made upon their virtue!" Such judgments, when barbed with a sufficient measure of truth, are apt to rankle.

It must not be thought for a moment that Morier was incorrect in his official relations in Berlin, but his remarkable ability and strength of character gave importance to his known Liberal and Constitutional sympathies. Had he been a diplomatist of merely ordinary qualifications, there would have been hardly need to mention him at all, but as a matter of fact he was an important factor in the complex situation of the Crown Prince and Crown Princess at this period.

A passage in Theodor von Bernhardi's diary, written in November, 1862, exhibits the feeling in Berlin aroused by the Crown Princess's visits to England :

"Conversation with Frau Duncker. I showed myself very impatient and discontented over the repeated long visits the Crown Princess made to England. 'She has nothing to do there and nothing to seek,' I exclaimed. Frau Duncker replied : 'The Crown Princess has her own views and her own will; her views and resolutions are very quickly formed—but when formed, there is nothing to be done against them.' Further conversation showed me that the Crown Princess cannot distinguish between our Three-thaler Diets

and the English Parliament; that she thinks everything here must be just as in England; the
Government must ever be by majority, the
Ministry always chosen by the majority—that she
tries to force these views on her husband, and
that Max Duncker fights against it as much as he
can.   Max Duncker let me see that he is ever
trying to set this young couple by the ears; their
ideas cannot be acted upon here."

The formation in the spring of a new Prussian
Cabinet composed entirely of Conservatives placed
the Crown Prince in a considerable difficulty,
because he had openly given his support to the
late Liberal Ministry.   Duncker's advice to him
was that he should absent himself for a time, and
that he should thereafter be present at the Ministerial councils without himself taking part in the
discussions.   This advice was accepted, and when
the Ministry endeavoured to remove Duncker to
an appointment at Bonn University, the Crown
Prince prevented it by emphatically declaring that
he did not wish to lose his counsellor.

The events which followed—the crisis on the
subject of military reforms, and the accession of
Bismarck to office—were regarded by the Crown
Prince with something like dismay, but he was
disarmed by the King's threats of abdication.   The
Crown Princess's secretary, the younger Stockmar,
in particular, strongly urged that the Crown Prince
should not intervene, as it was essential that he

should preserve his position removed from party strife.

The Crown Prince saw the wisdom of this advice, and on October 15, 1862, he started with his wife on a long visit to Italy. As the guests of the Prince of Wales, they joined the English Royal Yacht *Osborne* at Marseilles, and went to Sicily and the coast of Africa, including Tunis, where they visited the Bey at his castle, and the ruins of Carthage. At Naples the Crown Princess enjoyed herself particularly, sketching and taking long walks and excursions in all the delights of *incognito*. November 21, the Princess's twenty-second birthday, was spent by her in Rome, where the party made a long stay. After visiting other Italian cities, they returned to Berlin by way of Trieste and Vienna, having been away altogether rather more than three months.

It was this tour which laid the foundation of the great love for Italy and for Italian art which henceforth was a marked characteristic of the Crown Princess.

In the December of 1862 the Crown Prince and Princess made a short stay in Vienna. The American historian, Motley, was visiting Austria at the time, and it was characteristic of the Princess that the only person, outside the Imperial family, whom she desired to see was this brilliant writer. He gives a charming account of the interview in a letter to his mother :

L

" She is rather *petite*, has a fresh young face with pretty features, fine teeth, and a frank and agreeable smile and an interested, earnest and intelligent manner. Nothing could be simpler or more natural than her style, which I should say was the perfection of good breeding."

The Crown Princess told Mr. Motley that she had been reading Froude with great admiration, and she was surprised to find that, though Motley admired Froude and had a high opinion of him as an historian, he had been by no means converted to Froude's view of Henry VIII. " The Princess was evidently disposed to admire that polygamous party, and was also a great admirer of ·Queen Elizabeth." The Princess also spoke of Carlyle's *Frederick the Great*, which she had just read, but we are not told whether she agreed with Motley's view that Carlyle was a most immoral writer, owing to his exaggerated reverence for brute force, so often confounded by him with wisdom and genius.

CHAPTER IX

FIRST RELATIONS WITH BISMARCK

AFTER the death of Prince Albert, the relations between the Crown Princess and Bismarck become of absorbing interest to the student both of politics and of human nature.

Bismarck seems to have first met Prince Albert in the summer of 1855, when Queen Victoria and the Prince paid their state visit to Paris. In his *Reminiscences,* Bismarck says that in the Prince's manner to him there was a kind of "malevolent curiosity," and he convinced himself —not so much at the time as from subsequent events—that the Prince regarded him as a reactionary party man, who took up sides for Russia in order to further an Absolutist and "Junker" policy. Bismarck goes on to say that it was not to be wondered at that this view of the Prince's and of the then partisans of the Duke of Coburg descended to the Prince's daughter.

"Even soon after her arrival in Germany, in February, 1858, I became convinced, through members of the Royal House and from my own observations, that the Princess was prejudiced against me personally. The fact did not surprise me so much as the form in which her prejudice against me had been expressed in the narrow family circle—'she did not trust me.' I was prepared for antipathy on account of my alleged anti-English feelings and by reason of my refusal to obey English influences; but, from a conversation which I had with the Princess after the war of 1866, while sitting next to her at table, I was obliged to conclude that she had subsequently allowed herself to be influenced in her judgment of my character by further-reaching calumnies.

"I was ambitious, she said, in a half-jesting tone, to be a king or at least president of a republic. I replied in the same semi-jocular tone that I was personally spoilt for a Republican; that I had grown up in the Royalist traditions of the family, and had need of a monarchical institution for my earthly well-being : I thanked God, however, I was not destined to live like a king, constantly on show, but to be until death the king's faithful subject. I added that no guarantee could, however, be given that this conviction of mine would be universally inherited, and this not because Royalists would give out, but because perhaps kings might. 'Pour faire un civet, il faut un lièvre, et pour faire une monarchie, il faut un roi.' I could not answer for it that, for want of such, the next generation might not be Republican. I further remarked that, in thus expressing myself, I was not free from anxiety at the idea of a change in the occupancy of the throne without a transference of the monarchical traditions to the successor. But the Princess avoided every serious turn and kept up the jocular tone, as amiable and entertaining as ever; she rather gave me the impression that she wished to tease a political opponent.

"During the first years of my Ministry, I frequently remarked in the course of similar conversation that the Princess took pleasure in provoking my patriotic susceptibility by playful criticism of persons and matters."

In this passage we have evidently a perfectly frank expression of Bismarck's real feeling, and it gives an extraordinarily vivid picture of these two remarkable personalities, facing one another with watchful, guarded, measuring glance, like two duellists awaiting the signal for combat.

That Bismarck to a great extent misunderstood the Princess is plain enough, and indeed it would have been extraordinary if he had understood her, so different was she from any normal type of German lady. But there is abundant evidence that he did not underrate her intellectual ability, though it must have been a perpetual astonishment to him to find such mental powers in a woman, and there were even moments when the aims of the two, generally so wide apart, seemed actually to converge. It is curious to speculate how different the course of history might have been if the Princess had added to her other qualities that tact, prudence, and power of judging human character, which were surely alone wanting to make her one of the most remarkable women who have ever held her exalted rank.

The greatest injustice which Bismarck did the Princess lay in his suspicion—to use a mild term —of her German patriotism. The Prince Consort had consistently pursued the ideal of a union of the German States under the leadership of Prussia as the champion of German Liberalism. Such a new-born Germany might, or might not, have become the ally of England, but the Prince Consort must certainly be acquitted of any Machiavellian designs for the benefit of his adopted country; the supreme end he had in view was undoubtedly the happiness and greatness of Germany, and both his wife and his daughter knew and shared his aims.

From 1858 to 1861 the Prince Consort's influence in Prussian politics may almost be described as paramount; but the happy relations between England and Prussia were broken, partly by the inability of King William to share the liberalism of Queen Victoria and Prince Albert, which seemed to him positively anti-monarchical, partly by anti-Prussian feeling in England, and partly by the claim of the Prussian Liberals to dictate to the Crown on the question of army reorganisation.

Prince Albert did not live to see how completely his hopes had been shattered, and his premature death deprived his daughter of his counsel at the very moment when Bismarck came into office in the full tide of Russophil reaction and Anglophobia.

It is difficult to realise, in view of later events, how strong was the distrust which Bismarck inspired at the beginning of his accession to power. It was known that he desired an alliance with Napoleon III, and it was even believed that he would be capable of ceding German territory to France.

The trend of popular opinion was significantly shown on March 17, 1863, when the fiftieth anniversary of the Proclamation " To my People " was celebrated, and the foundation-stone of a memorial to Frederick William III was laid in Berlin.

Nothing that the authorities could do to give distinction to the occasion was omitted. The Crown Prince, who had just been appointed to a high post on the staff, commanded the military parade, and was present with his father at the festivities in honour of the survivors of the War of Liberation and the Knights of the Iron Cross. The citizens of Berlin, however, were conspicuous by their absence, and the popular feeling was expressed by the great writer, Freytag, who said in an article in a Liberal newspaper: " All good Prussians will pass this day quietly, seriously, and will consider the means by which they may best preserve the illustrious House of Hohenzollern for the future welfare of the State."

The first real efforts made by Bismarck to alienate the King from the Crown Prince and Princess date from the year 1863, just when the Princess was beginning to recover her spirits and normal state of mental health.

"Every kind of calumny was spread," wrote Morier, "respecting the persons supposed to be the Prince's friends. Spies were placed over him in the shape of aides-de-camp and chamberlains; conversations were distorted and imagined, till the Dantzig episode brought matters to a climax, and very nearly led to the transfer of the Prince to a fortress."

This episode, a speech delivered by the Crown Prince at Dantzig, possessed all the importance that Morier attributes to it, and it must be admitted that it was in the circumstances a highly imprudent utterance, for it dragged the differences between the Crown Prince and his father into the light of day.

The speech was delivered to the municipality of Dantzig on June 5, 1863. In it the Crown Prince referred to the variance which had occurred between the Government and the people, by which he meant a new ordinance restricting the freedom of the Press. This variance, he said, had occasioned him no small degree of surprise; and he added:

" Of the proceedings which have brought it

about I know nothing. I was absent. I have had no part in the deliberations which have produced this result."

Although the Crown Prince went on to pay tribute to the noble and fatherly intentions and magnanimous sentiments of the King, nevertheless the speech naturally created a great sensation, not only in Germany, but in other countries too. A correspondence followed between the Prince and his father, in which the former, while asking pardon for his action, offered to resign all his offices. Bismarck professes to have himself succeeded in making peace between the two, quoting to the King the text, "Deal tenderly with the boy Absalom," and urging that it was not advisable to make his Heir Apparent a martyr.

Bismarck's own account of the circumstances which led up to the speech is significant for its emphasis on the dates. He says that the Royal ordinance on the subject of the Press appeared on June 1; that on June 2 the Crown Princess followed the Prince to Graudenz; and that on June 4 the Prince wrote to the King expressing disapproval of the decree, complaining that he had not been summoned to the councils in which the step had been discussed, and enlarging on his view of his position as Heir Apparent. This obviously suggests, without exactly saying so in plain words, that the Crown Prince's speech on June 5 was inspired by his wife. But behind both the Crown

Prince and the Crown Princess, Bismarck thought that he detected the hand of Morier. And yet it is on record that Morier had not seen the Crown Prince or had any kind of communication with him at the time, before, or after, the Dantzig episode; in fact, it is quite clear, from letters Morier wrote to Ernest von Stockmar, that both he and his German correspondent sincerely regretted the Crown Prince's action.

The Crown Princess, however, seemed doomed to be associated with this unlucky speech. Not long after the affair was apparently settled, a remarkable and obviously inspired statement appeared in the *Times* to the following effect:

" While travelling on military duty, the Prince allowed himself to assume an attitude antagonistic to the policy of the Sovereign, and to call in question his measures. The least that he could do to atone for this grave offence was to retract his statements. This the King demanded of him by letter, adding that, if he refused, he would be deprived of his honours and offices. The Prince, in concert, it is said, with her Royal Highness the Princess, met this demand with a firm answer. He refused to retract anything, offered to resign his honours and commands, and craved leave to withdraw with his wife and family to some place where he would be free from suspicion of the least connection with the affairs of State.

" This letter is described as a remarkable performance, and it is added that the Prince is to be congratulated on having a consort who not only shares his liberal views, but is also able to render him so much assistance in a momentous and critical juncture. It is not easy to conceive a more difficult position than that of the princely pair placed, without a single adviser, between a self-willed Sovereign and a mischievous Cabinet on the one hand, and an incensed people on the other."

Naturally this version of the affair, with its open reference to the influence of the Crown Princess, aroused fresh excitement. Ernest von Stockmar, the private secretary of the Crown Princess, was said to have communicated the substance of the statement to the *Times*. Who really did so has never been revealed.

The unfortunate Stockmar, in any case, knew nothing of the matter; he would have given much to find out who was responsible. Indeed, this new complication to an already painful and suspicious affair so distressed Stockmar that he fell ill, and had to resign his position as secretary to the Crown Princess. This was for her a real misfortune, as even the most spiteful and prejudiced of her critics could not accuse the old Baron's son and pupil of being anything but a sound and patriotic German.

Bismarck was good enough to accept the Crown Prince's assertion that the statement was

inserted in the *Times* entirely without his cogniz-
ance, and he thought it was inspired by Geffcken;
in fact, he attributed it to the same quarter to
which, as he believed, the Crown Prince owed the
bent of his political views, namely, the school of
writers who extolled the English constitution as
a model to be imitated by other nations, without
thoroughly comprehending it.

What wonder, then, observed Bismarck, that
the Crown Princess and her mother overlooked
that peculiar character of the Prussian State which
renders its administration by means of shifting
Parliamentary groups a sheer impossibility? The
party of progress were then daily anticipating
victory in their struggle with prerogative, and
naturally took every opportunity to place the
situation "in the light best calculated to influence
female minds."

In the following August, Bismarck says, the
Crown Prince visited him at Gastein, and there,
"less under the sway of English influences,"
"used the unreserved language of one who sees
that he has done wrong and seeks to excuse himself on the score of the influences under which he
had lain."

This attitude, however, if it was ever really
adopted, was certainly short-lived. A fresh difference broke out between the Crown Prince and
the King on the subject of the former's attendance
at Cabinet Councils, and on this point the Crown

Prince undoubtedly held firm. Bismarck prints his marginal notes on a memorandum sent by the Crown Prince to his father. In these notes the whole constitutional position of the Crown Prince is discussed, but we are here only concerned with the following references to the Crown Princess:

" Especially necessary is it that the inter-mediary advisers, with whose aid alone his Royal Highness can be authorised to busy himself with the consideration of pending affairs of State, should be adherents, not of the Opposition, but of the Government, or at least impartial critics without intimate relations with the Opposition in the Diet or the Press. The question of discretion is that which presents most difficulty, especially in regard to our foreign relations, and must continue to do so until his Royal Highness, and her Royal Highness the Crown Princess, have fully realised that in ruling Houses the nearest of kin may yet be aliens, and of necessity, and as in duty bound, represent other interests than the Prussian. It is hard that a frontier line should also be the line of demarcation between the interests of mother and daughter, of brother and sister ; but to forget the fact is always perilous to the State."

In the autumn of 1863 Queen Victoria was staying at Coburg. She sent for Morier and had a long talk with him on the growing difficulties which seemed to encompass the Crown Prince and Princess. The fact that Morier ventured to hint that any appearance of interference on the part of England would be very prejudicial to the interests of their Royal Highnesses, and that a suspicion that the Crown Prince was being prompted from over the water would materially diminish in the eyes of the Liberal party the value of his opposition, shows that there was something, even then, to be said for the feeling which Bismarck so sedulously fostered.

During the summer of 1863, the Crown Princess accompanied her husband on a long tour of military inspections in the provinces of Prussia and Pomerania, and her Royal Highness performed the ceremony of naming a warship, the *Vineta*, at Dantzig.

This tour caused a good deal of discomfort to the Crown Prince and Princess, for in most of the towns they visited the municipal authorities ostentatiously refrained from celebrating the occasion; on the other hand, the populace as a rule received the Royal pair with abundant loyalty.

We have a curious glimpse of the sort of impression made in East Prussia by the Crown Princess in a private letter written by a member of the Progressive party, who afterwards became a confidential friend of the Crown Prince. This gentleman says that everyone was pleased with the Crown Princess, for she showed that she had a mind of her own. She informed a certain official that she read the *Volkszeitung*, the *National-*

zeitung, and the *Times* every day, and that she agreed entirely with those newspapers—in the circumstances an amazingly imprudent statement. It was, indeed, such a shock to the official that it reduced him to blank silence.

The breach between the Crown and Parliament was not the only question with which Prussia was troubled at this time. The summer of 1863 was also marked by the attempt of Austria to take the solution of the German question into her own hands by initiating a scheme for reforming the Federal Constitution.

The Emperor Francis Joseph invited the Princes and the free cities of Germany to a conference at Frankfort to discuss the reorganisation of the Germanic Confederation. King William was inclined to accept this proposal, but Bismarck held other views; and a further invitation from the Emperor that the King should send the Crown Prince to the Congress of Princes, was also declined.

Nevertheless the Congress was held, and there was also held a sort of family gathering of what Bismarck would have designated " the Coburgers " at Coburg. Queen Victoria was there, and in August the Crown Princess joined her, quickly followed by the Crown Prince.

Lord Granville, who was a close observer of the complicated intrigues of the Congress, wrote to Lord Stanley of Alderley: " The Princess

Royal is very Prussian on this Confederation question."

The Crown Prince's views on the subject were expressed in a letter which he sent to his wife's uncle, Duke Ernest, early in September. From this letter it seems clear that, whereas at first he had been inclined to favour the Austrian move, he altered his views when Austria showed her hand by demanding from the Congress a simple vote of assent or dissent to her project of reform. He mentioned that he had asked the King for permission to be absent from the meetings of the Cabinet, and indeed he paid with his family a long visit to Italy.

From Italy the Crown Prince and Princess proceeded to England, and that, with visits to Brussels and Karlsruhe, took up the rest of the year.

It must not, however, be thought that during this absence from Germany the Crown Prince and Princess ceased to take an interest in politics; on the contrary, they followed with the closest attention what was indeed a serious constitutional crisis in the autumn of 1863.

In October, after they had started for Italy, the Crown Prince wrote to Bismarck:

"I hope that, to use your own words, your efforts in the present difficult position of the constitutional life of our country may be successful, and may accomplish that which you yourself describe as the urgent and essential understanding with the national representatives. I am follow-ing the course of events with the deepest interest."

The constitutional crisis turned on the rejec-tion, by the Upper House and the Crown, of the Budget which had been adopted by the Lower House. The King, as advised by Bismarck, was for governing without a constitution, but the Crown Prince, with his strong predisposition in favour of the English constitutional system, which had ·by this time been developed by Queen Victoria, could not help regarding his father's attitude as jeopardising the security of the Crown.

The Crown Prince's position was particularly difficult because he was appealed to by all parties —by the Liberals, who looked forward to the day when he would be King of Prussia as perhaps not very far distant; and by the Conservatives, who ad-jured him to support the Government on dynastic grounds.

Of the two parties, the Liberals appeared to have the best of it, for the prolonged absence of the Crown Prince and Crown Princess was naturally interpreted in Germany as indicating, if not their sympathy with the Liberal party, at any rate their dislike of the existing Government.

But events were shaping themselves in such a way that the Dantzig affair, with all that had led up to it and had followed it, was soon to be for-gotten in a crisis of much greater moment, and

M

one which brought to the Crown Prince his baptism of fire.

It was during the visit of the Crown Prince and his family to England that King Frederick VII of Denmark, the last of his dynasty, died, and the question of the succession to the Duchies of Schleswig-Holstein immediately became acute.

CHAPTER X

THE WAR OF THE DUCHIES

PALMERSTON is reported to have said on one occasion, that there had been only three men in Europe who really understood the Schleswig-Holstein question. One of them was himself—and he had forgotten it; the second man was dead; and the third was in a mad-house.

The members of the Royal Houses of England, Prussia, and Denmark, however, considered that, without being either jurists or diplomatists by profession, they understood the question quite well enough to take different sides with ardent enthusiasm. The question came, in fact, like a dividing sword, and not for the first time it brought war in its train between Prussia and Denmark. The British Royal family was placed by its intimate ties with both combatants—the Prince of Wales had married Princess Alexandra of Denmark in March, 1863—in a position of peculiar delicacy, which was not rendered easier by the fact that public opinion in England warmly espoused the cause of Denmark.

If it was not easy for Queen Victoria and her advisers to steer a prudent course, the position of the Crown Princess in Berlin was even more difficult. She met the crisis with her customary courage, and she applied to its solution the teachings of that constitutional liberalism which she had imbibed from her father.

The Princess felt very strongly that the honour as well as the interest of Prussia—or perhaps one should say her interest as well as her honour—required the nation to play an unselfish part, and to seek indemnity in the moral prestige to be derived from the settlement of this ancient racial feud. As future Queen of Prussia, the Princess wished to see the interests of the Crown identified with the constitutional rights of the people ; she desired to see the inhabitants of the duchies once more contented, loyal subjects of Duke Frederick of Schleswig-Holstein. It was not her fault, nor was it within her knowledge, that the solution which Bismarck even then contemplated, and which he was ultimately able to carry out, belonged to a wholly different order of ideas.

It is necessary, in a brief retrospect, to show how this question of the duchies had become like an open sore, poisoning the relations between Denmark and Prussia. Perhaps the most fertile cause of trouble lay in the fact that Schleswig and Holstein, though grouped together by historical circumstances, were each very different in the character of its population and their real or supposed rights.

We need not go back further than 1846, when King Christian of Denmark declared the right of the Crown to Schleswig-Holstein. His son and successor, Frederick VII, on his accession in January, 1848, proclaimed a new constitution uniting the duchies more closely with Denmark. This step caused an insurrection and the foundation of a provisional government. Prussia thereupon came to the help of the duchies and defeated the Danes near Dannawerke. After a fruitless attempt at intervention by the Powers, hostilities were renewed, and in April, 1849, the Danes were victorious over the Holsteiners and Germans. There was further fighting and further diplomacy, until in July, 1850, the integrity of Denmark was guaranteed by England, France, Prussia, and Sweden. This was quickly followed by the defeat of the Schleswig-Holsteiners by the Danes at the battle of Idstedt. Early in the following year the Stadtholders of Schleswig-Holstein issued a proclamation placing the rights of the country under the protection of the Germanic Confederation.

This led to the Treaty of London of 1852, by which the possession of the duchies was assured to Denmark conditionally on the preservation of their independence and the rights of the German population in them. Now, Holstein belonged to the Germanic Confederation, but the treaty stipulated that Schleswig was not to be separated from

Holstein, though it was a point of honour with Denmark not to give up Schleswig.

The natural successor of King Frederick VII in the duchies was his kinsman, Duke Christian of Sonderburg-Augustenburg, who, in May, 1852, resigned his hereditary claim in return for a sum of two and a half million thalers. This settlement might have been excellent but for two facts—first that it had not received the assent of the Germanic Confederation; and secondly, that Duke Christian's two sons violently objected to it—indeed, the elder son, the Hereditary Prince Frederick, made a formal declaration of his rights of succession. Moreover, it must be admitted that Denmark showed a cynical disregard of the conditions in the Treaty of London respecting the independence of the duchies and the rights of their German population. The Schleswig Assembly complained and protested, and even petitioned the Prussian Chamber of Deputies, who actually promised aid to the duchies.

At last the crisis came in March, 1863, when the King of Denmark granted to Holstein a new and independent constitution, but annexed Schleswig, which did not belong to the Germanic Confederation. Thereupon the Confederation invited Denmark to withdraw this constitution. So far from doing so, however, the Danish Parliament proceeded to ratify it only two days before the death of King Frederick VII, whose successor,

King Christian IX, was forced on his accession, owing to a menacing uprising of popular feeling in Denmark, to sign the new constitution annexing Schleswig.

The glove was thus thrown down for Germany to pick up; the Hereditary Prince Frederick assumed by proclamation the government of the duchies, and appealed to the Germanic Confederation for the support of his rights. The majority of the German Governments sided with him, especially the Grand Duke Frederick of Baden, brother-in-law of the Crown Prince; while the Lower House in Prussia declared by a large majority that the honour and interest of Germany demanded the recognition and active support of the Hereditary Prince. It will be evident from what has been said above that Prussia had plausible and even sound reasons for her intervention, the chief of which was the popular feeling prevailing in Schleswig.

Now, it so happened that the Crown Prince and Princess had a strong personal as well as political interest in the question of the duchies. The Crown Prince and the Hereditary Prince Frederick were old friends. They had first met as fellow-students at the University of Bonn. The Hereditary Prince had afterwards served in the First Regiment of the Prussian Guards, he had been often at the Prussian Court, and the Crown Prince was the godfather of one of his children.

Naturally, therefore, the Crown Prince and Princess were favourable to his claims.

There is now no doubt that Bismarck had some time before resolved in principle on the annexation of the duchies, but of course he did not show his hand until it suited him, and above all he studiously concealed his plans from the Crown Prince. Indeed, the Crown Prince's personal relations with Bismarck were at this time practically suspended, if only because he happened at the time to be in England, where, however, the prevailing sympathy with Denmark did not influence him or the Crown Princess. In a letter written to Duncker from Windsor in December the Prince says that he has " daily defended the cause of my dear friend Duke Frederick, well backed up by my wife, who exhibits warm and absolutely German feelings in a most moving degree."

The Crown Prince and Princess would certainly have recoiled with horror from Bismarck's secret design of annexing the duchies. How little they understood the Minister's plans is curiously shown in the letter of the Crown Prince just referred to. He took the view that Prussia ought at once to occupy the duchies in order to establish the Hereditary Prince there. Bismarck, he says, hated the Augustenburg family and considered the national aspirations of Germany as revolutionary, desiring on the contrary to maintain the Treaty of London and strengthen Denmark.

The Crown Prince in fact thought that Bismarck had been too late, and that his policy was opposed to the proper assertion of Prussia's position.

Events now moved fast. The troops of the Germanic Confederation expelled the Danish troops from Holstein, and the Hereditary Prince was proclaimed throughout the duchy. The Augustenburg party, who were aware of the hostility of Bismarck to their candidate, endeavoured to win over the King of Prussia through the medium of the Crown Prince ; but ultimately, aided no doubt by certain imprudences on the part of the Hereditary Prince, Bismarck had his way. Both Austria and Prussia separated from the majority of the Diet, demanding that the King of Denmark should annul the new constitution annexing Schleswig, already mentioned, and announced that they would jointly manage the affairs of the two duchies.

In January, 1864, Austria and Prussia issued an ultimatum to Denmark, and in February began the war, which was somewhat euphemistically described as " undertaken by Austria and Prussia to protect the ancient rights of the German province of Schleswig-Holstein, in danger of extinction from Denmark."

It was considered essential in Berlin that a Prussian officer should be in command of the allied troops, and this could only be effected by calling on the venerable Field-Marshal von

Wrangel, as he alone was of superior rank to the officer at the head of the Austrian forces.

Von Wrangel, therefore, although he was much too old and eccentric for such responsibility, took the supreme command in right of his rank, but the Crown Prince was attached to his staff, with the understanding that he was to prevent the aged Field-Marshal from coming to any unfortunate decisions. Events showed that this was extremely necessary—indeed, nothing could have been more useful than the Crown Prince's tact in dealing with the rivalries among the divisional commanders, and also in altering the extraordinary, and sometimes positively insane, orders given by Von Wrangel himself. As a rule the Crown Prince was able to persuade the old man to make the necessary alterations, but there were occasions on which he was compelled on his own responsibility, either to suppress an order altogether, or in some other way to prevent it from being carried out.

The English Royal family were deeply divided in their sympathies in this war, but the Crown Princess, as her husband had written to Duncker, was wholly German in her feelings. She wrote to her uncle in Coburg: " For the first time in my life I regret not being a young man and not to be able to take the field against the Danes," and there is reason to believe that it was her influence which decided Queen Victoria to restrain the bellicose Palmerston, who would have liked England to support Denmark by force of arms.

In these circumstances it seems all the more monstrous that Bismarck's friends actually charged the Crown Princess with betraying the secrets of the Prussian Government to the English Ministers. Her complaints to the King only received as answer that the whole thing was nonsense, and that she should not treat it seriously. But the fact that the slanderers were never punished caused these calumnies to be long repeated, and even in part believed.

By the side of the Crown Prince and Princess there stood, in Bismarck's estimation, Queen Augusta, who had ever been the energetic champion of the Coburg doctrine of a liberated and united Germany under the leadership of Prussia. In his profound disbelief in Liberalism, Bismarck played the obvious game of raising the cry of foreign dictation. By means of his instruments in the Press and elsewhere, he set himself to exhibit England as at all times seeking to influence Germany for her own ends and often against German interests, for promoting her own security and the extension of her power, "lately through women, daughters and friends of Queen Victoria."

This campaign was only too successful, and it must soon have become obvious, both to Queen Victoria and to her daughter, that the unification of Germany by means of Prussian Liberalism was not in the range of practical politics. At the same time Bismarck risked a great deal. Nothing would have more completely upset his plans than a war with England over the duchies, and, as we have said, he was saved from that danger largely owing to the fact that Queen Victoria was influenced by the Crown Princess to withstand the chauvinism of her Ministers.

Throughout the campaign of 1864, the Crown Prince won the deep affection of the troops, not only by himself sharing their hardships, but also by his constant kindness and care for their comfort. Though he showed himself a true soldier and even a strategist of no small ability, the Crown Prince had no illusions about the horrors of war, which he now saw for the first time. He was deeply moved by the terrible sights he witnessed on the field of battle and in the hospitals. After the victory at Düppel in April, he would have been glad if an armistice had been concluded, and he wrote to Duncker: "You will understand how heavily my long absence weighs on me, for you know what a happy home I have waiting for me."

He had not long to wait, however, for on May 18 the supreme command was transferred from Field-Marshal von Wrangel to Prince Frederick Charles, the "Red Prince," and so the Crown Prince's mission came to an end. He joined the Crown Princess at Hamburg. She had originally meant to proceed as far as Schleswig in order to do what she could for the wounded in the hospitals, but, in obedience to urgent advice, she did not go further than Hamburg. The Crown Prince's journey thither, covered with all the laurels of successful warfare, was a triumphal progress.

As this campaign was the Crown Prince's baptism of fire, so to the Crown Princess it was a revelation and a call to action. On the occasion of the King of Prussia's birthday in March, the Crown Prince and Princess had presented him with a sum of money as the nucleus of a fund for helping the families of soldiers who had fallen or been disabled in war, and on the 'eve of the battle of Düppel the Crown Prince drew up an appeal on behalf of this institution, which afterwards bore his name.

But the war with Denmark revealed an even greater need than that of the care of the soldiers' wives and families. The Crown Princess saw with surprise and horror that the medical service of the troops in the field was practically non-existent. She remembered the achievements of Florence Nightingale in the Crimean War, and, though she was at the time herself more or less disabled, she undertook the heavy task of organising some sort of an army nursing corps. For this work, so appropriate for a soldier's wife, she was admirably fitted. Indeed, the War of the Duchies gave the Princess for the first time real scope for the exercise of her remarkable powers of organisation.

The Crown Princess, however, does not seem to have grown more prudent as time went on. There is a curious revelation in Bernhardi's diary in May, 1864, of her unfortunate habit of praising England to the disadvantage of Prussia. Says Bernhardi :

" After dinner conversation with the Crown Princess. She asked after England ; supposed that I had enjoyed England very much ; once there, one always longed to go back. I said : ' Yes, life is full in England.' She said with a very peculiar expression : ' Yes, one misses that here.' I thought to myself, however, that only the material interests are greater and more far-reaching than with us ; in many ways life is richer here than there."

Fighting, with intervals of diplomatic action, went on after the Crown Prince's return from the front, until peace was signed at Vienna on October 30. By this instrument the King of Denmark surrendered the duchies to the allies, and agreed to a rectification of the frontier and the payment of a considerable war indemnity. It was understood that Schleswig and Holstein were to be made independent, but differences of opinion arose between Austria and Prussia on this point, which led ultimately to the dissolution of the Germanic Confederation and the Austro-Prussian war of 1866.

Delightful glimpses of the family life led in the summer, of 1864 by the Crown Prince and Princess, and of her musical, literary, and artistic tastes, are given in letters written by Gustav Putlitz, the dramatist, to his wife. Putlitz was at this time chamberlain to the Crown Princess. His letters are too long and detailed to be quoted in full, but the following extracts will give a good idea of how deeply impressed this distinguished writer was with the vivid, eager personality of the Princess:

"*June* 26.—I passed a most delightful hour yesterday in this way. As I was going through the drawing-room, I found the Crown Princess with Countess Hedwig Brühl, the former looking for the words of a song of Goethe's, which she remembered in part, while Hedwig played the air. I found the song in Goethe for them. Thereupon we had a most interesting conversation about books. The Crown Princess is wonderfully well read; she has absolutely read everything, and knows it all more or less by heart. She showed us a reproduction of a drawing she had done in aid of the Crown Prince's Fund. It is a memorial of the victory at Düppel, and represents four soldiers, each belonging to a different arm of the service. The first is shown before the attack in the morning; the second is waving the flag at noon; the third, wounded, is listening to a hymn in the afternoon; while the fourth, victorious with a laurel wreath, stands in the evening at an open grave. The last is extremely natural and impressive, without any sentimentality. The conception shows real genius, and it is carried out most artistically. This youthful princess is more cultivated than any other woman I know of her age, and she has such charming manners, which put people entirely at their ease in spite of etiquette. She is not allowed to ride, and so she is accustomed to drive out daily for several hours, and practises pistol-shooting. In fact she possesses a wonderful mental and physical energy."

" *June* 27 (after dinner).—This morning the Crown Princess sent for me in the garden. I do not know what she is not devoted to—art, music, literature, the army, the navy, hunting, riding. On leaving she went down the mountain on foot, and I went with her through woods soaked with rain. She took out of her pocket the last issue of the *Grenzboten*, and gave it to me. It is amazing that she remembers everything she reads, and she debates history like a historian, with admirable judgment and firmness. After dinner she sang English and Spanish songs with a charming voice and correct expression."

" *June* 29.—After breakfast we went for a four hours' drive. The Crown Princess wanted every variety of wild flower we could find, and she knew the Latin, English, and German names of each kind. Every time we stopped she got out of the carriage and picked a flower which her sharp eye had detected, and which was not in the bouquet."

The party moved to Stettin, and Putlitz describes how the Crown Princess beguiled the journey with a constant stream of brilliant conversation on politics, literature, and art, as well as on more frivolous subjects.

When they arrived at headquarters and found the Crown Prince, she saw that everything was in disorder, and immediately, with characteristic energy, she began directing the rearrangement of furniture and the hanging of pictures. She herself was going on to Potsdam, but she was determined that her husband should be as comfortable as possible at Stettin. Says Putlitz :

" Furniture was put in its place, pictures were hung, wall-paper was selected—all the things having been brought from Berlin. Afterwards we went all over the house with the architect, and the Crown Princess issued her orders in the most practical and business-like way. Then we drove out and bought more furniture, and the things required for the Prince's washstand and writing-table. All the things were suitable, and chosen with care. We had an interesting conversation about English literature and drama. I am kept in perpetual astonishment by her natural behaviour, so many-sided, and full of judgment and sense."

When they arrived at the New Palace, Putlitz

happened to say that he had never seen more of it than the room where people wrote their names in the visitors' book.   At once the Princess showed him all over it.

He draws a charming picture of a tea-party at the Palace.   The young mistress, wearing a simple black woollen dress, sat at a spinning-wheel, and as she span she sang snatches of all kinds of songs, accompanied by one of her ladies.   Not far off, a chamberlain was reading poems by Geibel, or prompting others by Goethe and Heine which were recited by the Princess.

Putlitz cannot help recalling historical memories of the palace which was built by Frederick the Great in ridicule of Austria and France; which had seen the curious entertainments of his successor; had been decorated by Frederick William III in the stiff fashion of his day; had been opened by Frederick William IV to an intellectual and artistic audience at representations of *Antigone* and *A Midsummer Night's Dream;* "and was now the home of modern cultivation freed from formality."

The Princess, indeed, wanted a sort of history of the New Palace to be written, and she consulted Putlitz about it.   A few days later they discussed Frederick William III and Queen Louise, how the latter was always idealised, and how the former had become popular in spite of his roughness.

In his delightful book, *My Reminiscences,* Lord

Ronald Gower gives a most interesting account of a visit which he paid in this summer of 1864 to the Crown Prince and Princess, "two of the kindest and most amiable of Royalties," as he calls them. They met Lord Ronald and his mother at the station, in defiance of Royal etiquette, and took them off to the New Palace:

"We dined at two P.M. and we had to dress in our evening things for this repast. It took place upstairs in a corner room, with the walls of blue silk, fringed with gold lace. The Princess very smart, in a magenta-coloured gown with pearls and lace. The Crown Prince in his plain uniform, with only a star or two, which he always wears. 'It is a custom,' he said, 'and looks so very officered.' After dinner we went to the Crown Princess's sitting-room; the furniture there is covered with Gobelins tapestry—a gift of the Empress Eugénie."

Here Lord Ronald found some of the Princess's own paintings, including those lately finished, representing Prussian soldiers, his account of which it may be interesting to compare with that of Putlitz:

"One of these paintings was of a warrior holding a flag, inscribed *Es lebe der König*. The second a soldier looking upward. He has been wounded, and he wears a bandage across his brow; a sunset sky for background. This is inscribed *Nun danket alle Gott*. The third is another soldier looking down on a newly-made grave. Of these three I thought the second by far the best. There was another painting, also by the Princess, representing the Entombment."

The visitors were taken out driving : " We could judge of the popularity of our hosts, for everyone that we passed stopped to bow to them, and those who were in carriages stood up in them to salute as the Prince and Princess passed by."

The arrangements about meals seem extraordinary to modern taste. Lord Ronald says :

" Tea was served at ten in the evening in one of the rooms on the ground floor of the Palace. They call it the Apollo Room, I believe. It was a curious meal, beginning with tea and cake, followed by meat, veal, and jellies, and two plates of sour cream. For this repast one was not expected to don one's evening apparel a second time."

The visitors breakfasted upstairs with the Crown Prince and Princess and their children, in a room lined with pale blue silk framed in silver—not, perhaps, the best possible background for " the Princess in her favourite pink-coloured dress." Then, " the Princess showed us her private garden, and here she picked a clove, which she gave me with her own little hand."

Lord Ronald mentions the children with approval, but Putlitz, whose visit was much longer, got to know them really well :

" *July* 2.—The Royal children are very charming and well trained. The Crown Princess is strict with them, which is very praiseworthy in so young a mother, who is relieved by her rank of the duty of taking an active part in their education, for which she has not the time. People will indeed be surprised at this talented and cultured nature, when once her will has full scope."

The children on their side seem to have taken to Putlitz with enthusiasm. He gave the boys rides on his head, and he records with pride that " they came running from quite a long way off when they caught sight of me." He also records an accident—little Prince William being thrown from his pony—which must have reminded the mother of that day at Windsor when she was so distressed at a similar though more dangerous mishap to her brother, the Prince of Wales.

One morning after breakfast, says Putlitz, he met the Crown Prince and Princess on the terrace, " both full of almost infantile gaiety." Soon afterwards the children appeared. Prince William was riding his pony, when his hat fell off and hit the pony between its ears; the animal reared, and the Prince was thrown off on his back. Both parents remained quite calm, and apparently took no notice; whereupon the Prince mounted again and went on riding. It is not difficult to imagine the mother's pang of terror beneath that outward calmness. Well may Putlitz praise the sensible upbringing of the children, which made them perfectly natural, well-behaved, and obedient.

But it is the remarkable personality of the Crown Princess which chiefly interests this literary man turned courtier. One moment she is instructing him to write to a poet and thank him for a copy of verses ; at another she is arranging a picnic party in her own little garden near the Palace. Some one, generally Putlitz himself, reads aloud after tea, and if the poem or story is pathetic the Crown Princess is moved to tears. At other times they have music, generally glees, followed by good talk on literature or on contemporary politics and personages, about whom both the Crown Prince and the Princess speak with a candour which astonishes Putlitz. He cannot praise enough this delightfully informal, unaffected, and yet exquisitely cultivated and intellectual family life :

" Here one feels absolutely secure from intrigue, and only meets with frankness and clear intelligence. All evil designs must necessarily fail in the end before such qualities."

The dramatist felt also the great charm of the Crown Prince's personality. He says that the two natures of husband and wife are each a perfect complement of the other, and each exercises on the other an unmistakably happy influence. It is at the same time significant that, while emphasizing the perfect harmony of the marriage, he does not hesitate to say that the Crown Prince, notwithstanding the more brilliant qualities of the Princess, still preserves his simple and natural attitude and his undeniable influence.

And when the time comes to say good-bye, Putlitz sums up his experiences to his wife: "I have been entertained by a most highly dowered Princess and a most marvellous woman, full of intellect, energy, culture, kindness, and benevolence."

On September 11, 1864, a third son was born, Prince Sigismund. This little Prince was destined to have but a brief life. He was born the child of peace, the Emperor Francis Joseph becoming his godfather, but he died almost on the very day that Prussia drew the sword against Austria in the war of 1866.

That same autumn the Crown Princess paid her first visit to Darmstadt, to stay with her best loved sister, Princess Alice. The latter wrote to Queen Victoria a charming account of the visit, in which she said: "I always admire Vicky's understanding and brightness each time I see her again. She is so well, and in such good looks as I have not seen her for long. The baby is a love and is very pretty."

In October the Crown Prince and Princess, with their four children, started for La Farraz, in Switzerland. They left immediately after the birthday of the Crown Prince, which day was also that of the baptism of Prince Sigismund. The

Prince wrote just before leaving Potsdam to an intimate friend :

" The older I grow, the more I come to know of human beings, the more I thank God for having given me a wife like mine. What happiness it is to leave behind one all one's anxieties and all the troubles of this life, to be alone with those we love ! I trust that God will preserve our peace and domestic happiness. I ask for nothing else."

CHAPTER XI

HOME LIFE AND RELIGION

THE successful campaign against Denmark had drawn all German hearts together. Neither the Crown Prince nor the Crown Princess had ever been unpopular with the army, who felt really honoured by that honorary colonelcy which had so much amused the Princess. The Danish War greatly increased their popularity, and the year that followed was probably one of the happiest of their lives. They adored their children, who were being thoroughly well brought up, and, with the one paramount exception of the Prince Consort's death, no great bereavement had cast its shadow over their family circle.

The Crown Princess had early determined in her social life to consider neither party spirit nor high official position ; she preferred to gather round her a remarkable society of interesting and distinguished people,—scholars, theologians, archæologists and explorers, artists, and men of letters. She was always passionately fond of music, and many a young performer owed his or her first introduction to the public to the winter concerts which she organised, while no British painter or writer of eminence ever came to Berlin without receiving an invitation to the New Palace.

One of the most striking testimonies to the Crown Princess's intellectual interests is to be found in a letter written to Charles Darwin, in January, 1865, by Sir Charles Lyell. The great geologist says that he had had,

" An animated conversation on Darwinism with the Princess Royal, who is a worthy daughter of her father, in the reading of good books and thinking of what she reads. She was very much *au fait* at the *Origin* and Huxley's book, the *Antiquity*, &c. &c., and with the Pfahlbauten Museums which she lately saw in Switzerland. She said that, after twice reading you, she could not see her way as to the origin of four things ; namely, the world, species, man, or the black and white races. Did one of the latter come from the other, or both from some common stock ? And she asked me what I was doing, and I explained that, in re-casting the *Principles*, I had to give up the independent creation of each species. She said she fully understood my difficulty, for after your book ' the old opinions had received a shake from which they never would recover.' "

It may seem an intrusion on what should be sacred ground to touch on the religious belief of the Crown Princess, but it is a subject on which there have been a certain number of mis-statements, and it may therefore be well to set forth plainly the material facts.

The present generation perhaps hardly realises what a period of intellectual ferment had set in just at the time when the Princess's mind was most eagerly absorbing all that she could read and hear on the subject of religion and philosophy. She was twenty when *Essays and Reviews* appeared: she was twenty-two when Colenso published his book on the Pentateuch: twenty-three when Renan's *Vie de Jésu* appeared: twenty-four when Strauss's shorter *Leben Jesu* was published: and in one year from the time in her life at which we have now arrived *Ecce Homo* was to appear.

Most important of all, Darwin had published his *Origin of Species* in 1859, when the Princess was nineteen, and it is evident from Sir Charles Lyell's letter that she had not only read but understood that epoch-making book. Of all the giants of those days Darwin alone remains a giant; the lapse of time, as well as the work of other scholars and thinkers, has reduced the intellectual stature of those other writers whose work seemed of such crucial importance when the Princess was a young woman.

It was indeed a period when many thought that the old sound, even impregnable, position of Christianity had been not only undermined but overthrown. Strauss, for example, honestly believed that he had entirely destroyed the historical credi-

bility of the four Gospels.   The Princess herself
came to Germany at a moment when the Tübingen
school were the intellectual leaders, and Strauss
was their prophet, and the training which she had
undergone under the superintendence of her father
had prepared her to sympathise rather with the
attack than with the defence.   It is easy now to
see that orthodoxy was not then very fortunate in
its champions, and that the overwhelming weight
of the scholarship and intellectual strength of the
time belonged to the advanced thinkers.   Moreover, it must be remembered that much of the
religion of that day was mere lip-service, a conventional orthodoxy which, while it resisted investigation and inquiry on the one hand, failed to bear
practical fruit in conduct and life.

Only a few months after the Princess had
arrived in Prussia as a bride, the then Prince
Regent, her father-in-law, made a speech which
attracted great attention, not only in Germany
but in Europe generally.   In it he said it could
not be denied that in the Lutheran Church, the
established church of Prussia, an orthodoxy had
grown up which was not consistent with the basic
principles of the church, and the church, in consequence, had dissemblers among its adherents.   All
hypocrisy, the Prince continued—and he defined
hypocrisy as ecclesiastical matters which are utilised
for selfish purposes—ought to be exposed wherever
possible.   It was in the whole conduct of the in-

dividual that real religion was exhibited, and that must always be distinguished from external religious appearance and show.

When such language could be used from the very steps of the throne, it may be imagined how great was the intellectual ferment in which everyone who thought and read at all was necessarily involved. Naturally the eager, impulsive Princess, with the intellectual courage and sincerity which her father had implanted in her, could not stand aloof. But if, at this time of her life, she seemed to abandon the old orthodox positions, it is not less true to say that, while paying the penalty at the time in unhappiness and spiritual disquiet, she ultimately reaped the reward of an even firmer faith. She came to see, indeed, that the deepest religious convictions are not the fruit of philosophical speculation or of textual criticism, but of experience.

In the years that followed, the Princess was destined to be a near spectator of great events—of the progress and ultimate triumph of Bismarck's policy of blood and iron; while in her own home she suffered the bitter pain of the death of children, of sister, of brother. Even what seemed surely the crowning tragedy of her husband's brief reign and swift end was not all. That cruel malady, the origin of which still defies research, and which often, as in her case, kills slowly with lingering torture, seized upon her in her stricken widowhood.

Yet the successive ordeals through which she passed seemed but to strengthen her grasp upon the realities of life, and the Christian faith took on for her a new meaning and became the rock to which alone she clung. She left a most striking expression of her religious belief, written in the summer of 1884, at a time when she had no prevision of the fiery trials which were still in store for her. Long as the passage is, it is worth quoting in full:

"When people are puzzled with Christianity (or their acceptance of it), I am reminded of a discussion between an Englishman and an advanced radical of the Continent (a politician). The latter said, 'England will become a republic as time advances.' The Englishman answered, 'I do not see why she should. We enjoy all the advantages a republic could give us (and a few more), and none of its disadvantages.' Does not this conversation supply us with a fit comparison when one hears, The days of creeds are gone by, &c.? I say 'No.' You can be a good Christian and a Philosopher and a Sage, &c. The eternal truths on which Christianity rests are true for ever and for all; the forms they take are endless; their modes of expression vary. It is so living a thing that it will grow and expand and unfold its depths to those who know how to seek for them.

"To the thinking, the hoard of traditions, of legends and doctrines, which have gathered around it in the course of centuries remain precious and

sacred, to be loved and venerated as garbs in which
the vivifying, underlying truths were clad, and beyond which many an eye has never been able to
penetrate. It would be wrong, and cruel, and
dangerous to disturb them; but meanwhile the
number of men who soar above the earth-born
smallness of outward things continues to increase,
and the words in which they clothe their souls'
conception of Christianity are valuable to mankind; they are in advance of the rest of human
beings, and can be teachers and leaders by their
goodness and their wisdom. So were the Prophets
and the Apostles in their day, and so are all great
writers, poets, and thinkers. That the Church of
England should now possess so many of these men
is a blessing for the nation, and the best proof that
the mission of the Church on earth has not come
to an end."

Side by side with this we may quote some lines
which brought the Empress Frederick comfort in
her last hours of suffering :

> " All are stairs
> Of the illimitable House of God.
> . . . And men as men
> Can reach no higher than the Son of God.
> The perfect Head and Pattern of Mankind.
> The time is short, and this sufficeth us
> To live and die by ; and in Him again
> We see the same first starry attribute,
> ' Perfect through suffering,' our salvation's seal,
> Set in the front of His humanity.
> For God has other words for other worlds,
> But for this world the word of God is Christ."

We must now take up again the thread of the Crown Princess's life, when, unshadowed by any sense of impending doom, she was absorbed in her husband and children and in her intellectual and artistic pursuits.

Early in the year 1865 the Crown Princess had the joy of welcoming her sister, Princess Alice, on a visit to Berlin. Princess Alice wrote to the Queen: "Vicky is so dear, so loving! I feel it does me good. There is the reflection of Papa's great mind in her. He loved her so much and was so proud of her;" and she adds a vivid little picture of the baby: "Sigismund is the greatest darling I have ever seen—so wonderfully strong and advanced for his age—with such fine colour, always laughing, and so lively he nearly jumps out of our arms."

It was a great pleasure to the Crown Princess when her husband was appointed to the curious office of Protector of Public Museums. Thenceforward they both took a very active part in the management of these institutions, and it was owing to their efforts that the Old Museum has but few rivals in Europe in completeness and arrangement.

Prussia was then very backward in the practical application of art to industry, but the Crown Princess, who had seen how much her father had achieved in this direction in England, was determined to do all she could to secure a similar improvement in her adopted country. Early in

1865 she caused a memorandum to be drawn up setting forth the necessity of founding a School of Applied Art on the model of similar institutions in England. The movement thus started by the Crown Princess led eventually to the foundation of the Museum of Industrial Art at Berlin, which is connected with the School of Applied Art.

It was largely due to the active support and interest of the Crown Prince and Princess that applied art not only found a home in Prussia, but in the course of time reached so high a pitch of excellence that other countries are now fain to learn from Germany. The Crown Prince and Princess also both suggested and themselves supervised the collection and arrangement of an exhibition of artistic objects in the Royal Armoury at Berlin. This, by showing Prussian craftsmen what had already been done, greatly promoted the development of applied art.

But all was not sunshine during this peaceful, happy year, for during its course the Crown Princess lost the constant support and loyal help of Robert Morier. Although the whole of his diplomatic career had been given up to Germany, although he had devoted himself entirely to the study of the political, social, and commercial conditions, and of the relations between Prussia and England, it was arranged that he should be transferred to Athens.

Morier parted with the Crown Prince and

Princess on December 15, and it is on record that the Princess wept bitterly on saying good-bye to him.   Bismarck and his followers were proportionately delighted at getting rid of him.   But their joy was premature, for the Athens appointment fell through, and Morier was finally transferred to Darmstadt as Chargé d'Affaires, a change due to the personal intervention of Queen Victoria.

It must be remembered that Bismarck generally looked at things from a personal point of view. He had found by experience the value of secret agents, of whom he made constant use, and so he believed that every one whom he disliked, whom he feared, whom he wished to conciliate, made use of them too.   To his mind Robert Morier was a secret agent, and it was his great desire to isolate the Crown Prince and Princess from everyone who did not belong directly to his own party.

While at Darmstadt Morier remained in touch with the Crown Prince and Princess, and it was he who advised the selection of Dr. Hinzpeter as tutor to their eldest son, afterwards the Emperor William II.   Dr. Hinzpeter, who had been a friend of Morier for some time, was an authority on national economy and social reform, as well as a man of the highest personal character.

In the summer of 1865 Frau Putlitz and her husband were the guests of the Crown Prince and Princess at Potsdam.   This time it is the wife who records her impressions in a series of letters to her sister. She was quite as fervent an admirer of the Crown Princess as Putlitz was, and her letters really supplement and complete his letters, for they supply the feminine point of view.

Frau Putlitz was perhaps most impressed by the Crown Princess's versatility—the ease with which she could turn from a gay and smiling talk about bulbs, for instance, to the serious discussion of the profoundest subjects of philosophy. Naturally, this feminine observer notes the Princess's style of dressing, which she greatly admires as being both simple and perfect. "There is," she says, "a charm about her whole presence which it is impossible to describe." Her way of speaking, too, was fascinating, and though she declared that her German had an English accent, Frau Putlitz found it delightfully soft. Shakespeare the Princess frequently quoted, and one morning she read long passages with an expression which was warmly approved by the dramatist, Putlitz himself, who might be allowed to be a good judge. Frau Putlitz thought that the special charm of the Princess consisted in her entire simplicity and naturalness, which was exemplified in her never uttering banal, used-up phrases.

Of the children we have some glimpses; they are described as perfectly charming and very lively. The Princess told Frau Putlitz how anxious she was to have Prince William educated away from home with other boys of his own age, and this intention, as we know, she afterwards carried out in the case of both Prince William and Prince Henry. Little Prince Sigismund is pronounced to be really a delightful child. The Princess spoke with deep feeling of her father, whom she scarcely mentioned without tears, and she brought out all her souvenirs of him which she kept with loving care.

We are also shown the Princess among her books and pictures, the Princess singing old Scottish ballads and English hymns, the Princess painting flower-pieces, and above all the Princess as a gardener. Frau Putlitz compares the neatness of the Princess's own little garden, laid out by herself, to that of a little jewel-box. Enormous strawberries grew on beds of white moss under the beech hedges, and a gigantic lily brought by the Crown Prince from Hamburg was exhibited with pride. Frau Putlitz was surprised at the Princess's practical knowledge of horticulture, and the thoroughness with which she set about it.

These are, to be sure, not matters of great importance in themselves, but it is interesting to see how completely the charm of the Princess's personality fascinated both husband and wife, who were by no means ordinary observers.

CHAPTER XII

THE AUSTRIAN WAR: WORK IN THE HOSPITALS

WE come now to the outbreak of the war with
Austria, which arose directly out of the war with
Denmark, and which, as we now look back upon
it, seems to fall naturally into its place as part
of Bismarck's *politique de longue haleine* for the
unification of Germany.

The Royal personages of his time were to
Bismarck only pawns in the great game on which
he was ever engaged. It is impossible to read
his life and other literary remains without being
struck by the contempt which he entertained for
at any rate the great majority of those belonging
to the Royal caste, though the management
of them sometimes tried all his powers. It is
significant that at one moment Bismarck had
practically made up his mind to espouse the cause
of the Prince whom he habitually called "the
Augustenburger" in the Elbe duchies, and it was
only after a prolonged interview with the Prince
himself that he changed his mind, finding him
to be, from his point of view, quite impracticable.

As a rule, however, those Royal personages
whom Bismarck looked upon as pawns were actu-

ally not only content but proud of the position; the capital exceptions were of course the Crown Prince and Princess, who steadily resented and fought — sometimes successfully — against Bismarck's efforts to relegate them to a position in which they would not count at all.

It is curious to observe how Bismarck always managed to turn to account even circumstances which seemed at first sight most prejudicial to his designs. Thus in June 1865 the Budget, which included the payment of the bill for the Danish War, was rejected by the Liberal Deputies in the Chamber, but it was this which enabled Bismarck to take the plunge and govern without the constitution.

This rejection of the Budget was followed by the Convention of Gastein in August, by which Austria was to have the temporary government of Holstein, and Prussia that of Schleswig. Such an arrangement contained no element of permanence, and was indeed an obvious step on the way towards annexation. To the hereditary claims of "the Augustenburger," which the Crown Prince had most loyally continued to support, it dealt a fatal blow, and it is particularly interesting to note that Bismarck implored the King to keep the negotiations which led up to the Convention absolutely secret from the Crown Prince. He frankly told his sovereign that if a hint should reach Queen Victoria, the suspicions of the Emperor Francis

Joseph would be aroused, and the whole negotiations would fail, and he added, " Behind such
failure there lies an inevitable war with Austria."

The secret was duly kept from the Crown
Prince; he received the news of the Convention
with amazement, and it served to increase—if that
was possible—his detestation of Bismarck's policy.

The year 1866 therefore began with the
gloomiest prospects from the point of view held
by the Crown Prince and Princess. The Chambers
were opened, but quickly prorogued, and Prussia
openly prepared for war. Bismarck saw that the
moment was most favourable, for Austria was in
want of money, and was also beset with domestic
difficulties in Hungary, while he himself had
already practically arranged for the support of
Italy. Austria was thus driven to demand the
demobilisation of Prussia, and this was supported
in the Federal Diet by Bavaria, Saxony, Hanover,
Hesse-Cassel, and other States. Thereupon, on
June 14, Prussia declared the Germanic Confederation dissolved, and war began on the 18th.

We have become so much accustomed to the
conception of a united Germany that it seems now
extraordinary that in this war Prussia, with the
Northern States, should have been ranged against,
not only Austria, but Hanover and Hesse-Cassel,
with Saxony and Bavaria.

It thus fell out that the Crown Princess and
her sister, Princess Alice, were on opposite sides—

a singular penalty which Royal personages are liable to pay for the privileges of their rank. The circumstance naturally increased the maternal anxiety of Queen Victoria. There is no doubt that she believed that Austria would win, and when the result proved that she was wrong, her distrust of Bismarck was increased, not by his success, but by the use which he made of it.

Princess Alice's correspondence with her mother reveals how much she was affected by the prospect of this civil war, as she calls it. There are constant references to " poor Vicky and Fritz." On the eve of the outbreak she told her mother that her husband, Prince Louis of Hesse, intended to go to Berlin for a day just to see Fritz and explain how circumstances now forced him to draw his sword against the Prussians in the service of his own country.

We have already noted the extent to which the Crown Prince was excluded at this time from State policy, but as far as he possibly could, even up to the eleventh hour, he continued to oppose the idea of war. The moment, however, that the die was cast and war was declared, he became the simple soldier, intent only on his military duties and ardently desiring a victory for Prussia.

The Crown Princess's second daughter was born on April 12, and was christened Frederica Amelia Wilhelmina Victoria.

In May, the Prussian Army was divided into

three Corps, of which the second was placed under the command of the Crown Prince, who was also appointed Military Governor of Silesia during the mobilisation.

Immediately after the christening of the little Princess, the Crown Prince joined his staff at Breslau. But he left under the most mournful auspices. Just before his departure the baby Prince Sigismund, whom Princess Alice had described as " that beautiful boy, the joy and pride of his parents," fell suddenly ill, and, what seemed particularly cruel and unnecessary, even the doctor in attendance on the sick child had to leave for the front.

There is a very sad reference to the illness of her little nephew in a letter written by Princess Alice on June 15: " The serious illness of poor little Sigismund in the midst of all these troubles is really dreadful for poor Vicky and Fritz, they are so fond of that merry little child."

Prince Sigismund's disease was at first difficult to diagnose. As a matter of fact it was meningitis, and very soon it became clear that there was no hope. On June 19 the child died, at the very moment when his father was addressing his troops at Niesse, and the Crown Princess found herself alone, without anyone near or dear to her to share her bitter grief in this, the second great loss of her life.

Queen Augusta journeyed to the front to tell

her son of his bereavement.   He, however, more
fortunate than the Crown Princess, had much to
absorb every moment of his time and thoughts.
But after the war was over, in a speech made to
the Municipality of Berlin, the Crown Prince
alluded briefly to his loss.   " It was a heavy trial
to be separated from my wife and my dying boy.
It was a sacrifice which I offered to my country."

In the *Reminiscences of Diplomatic Life* published by Lady Macdonell, widow of Sir Hugh
Macdonell, a fact is revealed which shows how the
mother's heart must have hungered for Prince
Sigismund.

Lady Macdonell became on terms of considerable intimacy with the Crown Princess, who was
evidently impressed by her sympathetic nature.
One day, when they were going down a corridor
in the New Palace, the Princess suddenly unlocked
a door, and in the room to which the locked
door gave access was preserved surely one of the
strangest and most pathetic forms of consolation
to which a bereaved mother ever had recourse.
Lady Macdonell writes :

" I saw a cradle, and in it a baby boy, beautiful
to look upon, but it was only the waxen image
of the former occupant, the little Prince Wenceslau
[a mistake for Sigismund], who had died when the
Crown Prince went to the war of 1866.   How
pathetic it was to note the silver rattle and ball
lying as though flung aside by the little hand,

the toys which had amused his baby mind arranged all about the cradle, his little shoes waiting, always waiting—at the side."

When, five years later, Prince and Princess Charles of Roumania lost their only child, Princess Marie, at the age of three and a half, the Crown Prince wrote a letter of condolence to Prince Charles, who was Prince Sigismund's godfather, in which he said:

"May the grace of God give you strength to bear the hopeless grief, the weight of which we know from our own knowledge! In imagination I place myself in your attitude of mind, and realise that you must both be benumbed with sorrow at seeing your sweet child dead before you, knowing that you can never again see a light in her dear eyes, never again a smile on her face! Certainly it is hard to say: 'Thy will be done!' I put this text on the tomb of my son Sigismund, your godchild, because I know of no other consolation; and yet I cannot overcome that pain to-day, though many years have already gone by, and though God has given me a large family. Time does undoubtedly blunt the keenest edge of a parent's anguish, but it does not take away the weight of sorrow which goes with one for the rest of one's life. That my wife is united with me in these sympathetic thoughts you know."

The course of the war of 1866 is well known, and there is no need to trace it in detail. The

operations of the Crown Prince with the Second,
or Silesian, Army exercised a crucial influence on
the whole campaign. Field-Marshal Count von
Blumenthal, who, as Chief of the Staff, saw the
whole of the operations, bears testimony to the
brilliant strategic dispositions of the Crown Prince,
which were particularly exhibited in the defeat
of the Austrians at Nachod and the subsequent
engagements. Von Blumenthal notes that the
Crown Prince possessed, not only an extraordinary
power of self-control and coolness, but also, what
is not always found even in the greatest military
leaders, an instinctive perception of how much he
could leave to subordinates, while himself keeping a firm hand on the general course of action.
The soldiers themselves adored him, for he always
managed to find time to visit the wounded in the
field hospitals, as well as to encourage by his in-
spiring utterances the troops in line.

The manner in which the Crown Prince effected
a junction with Prince Frederick Charles and the
First Army was most masterly; he came up exactly at the right moment and at the right place.
Unfortunately, as generally happens, politics inter-
vened, and the Crown Prince was prevented from
following up the victories with as much energy as
he desired—indeed, it seemed to him that there
was a conspiracy to tie his hands and control his
movements. He even dropped a hint in the
sympathetic ear of Von Blumenthal that if this

treatment continued he would ask the King to relieve him of his command. Happily this was not necessary. The King himself assumed the supreme command on July 1, and two days later there came the crowning mercy of Königgrätz, or Sadowa, when the Austrians, under Benedek, were totally defeated. It was for his services at this great battle that the Crown Prince was decorated with the Order " Pour le Mérite."

Of Bismarck's exertions in this war, an English observer who was with the Prussian Army has left the following striking picture : .

" Bismarck believes in himself and fully so. He believes he was called on to do a certain work, and that he is quite able to accomplish it. His power of endurance is very great. He often sits up night after night working hard. During this campaign he has never slept more than three hours out of the twenty-four : this is less than the great Napoleon, who under similar circumstances took four hours' sleep. But constantly continued work has had an effect upon him : his face is seamed all over, he has dark lines under his eyes, and the eyes themselves are bloodshot. He looks like a man who is knocked up by overwork, and yet he is gay and jovial, pleasant and cheery. What surprised me most was his thorough openness in conversation. Without the least reserve he spoke of his intentions, of the future of Prussia and of Germany. For an hour and a half he thus went on.   His resolve is indomitable, and he also feels certain of going through with the work before him.   The King is of course a mere tool in his hands; but it shows his great skill and dexterity in turning such an instrument to serve his purpose. I do not think him Liberal in the sense that you or I are Liberal.   There is no doubt but what he thinks best he will enforce, and that what he does is, he believes, for the good and glory of Prussia."

Further Prussian victories followed, and the negotiations for peace exhibited a curious re-arrangement of the three personalities concerned.

Bismarck was strongly in favour of concluding peace very much on the terms offered by Austria, partly because he feared French intervention, and partly because he saw the imprudence of pressing home her defeat so deeply upon Austria as to leave her with a burning desire for revenge.   He wanted to look forward, in the diplomacy of the future, to a friendly Austria.   The King, however, could not bear to sacrifice, as it seemed to him, the result of the expenditure of so much blood and treasure, and he wished to follow up the Prussian victories, without having any very clear idea of what further gains could thereby be made.

In these circumstances it was the Crown Prince who came forward as the mediator between the King and his Minister; it was the Crown Prince who supported Bismarck against his father.   What really clinched the matter with the King was Bismarck's threat to resign. At the critical Council of War there was a dramatic scene. The King turned to the Crown Prince and said, "You speak, in the name of the future;" and when he found that his son agreed with Bismarck he gave in, and consented, as he himself described it, to bite into the sour apple.

Nevertheless, the terms of peace were not at all bad for Prussia. Her great object, namely, the dissolution of the Germanic Confederation, was secured; she obtained a considerable accession of territory, including Schleswig and Holstein, Hanover, the Electorate of Hesse, and other territories, which covered more than 1300 square miles, with a population of over four millions. Moreover, in August, 1866, on the invitation of the King of Prussia, the Northern States of Germany concluded a treaty of alliance, offensive and defensive. Thus was established the North-German Confederation, which was joined by Saxony in the following October, and formed an important step on the way to a united German Empire. Altogether the Confederation consisted of twenty-two States, and the first meeting of the Deputies was held at Berlin on February 24, 1867.

It was suggested that the Crown Prince should become Governor-General of Hanover, thus newly annexed to Prussia. It was thought that this plan would to a great extent console Hanover for losing her status as a kingdom, especially as the Crown Princess was closely related to the dispossessed monarch, King George V. The Crown Prince, however, insisted on arrangements which would have made Hanover altogether too independent to be agreeable to Bismarck, and so the idea was not carried out.

On the close of the war of 1866, the Crown Prince and Princess proceeded to Haringsdorf, a little village on the shores of the Baltic, to which the Princess and her children had been sent on account of the cholera, which was then very prevalent in Potsdam.

While there the Princess still busied herself with plans for the care of the wounded in the war. She had already assigned a great part of the palace at Potsdam for the nursing of wounded officers, and a little later on she proceeded with her husband on a long visit to Silesia. There they greatly improved the organisation of the war hospital at Hirschberg. Everything was under their personal supervision, and, thanks to their energy and kindly encouragement, the work was undoubtedly much more efficiently done than it would otherwise have been.

The Crown Prince had ridden with his father over the stricken field of Königgrätz, doing what they could to succour the wounded and the dying. How deeply the horrors of war had been impressed on the Prince's mind is shown by the words he wrote in his diary on the night of the battle : " He who causes war with a stroke of the pen knows not what he is calling up from Hades."

As for the Crown Princess, though she had been spared the sight of the worst horrors, she had nevertheless seen enough to enable her, with her eager, imaginative sympathy, to share in the fullest degree her husband's intense feeling. She never felt she could do enough to mitigate the sufferings of the soldiers, both on the battlefield and afterwards in the weary months of convalescence in hospital. This autumn she organised an enormous bazaar at the New Palace in aid of the wounded, to which contributions came from all over the world. The Crown Prince himself went round collecting money for the soldiers, and the whole enterprise brought in a large sum for the fund.

The years that followed up to the outbreak of the war with France were not very eventful.

At the beginning of 1867, the Crown Prince and Princess stayed a while at Dover, where they met Princess Alice and her husband, who went back with them to stay for a few weeks in Berlin. They afterwards went together to Paris, at the invitation of the Emperor and Empress of the French, in order to visit the great International Exhibition then being held there. The Crown Prince had served as president of the Prussian Committee for the Exhibition. Their stay in

P

France gave great pleasure to the Crown Princess; the two sisters visited many philanthropic centres, and made an exhaustive survey of French art. It was on this visit to Paris that the Crown Princess first conceived the idea of the School of Design in Berlin which now bears her name, for she was greatly impressed by the imaginative fertility of the Parisian craftsmen, and by the perfection of their work.

The Crown Princess left Paris before her husband. Princess Alice wrote to her mother on June 9: "Dear Vicky is gone. She was so low the last days, and dislikes going to parties so much just now, that she was longing to get home. The King [of Prussia] wished them both to stop, but only Fritz remained. How sad these days will be for her, poor love! She was in such good looks; every one here is charmed with her."

The Crown Prince had induced his father to visit the Exhibition, and the King, who brought Bismarck with him, had a magnificent reception from the Imperial Court. The Crown Prince and Princess did not abate their interest in politics, and they certainly shared Bismarck's view at this time ·that an arrangement with France was in every way desirable in order to avert war and to consolidate the gains of 1866.

In the autumn a terrible scarcity, almost amounting to famine, in East Prussia afforded a fresh opportunity for the practical sympathy of the Crown Prince and Princess. Together they organised a relief fund and relief works by which the sufferings of the population were much mitigated.

It was on February 10, 1868, the anniversary of Queen Victoria's wedding, and of the Crown Princess's christening, that another son was born, who seemed sent to fill the terrible gap which the death of Prince Sigismund had made two years before. The child was christened on the King of Prussia's seventy-first birthday, at Berlin, receiving the names of Joachim Frederick Ernest Waldemar. The Princess's fourth son was a beautiful and clever child, and his death, which was to follow when he was only eleven years old, was perhaps the deepest grief that fell on his parents. It is significant that when the Emperor Frederick chose his last resting-place, he desired to lie by the side of this child.

In the spring of 1868 the Crown Prince paid a visit to Italy in return for the visit paid to Berlin by Prince Humbert the year before. The Crown Princess did not go with him, but she followed with deep interest and pleasure the accounts of his reception, which were remarkably enthusiastic, and also politically useful, for it prevented the accession to power of a Ministry hostile to Prussia.

In 1869 the Crown Princess received a long visit from Princess Alice at Potsdam, and the two sisters spent their mother's birthday, May 24, together. Princess Alice spoke in a letter to Queen Victoria of the delightful life "with dear Vicky, so quiet and pleasant, which reminds me in many things of our life in England in former happy days, and so much that we had Vicky has copied for her children. Yet we both always say to each other that no children were so happy, and so spoiled with all the enjoyments and comforts children can wish for, as we were." Again, on June 19, " Vicky was very low yesterday ; she has been so for the last week, and she told me much of what an awful time she went through in 1866 when dear Siggie [Sigismund] died. The little chapel is very peaceful and cheerful and full of flowers. We go there *en passant* nearly daily, and it seems to give dear Vicky pleasure to go there."

The two sisters spent a happy time together at Cannes in the late autumn of 1869, while their respective husbands were abroad. The Crown Prince, with Prince Louis of Hesse, visited Vienna, Athens, Constantinople, and the Holy Land, and went on thence to Port Said for the opening of the Suez Canal. In Jerusalem the Crown Prince took formal possession in the name of his father of the ruined convent of St. John, ceded by the Sultan for the erection of a German Protestant Church. The two Princes joined their wives at Cannes shortly before Christmas.

On their way home the Crown Prince and

Princess spent a week in Paris, staying at an hotel. The Crown Princess was surprised to see how changed the Emperor Napoleon was since they had seen him last. She thought him ailing and dejected. In the course of conversation, the Emperor mentioned that he had a new Minister, a certain M. Ollivier.

The Crown Prince and Princess returned to Berlin on the morning of the New Year, 1870. The next time the Crown Prince met Napoleon III was on the morning after the capitulation of Sedan.

CHAPTER XIII

THE FRANCO-GERMAN WAR

THE year 1870 opened with no premonition of the tremendous events it was to bring forth.

Princess Victoria had been born on the eve of the Austrian War in 1866, and now, on the eve of this yet greater struggle, on June 14, 1870, the Crown Princess gave birth to her third daughter, Princess Sophia Dorothea Ulrica Alice, who was destined to become Queen of the Hellenes. The candidature of Prince Leopold of Hohenzollern-Sigmaringen for the throne of Spain was announced on July 4, and after fruitless attempts at intervention by the Crown Princess's old friend, Lord Granville, then the British Foreign Minister, war was declared between France and Prussia on July 15.

At the time of the little Princess's christening, which took place at the New Palace on July 25, there were few present at the ceremony who were not under orders for the front, and most of the men were already in their campaigning uniform. Emotion, anxiety, and excitement made the even then old King William feel unequal to the task of holding his little granddaughter at the baptismal font according to his wont, and this duty was performed for him by Queen Augusta. The fact that the Kings of Würtemberg and Bavaria were the child's godfathers marked the decision of those States, with Baden and Hesse-Darmstadt, to throw in their lot with Prussia in the war, as the deputies of the North-German Confederation had also done.

The christening was one of special splendour and solemnity, the two outstanding figures in the congregation being Bismarck, in his uniform of major of dragoons, and Field-Marshal Wrangel, now in his eighty-ninth year. Among the guests at the christening were Lord Ronald Gower and " Billy " Russell, the famous war correspondent. Two or three days before, they had been received by the Crown Princess at the New Palace, and Lord Ronald writes : " The Princess expressed almost terror at the idea of the war, and was deeply affected at the sufferings it must bring with it. She feared the brutality of Bazaine and his soldiers, should they invade Germany."

After the christening, King William and Queen Augusta held a kind of informal court in the curious hall known as the Hall of the Shells, full of memories of Frederick the Great. Early the next morning the Crown Prince slipped away out of the palace to spare his wife the agony of parting.

Even at such a moment as this, the Crown Princess's private and personal anxieties were em-

bittered by circumstances which she was unable
to modify or affect. Although England was not
only ignorant, but was to remain, like the rest
of the world, in ignorance for many years, of
the falsification of the famous Ems telegram,
sympathy with Germany as the supposed injured
party in the quarrel was by no means universal.

It is true that on the morrow of the declaration
of war the *Times* described it as "unjust but
premeditated—the greatest national crime that
we have had the pain of recording since the days
of the first French Revolution." Nevertheless,
France by no means lacked sympathisers in
England—indeed, the Crown Princess was much
distressed at the way in which her native country
interpreted the obligation of neutrality. The
Prussian Government considered that the exporta-
tion of coal and arms to France was a breach of
neutrality; and the attitude of England during
the Danish War was still remembered and resented
in Germany.

Bismarck, with what Europe has now become
aware was gross hypocrisy, observed to Lord
Augustus Loftus, the British Ambassador in Berlin,
that "Great Britain should have forbidden France
to enter on war. She was in a position to do so,
and her interests and those of Europe demanded
it of her," a sufficiently cynical observation on the
part of a man who, as we now know, had himself
forced on the conflict at the eleventh hour.

To Queen Victoria the Crown Princess confided her troubles : "The English are more hated at this moment than the French, and Lord Granville more than Benedetti. Of course, *cela a rejailli* on my poor innocent head. I have fought many a battle about Lord Granville, indignant at hearing my old friend so attacked, but all parties agree in making him out *French.* I picked a quarrel about it on the day of the christening, tired and miserable as I was. I sent for Bismarck up into my room on purpose to say my say about Lord Granville, but he would not believe me, and said with a smile, '*But his acts prove it.*' Many other people have told me the same. Lord A. Loftus knows it quite well. Fritz, of course, does not believe it, but I think the King and Queen do."

Meanwhile, France was complaining bitterly of Lord Granville's "cold, very cold" attitude. Then suddenly, on July 25, the *Times* published a draft secret treaty which had been proposed by the Emperor Napoleon to Prussia in 1866. The terms were—(1) that the Emperor should recognise Prussia's acquisitions in the late. war ; (2) the King of Prussia should promise to facilitate the acquisition of Luxemburg by France ; (3) the Emperor should not oppose a federal union of the Northern and Southern German States, excluding Austria ; (4) the King of Prussia, in case the Emperor should enter and conquer Belgium, should support him in arms against any opposing Power; and (5) France and Prussia should enter into an offensive and defensive alliance.

This disclosure caused an enormous sensation, and Queen Victoria was much shocked at the apparent revelation of French greed and duplicity. Writing to the Queen, the Crown Princess observed : " Count Bismarck may say the wildest things, but he never acts in a foolish way,"—an interesting pronouncement when one remembers how keen had been and was to be the struggle between these two powerful and determined natures.

As a matter of fact, Bismarck did not hesitate to admit that the document was authentic, but he insisted that he had never seriously entertained the proposal, which came entirely from the Emperor. Not long afterwards, on the day of the battle of Wörth, the game of "revelations" was taken up by General Turr, who disclosed proposals made by Bismarck in 1866 and 1867 for the annexation of Luxemburg and Belgium by France.

But already all such recriminations and discussions seemed merely of academic interest; already everything was swept from the mind of the Crown Princess save the necessity for hard work and intelligent organisation. With an ardour natural to her generous and sympathetic temperament she threw herself into everything that could mitigate the sufferings and promote the welfare of both combatants and non-combatants. Prussia's two former wars had given her an amount of experience which she was now able to turn to the best account. Spontaneously, without any advice or prompting from others, she wrote the following letter to the whole of the German world, her desire being to touch the hearts, not only of those Germans at home, but also of those who had settled overseas, in America and elsewhere :

"Once more has Germany called her sons to take arms for her most sacred possessions, her honour, and her independence. A foe, whom we have not molested, begrudges us the fruits of our victories, the development of our national industries by our peaceful labour. Insulted and injured in all that is most dear to them, our German people—for they it is who are our army—have grasped their well-tried arms, and have gone forth to protect hearth, and home, and family. For months past, thousands of women and children have been deprived of their breadwinners. We cannot cure the sickness of their hearts, but at least we can try to preserve them from bodily want. During the last war, which was brought to so speedy, and so fortunate, a conclusion, Germans in every quarter of the globe responded nobly when called upon to prove their love of the Fatherland by helping to relieve the suffering. Let us join hands once more, and prove

that we are able and willing to succour the families
of those brave men who are ready to sacrifice life
and limb for us! Let us give freely, promptly,
that the men who are fighting for our sacred rights
may go into battle with the comforting assurance
that at least the destinies of those who are dearest
to them are confided to faithful hands.

" VICTORIA CROWN PRINCESS."

This eloquent appeal met with the splendid
response which it deserved, and although practically
every German Princess of the time took a more
or less active part in the care of the wounded and
of the families of the soldiers, it was soon realised
that the Crown Princess was the master mind to
whom all must look for their orders.

Queen Augusta supervised the ambulance and
hospital services in Berlin, while the Crown
Princess moved to Homburg and started on the
organisation of a series of field-lazareths, being
most efficiently helped in her labours by her sister,
Princess Alice, who herself organised and actively
supervised four field hospitals in Darmstadt itself.

The Crown Princess began by turning the old
military barracks at Homburg into a hospital, the
existing hospital being set aside for the use of
wounded French prisoners. She also built at her
own expense two magnificent wards, and they—
doubtless partly because they were new buildings
—showed far more satisfactory results in lower

death-rate and shorter convalescence than did the wards in any other of the German military hospitals.

The Victoria Barrack, as the new wards were called, was built of wood on a brick foundation. In addition to the wards, the building contained a good ;store-room, lined with glass cupboards, in which was kept a quantity of old linen which Queen Victoria had sent for the wounded. Each ward contained twenty-four beds. A feature which the German doctors and nurses regarded with decidedly mixed feelings was a system of ventilation which enabled the whole building to be opened from end to end when required.

By the Crown Princess's orders, the very simplest and plainest appliances compatible with health and comfort were used. Thus the necessary furniture was all of varnished deal. By her wish, too, a great effort was made to give a bright and home-like appearance to each ward, and this, like the special ventilation, was quite a new idea to both German patients and German doctors. In the corners of each ward stood large evergreen shrubs, and on every table were placed cut flowers in glasses. Whenever the Crown Princess received a personal gift of flowers, she immediately sent it off to the hospital, often bringing a bouquet and arranging it herself. Nothing in the Victoria Barrack was used which could conceal any dirt; for instance, the crockery was white and the glass plain.

The Crown Princess attended the military hospitals daily. She went through every ward, and spoke to every patient; and she was quite as regular in her attendance on the wards containing the French prisoners as she was on those where the German soldiers lay. In this way she came into personal association with ordinary people of a class of whom Princesses see as a rule little or nothing. With many of the soldiers who were then tended under her supervision and care she kept in touch long after the war was ended— indeed, she was always eager to help in after life any of those whom she had known at Homburg, or who had fought under her husband's orders.

But the Crown Princess did far more than the work associated with her name at Homburg. It was owing to her promptness and her energy that a long line of military hospitals was rapidly organised along the whole of the Rhine Valley.

At the end of the campaign of 1866 the Crown Prince and Princess had founded the National Institution for Disabled Soldiers, and by the special order of the King it was given the name of the Victoria Institution, because the Crown Princess had suggested and instigated its creation. At the close of 1871, this Institution, again at her suggestion, was placed upon a wider footing, and applied to the whole of Germany instead of only to Prussia.

There is no need here to describe the course of the war itself. A vast literature, both technical and general, has grown up round it, and there are many people by no means yet old who remember vividly that immense and sanguinary struggle. To the Crown Prince was assigned the command of the Third Army, in which nearly every State of both North and South Germany was represented, including the Bavarian Corps and the Divisions of Würtemberg and Baden. Once more the Prince proved his fitness for high command, perhaps most notably at the battle of Wörth, when his admirable dispositions and his unhesitating resolve that even the last man must if necessary be staked were the main causes of the victory. Yet the Crown Prince said to the great German writer, Freytag, who was with him in this early part of the war:

"I hate this slaughter. I have never desired the honours of war, and would gladly have left such glory to others. Nevertheless, it is my hard fate to go from battlefield to battlefield, from one war to another, before ascending the throne of my ancestors."

Much as he hated war, the Crown Prince never hesitated, as weak commanders have always done, to pay the necessary price of victory in human lives. Among the troops, "Unser Fritz," as they called him, quickly became extraordinarily popular —indeed, their devotion to their leader formed a strong and politically useful link between men who had actually fought against one another so recently as the Austrian War.

Throughout the campaign, the Crown Prince and Princess corresponded daily. The siege of Paris had begun on September 15, and the Crown Prince was at Versailles on his birthday, on October 18, almost the first birthday he had spent away from his wife since their marriage. When he woke in the morning he found on his table a small pocket-pistol, and a housewife, filled with articles for daily use, from the Crown Princess.

There is a very interesting glimpse of the Crown Princess in December 1870, that is, during the middle of the war, in Prince Hohenlohe's Memoirs. He was asked to lunch with her, and they had a long talk about public affairs. The Princess was very dissatisfied concerning the proposed Convention with Bavaria, and it seemed to the statesman that both ʃshe and Princess Alice were enthusiastic for the idea of a united Empire without any exception, and that neither sister liked the proposal of federation. The Crown Princess listened attentively, however, to Hohenlohe's defence of the special nature and justification of the Bavarian claims, but it is evident that she agreed with her husband on the ʃquestion of coercing the Bavarians, if it should be necessary.

The two sisters were together as much as was possible during those terrible months of hard work and anxiety. Princess Alice spent half of the

December of 1870 in Berlin, and wrote to her mother: "It is a great comfort to be with dear Vicky. We spend the evenings alone together, talking or writing our letters. It is nearly five months since Louis left, and we lead such single existences that a sister is inexpressibly dear when all closer intercourse is so wanting!"

On Christmas Eve there arrived at the house at Versailles where the Crown Prince was then living a huge chest, and he asked his hostess and her family to share his Christmas cake, "for," said he, "this cake was baked by my wife, and you will much oblige me by tasting it." He then chatted to them about the Christmas festival in his own happy household, and translated the letters of the Crown Princess and of his two elder children. Long afterwards this lady wrote to a friend a letter which has since been published:

"In those fateful days we learnt to know the good and open heart of the late Emperor. We were fortunate indeed to be under the protection of that stately and friendly gentleman, who appeared to us, as we now think of him, to have been a good genius who warded off mischief from our household."

The Crown Princess was accused of having interfered to prevent the bombardment of Paris. Thus Busch writes on December 24, 1870:

"Bucher told us at lunch he had heard from Berlin that the Queen and the Crown Princess had

Q

become very unpopular, owing to their intervention on behalf of Paris; and that the Princess, in the course of a conversation with Putbus, struck the table and exclaimed : ' For all that, Paris shall not be bombarded ! ' "

As a matter of fact, though both Moltke and the Crown Prince considered that the right tactics would be to starve out Paris by a strict investment, the bombardment, which was urged by Bismarck for political reasons, was delayed, not by any slackness on the part of the Third Army, but simply by insufficient preparation of the siege-train in Berlin. The Crown Princess suffered bitterly from Bismarck. She knew well that he was indispensable, the man of the hour, but he would never trust her. He often held back important political news from the Crown Prince for fear it should leak out through the Crown Princess to England. In this he did her an injustice so gross that it could not be atoned for by his own tardy acknowledgment of the fact in *Thoughts and Remembrances.*

On January 25, 1871, we learn from Busch that Bismarck said of the English who wanted to send a gunboat up the Seine to remove the English families there :

" ' They merely want to ascertain if we have laid down torpedoes and then to let the French ships follow them. What swine ! They are full of vexation and envy because we have fought great battles here—and won them. They cannot bear to think that shabby little Prussia should prosper so. The Prussians are a people who should merely exist in order to carry on war for them in their pay. This is the view taken by all the upper classes in England. They have never been well disposed towards us, and have always done their utmost to immure us. The Crown Princess herself is an incarnation of this way of thinking. She is full of her own great condescension in marrying into our country. I remember her once telling me that two or three merchant families in Liverpool had more silver-plate than the entire Prussian nobility. 'Yes,' I replied, 'that is possibly true, your Royal Highness, but we value ourselves for other things besides silver.'"

After the capitulation of Sedan, the Crown Prince issued from Rheims an appeal for the wounded soldiers and the relatives of the killed and wounded. In it he spoke of his happiness in commanding in the field an army in which Prussians fought side by side with Bavarians, Würtembergers, and men of Baden, and declared that the war had created one German Army and had also unified the nation.

Later on, when the German armies sat down before Paris, the Crown Prince allotted some of the large rooms of the Palace of Versailles for a hospital, and himself supervised the arrangements. All through the war, indeed, he showed the keenest interest in the hospital service, and was constant in his visits to the wounded soldiers. Here we may trace the influence of his wife, who eagerly awaited all that he could tell her in his letters about the poor men to whom her woman's heart went out with such ardent sympathy. The Crown Prince took pains to supply the patients with interesting reading, and at his suggestion the editor of a Berlin Liberal paper sent many hundreds of copies of it daily to the military hospitals. This, however, was not approved at headquarters, and an order was actually issued by von Roon, forbidding the distribution of the paper.

Such incidents illustrate the difficulties with which both the Crown Prince and the Princess had to contend. The presence at Versailles, not only of the King and Bismarck, but of a cohort of German princes with their retinues, as well as numerous diplomatists, Ministers, and other official personages, did not make the Crown Prince's position easier. He had been raised after the fall of Metz to the highest rank in the army, that of General Field-Marshal, the promotion being communicated to him in a letter from his father bearing grateful testimony to his brilliant successes in the field, notably the strategic advance by which he covered the left of the main army and enabled it to overcome Bazaine's forces. But this elevation in rank does not appear to have been of much practical value to him.

Naturally both the Crown Prince and the Crown Princess took the keenest interest in the question of the Imperial title.

By the end of November, 1870, Baden, Hesse-Darmstadt, Würtemberg, and Bavaria had all joined the North-German Confederation by treaty. Early in December, the King of Bavaria, in a letter to the King of Saxony which was really written by Bismarck, nominated the King of Prussia as Emperor of Germany, and the North-German Parliament, after voting large supplies for the continuance of the war, adopted by an overwhelming majority an address requesting the King to become Emperor. His brother and predecessor had refused the Imperial crown proffered him by the Frankfort Parliament, on the ground that the legal title was insufficient, but now that the dignity was tendered by the Sovereigns and the people of Germany, it was not possible for the King to refuse.

Neither the King himself, however, nor the older Prussian nobility liked the change, which, it was feared, might transform the almost parsimonious austerity of the Prussian Court into something like the pomp and extravagance with which other sovereigns had surrounded themselves. Bismarck, who considered all such matters as titles and heraldic pomp to be only important because they influence men's minds, was disposed to agree with his Sovereign's feeling, but it was the corner-stone of his policy to conciliate the South German States.

To the Crown Prince, on the other hand, with his strongly idealist nature and his highly developed historical imagination, the conception of the Empire won by the sword made an irresistible appeal. He was ready to see in it a revival of the old Empire, by which the King of Prussia should be, not first among his peers, but the overlord of all Germany.

It is significant, however, that King William was proclaimed, in the Hall of Mirrors at Versailles, not Emperor of Germany, but German Emperor. This was on January 18, 1871, the anniversary of the day on which the first King of Prussia had crowned himself at Königsberg. The Crown Prince supervised all the arrangements for the ceremony, and it was his idea to form a kind of trophy of the colours of the regiments which had won glory at Wörth and Weissenburg, Mars-la-Tour, Gravelotte, and Sedan. Before this trophy the King pronounced the establishment of the German Empire. On the same day by Imperial rescript the new Emperor conferred on the Crown Prince and on his successors as heir apparent the title of Imperial Highness.

The preliminaries of peace were not signed till February 26, and we have, in a letter written two days later by his friend, Herr Abeken, an interesting glimpse of the feelings with which the Crown

Prince regarded these great events, and also the reliance which he placed on the aid of his wife. The Crown Prince told Abeken that he was fully conscious of the tremendous responsibility now incumbent on him. It was thrice as great as that which lay on him as Crown Prince of Prussia, but he did not shrink from it. God had already given him a blessed help and support in his wife, by whose assistance he hoped to fulfil his great work.

The Crown Prince had the satisfaction of leaving behind him in France as friendly feelings towards him personally as could well be entertained by the vanquished for a victorious foe. He had distinguished himself among the German leaders by his moderation in victory, by his stern repression of excesses, and by his chivalrous tributes to the bravery of his enemies.

The Crown Princess, absorbed in her labours among the suffering soldiers, was scarcely aware at the time of the venomous feelings still cherished against her in Prussia, and it was with an exultant heart—as " German " as her most captious and suspicious critics could have wished — that she welcomed the conclusion of the great conflict.

Berlin was reached on March 17, 1871, and though no official reception then took place, the Royal carriage in which the new Emperor and the Crown Prince were to be seen side by side could only proceed at a foot's pace through the dense masses who crowded the streets.

Later, in response to the call of the great crowd who thronged about his palace, a window opened, and the Crown Prince was seen in the midst of his family beside the Crown Princess, with his youngest child, the little Princess who had been born at the beginning of the war, in his arms.

CHAPTER XIV

PUBLIC AND PRIVATE ACTIVITIES

WHEN the great struggle was over at last and peace was declared, the Crown Princess had a pleasant opportunity of exercising the generosity and delicacy which formed perhaps the most notable part of her many-sided and impulsive character.

M. Thiers had sent to Berlin as French Ambassador the Comte de Gontaut Biron. Although allied by birth to several great German families, M. de Gontaut, as he was generally styled, found his position in Berlin a very painful one. France lay in the dust at the feet of the only real conqueror she had ever known. The whole of the huge war indemnity had not yet been paid off, and French territory was not yet free from the foot of the invader. There were also all kinds of comparatively unimportant, yet vexatious and annoying, outstanding points which still awaited settlement, and till these were arranged Germany refused to give up certain prisoners confined in German fortresses.

Moreover, Bismarck, though outwardly conciliatory and courteous, did not seek to spare the

French Ambassador as a more generous and sensitive foe would have done. M. de Gontaut was actually expected to be present at each of the splendid Court and military fêtes which were then being given to celebrate the foundation of the new German Empire and the victorious return of the Prussian Army to the capital.

From the very beginning of his difficult task, the Ambassador found firm and kind friends in the Crown Prince and Princess. On the occasion of his first audience the Crown Princess came forward with kindly, eager words, telling him that she and her husband had just read with the greatest pleasure the memoirs of his grandmother, that Duchess de Gontaut who, as Gouvernante of the Royal children, played so great a part in the Revolution, and later, in the Restoration. The Princess went on to speak of her intense satisfaction and relief at the declaration of peace, and she concluded with the words: " We know that you have made a great sacrifice in coming to Berlin; and we will do everything in our power to make your task less painful."

When M. de Gontaut was later joined by his daughter, the Crown Princess did all she could to make the daily life of this young French lady as agreeable as was possible in the circumstances, and in this she had the warm sympathy and assistance of the Empress Augusta, who, as we know, had many old and affectionate links with the Legitimist world to which the Ambassador belonged.

The Crown Princess's youngest child, who afterwards married Prince Frederick Charles of Hesse, was born on April 22, 1872, and was christened Margaret Beatrice Feodora—Margaret after the Queen of Italy, whom the child's parents both regarded with warm affection.

Queen Margherita came to Berlin for the ceremony, and a great fête was given at the New Palace. It was more like an English garden party than anything previously known at the Prussian Court, but the Crown Princess had a way of making her own precedents. She caused invitations to be sent, not only to the nobility and the hosts of officials who had a prescriptive right to be present at such a function, but also to persons who were merely distinguished for their literary, artistic, or scientific achievements.

The months which followed ushered in a peaceful period of happiness and rest for the Princess. Her magnificent work during the war had won her warm friends and admirers in every class, but of more moment to her than her own personal popularity was that enjoyed by the Crown Prince, whose relations with the military party now became much pleasanter in consequence of his achievements in the field and the enthusiastic devotion felt for him throughout the army.

Unfortunately for the Crown Prince and

Princess, Bismarck's position had been even more radically transformed by the war, and the Minister's domination over his already ageing sovereign grew more and more obvious.   It was an open secret that the Emperor and his heir differed on many important questions, and the gulf between [them was sedulously widened by Bismarck's jealous prejudice against the Crown Prince.   Incidents that would have been in ordinary circumstances too slight to mention now revealed, even to strangers, the friction which was symptomatic of deeper disagreement.

The Crown Prince, as we have seen, set much store by the new Imperial honours which the war had brought to his House, and he was always very punctilious in speaking of his father as " Emperor " and of his mother as " Empress."   The Emperor, however, habitually still spoke of himself as " King " and of the Empress as " Queen." The story goes that on one occasion the Emperor, addressing some lady in the presence of his son, observed that it was extraordinarily mild for the time of year, and that " the Queen " had brought him some spring flowers which she had picked out of doors that morning.   The Crown Prince answered, " Yes, so the Empress told me."   " I did not know you had already seen the Queen to-day," remarked his father.

The experiences she had just gone through had shown the Crown Princess the inadequacy of the

existing⁚ hospital organisation in Germany. From
her point of view, and from that of the English
ladies who had rendered her such great assistance in
creating—it was nothing less—the Army Nursing
Service, a more scientific training for nurses was
evidently the first necessity ; and in securing this
she was particularly helped by Miss Lees, afterwards Mrs. Dacre Craven, who had been a friend
and associate of Miss Nightingale.

In 1867 the Crown Princess had drawn up a
memorandum in which she laid it down that the
best nurses would prove to be those who would
combine the obedience of the Catholic Sisterhoods
with a more scientific and comprehensive training. The Kaiserwerth Institution, where Florence
Nightingale had gained valuable experience, did
not give a sufficiently scientific education, and she
came to the conclusion that a nursing school must
be established in Berlin, where ladies, who should
be given a distinguishing dress and badge, should
be trained. The outbreak of the war of 1870
interrupted this scheme, but now that the pressing
emergency was over, the Princess returned to her
old scheme, the fundamental principle of which
was that it should be carried out by educated and
refined gentlewomen, preferably orphans. They
were to have a three years' theoretical and practical course, followed by a course of monthly nursing,
and were to pass an examination to test their
proficiency.

In the face of strong opposition, both on the part of the medical profession and of the middle classes in Germany, the Princess organised this society of trained lady nurses, who tended the sick poor in their own homes. The society began in a very quiet, humble way, but now you could not find a German, man or woman, who would not admit that this was a splendid addition to the philanthropic institutions of the country. The Princess also founded a society for sending the sick children of poor parents out of the larger towns into the country or to the seaside.

It need hardly be pointed out that in each of these cases the Crown Princess copied peculiarly British institutions, and this no doubt was partly why they aroused such indignant opposition.

All through her life one of the Princess's mental peculiarities was that of thinking it impossible that any reasoning human being could object to anything that was obviously in itself a good and wise measure. To oppose a scheme simply because the idea of it had first originated in England or in France was something that she could not understand, so far removed was she from certain littlenesses of human nature, as well as from the dominion of national and racial prejudice.

The Crown Princess, and in this also she was warmly supported by her husband's approval and sympathy, wished the new Empire to bestow

more recognition on those Germans who had
attained distinction in the arts of peace rather
than of war. Encouraged by the knowledge that
her work during the country's wars had at last
won a measure of national understanding and
gratitude, she again did everything in her power
to break down the old Prussian Court barrier
between the " born " and the " not born." But,
as might have been predicted, the Princess's
efforts were fairly successful as regards the latter,
though not as regards the former.

To German women of all classes, the Princess's
interest in science seemed both eccentric and un-
feminine. She had attended, when still a very
young woman, some lectures given in Berlin by
the great chemist, Hoffmann, who dedicated to
her, in later years, his book, *Remembrances of Past
Friends*—a compliment which pleased and touched
her very much.

Her practical love of art was also regarded as
uncalled for in a Royal lady, and indeed unnatural
in the mother of a large young family. She
had a studio built in the palace, where she worked
under the teaching of Professor Hagen, and she
also studied under Von Angeli. She was fond of
visiting the studios of Berlin painters, particularly
of the two Begas, of Oscar the painter, and Reinhold the sculptor, where she sometimes made
studies as a student, and where she sometimes
was herself the study. She and her husband were

always great friends of the various artists.   Among
the names that recur constantly in this connection
are those of Anton von Werner, to one of whose
children the Crown Prince was godfather, and
Georg Bleibtreu.

The New Palace in Berlin was nicknamed
"The Palace of the Medicis," because of the enthusiastic encouragement which its owners always
gave to what they believed to be genius, or even
talent.   The Crown Princess not only entertained
persons of distinction in art and literature, but,
what was less easily forgiven her, any foreign
scientists and artists of eminence who came to
Berlin were eagerly invited by her, generally to
informal tea-parties.

But in time even the Princess realised that it
was hopeless to try to blend the two elements.
Unfortunately, she never took the trouble to
hide her preference for people who interested and
amused her to those who were merely "hoffähig."
The Prussian nobility were amazed and affronted
that a Prussian princess should esteem so lightly
the possession of numerous quarterings, and it
was a bitter grievance that their future sovereign
and his consort actually preferred the society of
painters and musicians and similar persons whom
they regarded as nobodies.

At the same time, she was always on cordial
and pleasant terms with diplomatists, who as a
rule combine the advantages of good birth with

intelligence and culture and the most delightful of professions. For many years of her life her greatest personal friends were Lord Ampthill (at the time Lord Odo Russell) and his wife, a daughter of that Lord Clarendon who had expressed so high an admiration of the Princess Royal's mental gifts.

But perhaps the Crown Princess most surprised and offended her husband's future subjects by her pro-Jewish attitude. In this she showed extraordinary courage and breadth of view. For example, she accepted the patronage of the Auerbach schools for the education of Jewish orphans, and that at a time when the whole of Berlin, from the great official world to the humblest tradesman, was taking part in the Judenhetze.

The Crown Princess was indeed, as we have seen, extremely broad-minded in matters of religion. She heartily despised the type of mind which attacks Jews as Jews, or Catholics as Catholics. She showed this in March, 1873, when she spoke strongly to Prince Hohenlohe about the hostile policy the Prussian Government was then pursuing towards his Church. She observed that in her opinion those called upon to govern should influence the education of the people, as that of itself would make them independent of the hierarchy, and she added: " I count upon the intelligence of the people; that is the great

R

power." But Hohenlohe drily answered: ' " A much greater power is human stupidity, of which we must take account in our calculations before everything."

What we should call the middle classes were incensed by certain other activities of the future Empress. From the very first the Crown Princess had been ardently desirous of improving the position of the women of her adopted country. But the German woman of that day was quite content with the place she then held, both in the public esteem and in the consideration of her menfolk; the fact that in youth she was surrounded with an atmosphere of sentimental adoration made up, in her opinion, for the way she was treated in old age and in middle age.

Even so, the efforts made by the Crown Princess in time bore fruit. They comprised the Victoria Lyceum, founded in June, 1869, but placed—and here one reluctantly perceives a certain want of tact on the part of the foundress—under the direction of an English lady. There were also, under the special patronage of the Crown Princess, Fraulein Letze's school for girls of the upper classes, and the Letteverein. Other educational establishments which owed much to her sympathy and direct encouragement were the Victoria and Frederick William Institute, and the Pestalozzi-Froebel House, and these are only a few of the educational establishments in which she took an

active and personal interest. Perhaps the most
admirable of them all was the Victoria Fortbildung-
schule, which gave girls the means of continuing
their education after they had left school.

In another matter concerning the education of
women the Crown Princess was violently opposed
to German public opinion. She was a firm believer in the value of gymnastic exercises and
outdoor games for girls, and that at a time when
they were practically unknown in Prussia. The
first lawn-tennis net ever seen in Germany was
put up in the grounds of the New Palace at Potsdam, and she was unceasing in her efforts to
introduce gymnasiums into girls' schools.

In the winter of 1872, the Crown Prince fell
ill of an internal inflammation, and though the
critical period was soon over, he took a long
time to recover his strength. Margaretha von
Poschinger reproduces in her life of him an extraordinary utterance said by the *Rheinische Kurier*
to have been made by the Crown Prince to his
wife at this time :

"The doctors say that my illness is dangerous.
As my father is old, and Prince William is still a
minor, you may not improbably be called upon
to act temporarily as Regent. You must promise me to do nothing without Prince Bismarck,
whose policy has lifted our House to a power
and greatness of which we could not have
dreamed."

The interest of this is considerable if we could
be sure that it was authentic, and not simply what
the newspaper wished the public to believe that
the Crown Prince had said. It may well be that
Bismarck, who was in the habit of providing for
every contingency, was alarmed by the Crown
Prince's illness, and desired to consolidate his
own position in the event of the Crown Princess
becoming Regent.

After a long convalescence at Wiesbaden the
Crown Prince returned with his wife to Berlin in
the spring of 1873. In the summer they went
to Vienna for the International Exhibition, and
while there they called, quite without ceremony,
on Von Angeli, the painter. The Crown Princess
invited him to come to Potsdam to paint her
husband's portrait; he accepted the commission,
and it was the beginning of a long friendship.

Von Angeli speaks with enthusiasm of the
simple and charming home life of the Crown
Prince and Princess, who often entertained him.
He notes that, while there was much talk of a
literary, artistic, and scientific kind, politics and
military matters were never referred to. For the
Crown Princess the painter had the highest
admiration—indeed, he says she was gifted with
every adornment of mind and heart. She made
such progress in painting that Von Angeli declares
himself proud to call himself her instructor. The
Crown Prince took a keen interest in his wife's

success, and was himself encouraged to begin working both in charcoal and in colour.

As regarded the relations between England and Germany, the Crown Princess had an increasingly difficult part to play during the years that immediately succeeded the war. France and Germany—the former with far more reason—both considered that they had been badly treated by Great Britain during the conflict. Prince Bismarck either was, or pretended to be, watchful and apprehensive of the state of feeling in France, and Moltke, following his lead, spoke at a State banquet as if war might again be forced on Germany by France.

Urged, as Bismarck and his friends believed, by the Crown Princess, but really by the advice of Lord Granville, Queen Victoria, in 1874, made a personal appeal to the German Emperor. In her letter, after observing that England's sympathies would be with Germany in any difference with France, she added the significant qualification, " unless there was an appearance on the part of Germany of an intention to avail herself of her greatly superior force to crush a beaten foe."

In reviewing the life of the Empress Frederick as a whole, it must never be forgotten that the Emperor William was not expected to reach, as in fact he did, an extraordinary old age. After the Franco-Prussian War, everyone of any intelligence, from Bismarck downwards, attached great importance to the Crown Princess's views and feelings; they believed that she, had established a commanding influence over her husband, and that the moment he succeeded to the throne she would be the real ruler. Accordingly, the further intervention of Queen Victoria in 1875, when a German attack on France appeared imminent, was the crowning offence of the " British petticoats."

Queen Victoria, as is well known, wrote a personal letter to the Tsar, who responded by going himself to Berlin. The " British petticoats," it is true, had resented what appeared to be the act of aggression of France before the falsification of the Ems despatch had been revealed, but they were angered by Bismarck's conspiracy with Russia in denouncing the Black Sea Treaty; and his opposition to a law of Ministerial responsibility, which might have given the new Empire a constitutional basis, showed the impossibility of any real political sympathy between the Minister and the Princess who had been trained in the school of Prince Albert.

The consequence of Queen Victoria's successful intervention was indeed far-reaching. The ten years which followed were probably the most anxious of Bismarck's whole life. France, by the prompt payment of the indemnity and in other ways, had shown a most disquieting power of revival after the war. In addition, the understanding with Russia, which was the pivot of Bismarck's foreign policy, having broken in his hands, he was obliged to recast his policy from the foundations; and, though he succeeded in his immediate aims of separating England and France on the one hand, and France and Russia on the other, his resentment against the Crown Princess and her mother as the origin of all his troubles burned all the more fiercely.

After each quarrel—for quarrels there were—between the all-powerful Minister and his future sovereign, a peace, or rather a truce, was generally patched up, and Bismarck would be invited to some kind of festivity at the Crown Prince's palace. A shrewd observer has recorded that on such occasions his manner to the Crown Princess was always courteous, but to the Crown Prince he was often curt to the verge of insolence.

So intense was the feeling aroused among Bismarck and his followers, that the Crown Prince and Princess found life in Berlin almost intolerable, and they began spending a considerable portion of each year abroad.

The many philanthropic, social, and political interests of the Crown Princess were never allowed to interfere with her family life and duties. Very soon after the war, both she and the Crown Prince began to give much anxious thought to the education and training of their eldest son. We have a significant glimpse of how the question moved the conscientious father in a passage in the

Crown Prince's diary written on January 27, 1871, while he was still in the field :

"To-day is my son William's thirteenth birth-day. It is enough to frighten one to think what hopes already fill the head of this boy, and how we are responsible for the direction which we may give to his education; this education encounters so many difficulties owing to family considerations and the circumstances of the Berlin Court."

The Crown Princess was the victim of much malevolent and ignorant criticism when it was realised that the old traditions were to be broken in some important particulars. The civil element was to be at least of equal importance as the military in the training of Prince William, and he and Prince Henry were sent to the ordinary "gymnasium," or public school, as we should call, it, at Cassel, a little town in the old Duchy of Hesse, which the parents deliberately chose be-cause it was some distance from Berlin. The sanction of the Emperor William had to be ob-tained for this plan, and though he gave it there can be little doubt that he really disapproved. .

This "magnanimous resolve, heretofore un-exampled in the annals of our reigning families," was indeed regarded with mixed feelings by the country generally. It was not, as was supposed by many, an English idea to send the heir to the throne to an ordinary school. The Prince of Wales had not been educated at all on those lines, and there was certainly no precedent in the Royal House of Prussia. The plan was not without risks, but on the whole it succeeded admirably. By the special wish of the parents, the two princes were treated just like other boys; they were addressed as "you," and were called "Prince William" and "Prince Henry." "No one," said an English newspaper correspondent, "seeing these two simple, kindly-looking lads in their plain military frocks, sitting on a form at the Cassel Gymnasium among the other pupils, would have guessed that they were the two young Imperial Princes."

The Princes had one privilege accorded them; they lived with their tutor, Dr. Hinzpeter, but this circumstance certainly did nothing to reconcile Bismarck to the plan.

Bismarck gives a significant account of his meeting with Hinzpeter at a time when public opinion was busy with the Polish question, and the Alvensleben Convention aroused the indignation of the Liberals in the Diet. Hinzpeter was introduced to Bismarck at a gathering at the Crown Prince's. "As he was in daily communication with the Royalties, and gave himself out to be a man of Conservative opinions, I ventured upon a conversation with him, in which I set forth my views of the Polish question, in the expectation that he would now and again find opportunity of giving expression to it." Some days later Hinzpeter wrote to Bismarck that the Crown Princess had asked to know the subject of their long conversation. He had recounted it all to her, and had then reduced it to writing, and he sent Bismarck the memorandum with the request that he would examine it, and make any needful corrections. This was really courting a snub, which Bismarck hastened to administer, flatly refusing Hinzpeter's request.

The Princess's English ideas prevailed in the physical education of her children, and in her care to occupy them with such innocent pursuits as gardening. But the mother's desire that her eldest son should not be too much under the glamour of military glory was defeated, partly by the boy's own firmness of character, partly by the events of history. The three great wars which culminated in the foundation of the German Empire—the Danish, the Austrian, and the French—covered the period of his boyhood, and his earliest recollections of his father were of a great soldier going forth to win the laurels of victory over the successive enemies of his country. The young Prince in fact spent most of his impressionable years in the full influence of that hero-worship for Frederick the Great which formed the strongest link between the father and the son, though it is plain that each admired his great forbear for different reasons.

CHAPTER XV

THE REGENCY

In the January of 1874 the Crown Princess went to Russia to be present at the marriage of her brother, the Duke of Edinburgh, with the Grand Duchess Marie Alexandrovna. Unlike most Royal personages, many of whom regard such functions as weddings as duties to be endured, the Crown Princess thoroughly enjoyed the experience. The Emperor Alexander was charmed with her cleverness and enthusiasm, and gave her a ruby bracelet, which she was fond of wearing to the end of her life.

The Princess had the pleasure of entertaining the Prince and Princess of Wales on their way home from St. Petersburg. It was the first time the Princess of Wales had appeared at the Prussian Court since the War of the Duchies, and her wonderful beauty and charm of manner greatly impressed all those who were brought in contact with her.

The Crown Princess gave a splendid fancy dress ball at the New Palace in February, 1874. To some who were present it recalled the costume ball given by Queen Victoria and Prince Albert at Buckingham Palace nearly thirty years before. The Crown Princess, who was devoted to Italy and to Italian art, decided that the entertainment should be known as the Venetian Fête. She herself wore a replica of the dress in which Leonora Gonzaga was painted by Titian. A portrait of the Crown Princess in this dress was afterwards painted by Von Angeli.

The Crown Prince and Princess spent the spring of 1875 in Italy, including a long stay in Venice. There they entertained the painter Anton von Werner, who has left an enthusiastic account of their visit.

He records that the Princess drew and painted with real industry, now sketching the unequalled treasures of the past, now studying the effects of light or shade on the canals or in the square of St. Mark's. The painter was astonished, not only at the Princess's powers of technique, but also at her artistic sympathy and feeling. She seemed to know intuitively what would make a fine sketch. On the evening of her departure, he says, this artist Princess carried away with her an unforgettable picture. The Grand Canal was covered with a fleet of gondolas, each lighted with torches, while the full moon shed her radiance over the noble palaces and the Rialto Bridge.

Von Werner adds that the Princess, in spite of the many claims on her time, had since that time persevered in all her artistic studies, and he particularly mentions Von Angeli, Wilberg, Lutteroth, and Albert Hertel as painters who helped and inspired her. She did life-sized portraits of her children, Prince William and the Hereditary Princess of Saxe-Meiningen, in addition to numerous pencil and water-colour sketches of really remarkable artistic merit.

In the October of that year the Crown Prince, in a long letter to his old friend, Prince Charles of Roumania, mentions that the Princess is more industrious and successful than ever in painting and drawing, and does marvels in the way of portraits. He also describes how his wife led her Hussar regiment past the King. She did it, he says, magnificently, and looked extremely well in her simple yet becoming uniform.

The Crown Princess was of great assistance to her husband in his scheme of adding a Royal Mausoleum to the Berlin Cathedral, which should be a kind of Pantheon of the House of Hohenzollern. There were to be statues of all the Electoral Princes and Kings, with inscriptions relating the history and exploits of each. This involved a great deal of historical research, of which the Princess took her share, as also in the composition of the more detailed historical memoirs or character sketches of his ancestors to which the Crown Prince also devoted himself.

A visit to Scheveningen in 1876 enabled the Crown Princess to study, much to her delight, the historical and artistic treasures of the old cities of Holland.

It will be remembered that the Crown Princess, many years before, had had scruples about her husband's association with Freemasonry. She was perhaps reassured by a speech which he delivered in July, 1876, when Prince Frederick of the Netherlands celebrated his sixtieth anniversary as Grand Master. Freemasonry, he declared, aimed at love, freedom, and tolerance, without regard to national divisions, and he hoped it might be victorious in the struggle for intellect and liberty. This speech is particularly interesting because, only two years before, the Crown Prince had resigned his office in Grand Lodge in Berlin owing to the opposition he encountered in striving to carry out certain reforms in the craft.

1877 was an eventful year in the Prussian Imperial family. In February, Prince William received his commission in the Foot Guards; Princess Charlotte was betrothed to the Hereditary Prince Bernhard of Saxe-Meiningen; and Prince Henry made his formal entry into the Navy.

In April of this year it became known that Bismarck had made one of his not infrequent threats to resign, and Bucher wrote to Busch to tell him the news: "It is not a question of leave of absence," he said, "but a peremptory demand to be allowed to retire. The reason: Augusta, who influences her ageing consort, and conspires with Victoria (the Crown Princess)."

The year 1878 opened brightly for the Crown Princess, for in February her eldest daughter, Princess Charlotte, was married to Prince Bernhard of Saxe-Meiningen. Prince Bismarck, however, excused himself from appearing at the ceremony on the pretext of ill-health.

It was at this marriage, the first of the Crown Princess's family weddings, that her brother, the Duke of Connaught, made the acquaintance of his future wife.

In the month of May came the attempted assassination of the Emperor by a youth called Hodel. The Emperor then had a marvellous escape, but on June 2, which happened to be a Sunday, the aged Sovereign was driving down Unter den Linden when, from an upper window of an inn called " The Three Ravens," Nobeling, a Socialist, fired two charges of buckshot into the Emperor's head and shoulders. Violent hæmorrhage set in, and for some hours it was said, first, that he was dead, and secondly, that if not dead he could not survive the day.

The Crown Prince and Princess were then in England, and the news reached them at Hatfield, where they were staying with Lord and Lady Salisbury. Within a very short time of the receipt of the telegram, they started for Berlin, finding on their arrival that the Emperor had recovered sufficiently to sign an order conferring the Regency on the Crown Prince.

The Regency was hardly more than titular, for the old Emperor stipulated that his son was only to "represent" him, and that the government was to be carried on as before in accordance with the Emperor's known views. As to that, Bismarck had his own ideas, and he succeeded in overcoming the Crown Prince's natural hesitation at accepting such a position.

Nevertheless, it was an extraordinarily sudden and dramatic change in the whole position of the Crown Prince and Princess. In the first place it absolutely put an end to the plan, which had been seriously discussed and on the whole approved by Bismarck, that the Crown Prince should become Governor-General or Lieutenant-Governor of Alsace-Lorraine. Obviously this scheme was no longer practical. The Emperor was old and his wound was serious; the accession of his son seemed imminent.

It is curious to recall that, so far back as January, 1862, Queen Augusta, speaking to Prince Hohenlohe, had observed: "The King and I are old people: we can hardly hope to do more than work for the future. But I wish we could look forward to a happier state of things for our son." She was destined to live thirty years longer, and to survive the son to whom she ever proved herself a loyal and devoted mother, while her husband, whom even then she described as old, was destined to live more than another quarter of a century—almost as long, in fact, as the son who succeeded him for so tragically brief a reign.

But now, in 1878, it seemed as if the Crown Prince, even in the unlikely event of his father's recovery from his wound, must become virtual ruler of the German Empire.

A very few days, however, made it clear that Bismarck was determined to allow the new Regent as little authority as possible beyond that conferred by the signing of State documents, and that he was to have no practical influence on foreign politics. But fortune, then as always, seemed to single out Bismarck for special favour, for in the all-important matter of Russo-German relations the Crown Prince was far easier to manage, in so far as any management of him was necessary, than the old Emperor, who was fondly attached to his nephew, the Tsar Alexander II.

Those months, during which the Crown Prince exercised in theory a power which he certainly did not possess in reality, were among the most trying of all the trying months the Crown Princess ever passed through, the more so that the Berlin Congress, which she and the Prince had gone to England to avoid, opened on June 13. Among those who sojourned in Berlin during those eventful days, and whose presence must

s

have been a pleasure to the Princess, were Lord
and Lady Salisbury.

But during the Congress the Crown Prince
and Princess kept rigidly apart from even its social
functions, the only exception being that the Crown
Prince gave an official dinner in the King's name
to the plenipotentiaries. The Crown Princess
stayed out at Potsdam, while the Empress refused
to appear in any official way ; she treated her
son entirely as if he were already Emperor.

Most serious was the sharp division caused
between the father and son by the decisions of
the Congress. The Crown Prince, who had a lifelong dislike and suspicion of Russia and of Russian statecraft, was supposed to have favoured
England, and the old Emperor, to the very
end of his life, considered that Germany had
not done as well at the Congress as she should
have done. He ascribed the fact—probably most
unfairly—to the Crown Prince instead of to
Bismarck.

Meanwhile, all kinds of gossip were rife as to
the Crown Princess's efforts to influence her husband, for by the public at large the Regent was
regarded as all-powerful.

To give an example of how the Princess was
misunderstood and misjudged ; when Hodel
attacked the Emperor, the latter declared that
he did not wish the full severity of the law to be
exercised. But when Nobeling's far more serious

attempt at assassination followed, public opinion demanded that Hodel should be condemned to death. The Crown Prince, as Regent, had to sign the death-warrant, and it became known that he had told a personal friend how very painful it was to him to sign it. It was widely believed that this over-scrupulousness, for so the good Berliners considered it, was due to the influence of the Crown Princess; yet as a matter of fact she had been, from the first, of opinion that Hodel, who had certainly meant to kill his Sovereign, should be executed.

In spite, however, of Bismarck's determination to make him a cypher, the Crown Prince did not allow himself to be put wholly in the background. To the Minister's great annoyance, he opened a personal correspondence with the new Pope, Leo XIII, in the hope of putting an end to the Kulturkampf. Though at the time it did not seem as though the Prince had succeeded, it laid the foundations for the ultimate solution of the problem.

The Regent also appointed a certain Dr. Friedberg, a distinguished Jewish jurist, who belonged to the Liberal party, to a very high judicial post. Curiously enough, this was the only appointment the Crown Prince made which was not afterwards revoked. The Emperor William I retained Friedberg, but refused to bestow on him the Black Eagle even after he had served for nine years in office. Ten years later, when the Emperor Frederick was on his way home from San Remo after his father's death, he received a Ministerial delegation at Leipzig, and, on seeing Friedberg, he took the Black Eagle from his own neck and placed it about that of his old friend.

By the end of the year, the Emperor was quite himself again. On a certain memorable evening in December, he appeared at the Opera and was the object of an extraordinary popular demonstration. The next day he wrote an open letter to the Crown Prince, thanking him in the warmest terms for the way in which he had fulfilled his duties as Regent.

It was rumoured at the time—it is difficult to know with what truth—that the Crown Princess would have liked, after the recovery of her father-in-law, that a special post should be created for her husband. But on his side the Crown Prince said to an English friend that he had no wish to find himself the fifth wheel of the coach, and that he hated having only a semblance of authority.

During that visit to England which was so suddenly interrupted by Nobeling's attempt on the Emperor, Mr. Goschen, the statesman whom Lord Randolph Churchill afterwards "forgot" at the time of his dramatic resignation, was asked to arrange a meeting between the Crown

Prince and Princess and George Eliot. The novelist thus describes the party in a letter to a friend :

" The Royalties did themselves much credit. The Crown Prince is really a grand-looking man, whose name you would ask for with expectation if you imagined him no royalty. He is like a grand antique bust—cordial and simple in manners withal, shaking hands, and insisting that I should let him know when next we came to Berlin, just as if he had been a Professor Gruppe, living *au troisième*. *She* is equally good-natured and unpretending, liking best to talk of nursing soldiers, and of what her father's taste was in literature. We had a picked party to dinner—the Dean of Westminster, the Bishop of Peterborough, Lord and Lady Ripon, Dr. Lyon Playfair, Kinglake, Froude, Mrs. Ponsonby (Lord Grey's granddaughter), and two or three more 'illustrations'; then a small detachment coming in after dinner. It was really an interesting occasion."

This was the kind of party which the Crown Princess thoroughly enjoyed, though even then her shyness always struck those who met her for the first time. On this occasion she opened her conversation with George Eliot by saying, " You know my sister Louise ? "—and George Eliot's comment is " just as any other slightly embarrassed mortal might have done."

On December 14, the anniversary of the

Prince Consort's death, the Crown Princess suffered another, and a hardly less terrible bereavement.

Her beloved sister, Princess Alice, Grand Duchess of Hesse, after losing one child from diphtheria and devotedly nursing her husband and her other children, herself fell a victim to the malady, the treatment of which was not then so well understood as it is now. The sisters had been fondly attached to one another from childhood, and after Princess Alice's marriage the tie was drawn even closer. They had been inseparable during the Franco-Prussian War, and for many years the happiest days spent each year by the Crown Princess were those when she was able to pay a flying visit to the Grand Duchess, or when the Grand Duchess was able to spend a few days at Berlin or Potsdam.

But there was yet another and an even more bitter sorrow in store for the Crown Princess. In March, 1879, her third son, Prince Waldemar, died in his eleventh year. He was a clever, affectionate, merry-hearted boy, and would have been his mother's favourite child, if she had allowed herself to make differences between her children. Like the Princess herself, he had been intellectually far in advance of his years, and he had had as tutor a distinguished professor, Herr Delbrück, who succeeded Treitschke in the Chair of History at the Berlin University, and afterwards played a considerable part in German thought and even in German politics.

It is shocking to have to record an example of the prejudice which was even then still felt in certain circles in Germany against the bereaved Crown Princess. A minister of the sect who called themselves the Orthodox Protestants, when he heard of the death of the young Prince, observed that he hoped it was a trial sent by God to humiliate her hard heart. This monstrous utterance must have found its way into print, or to the ears of some singularly ill-advised human being, for the Princess came to know of it, and in her then state of anguish it gave her more pain than perhaps even the minister himself would have wished to inflict.

It was natural that the mother's heart should at this moment turn with keen anxiety to her son, Prince Henry, who was then serving abroad in a German warship. She imagined him in the midst of all sorts of perils, and she begged the Emperor to allow him to return home at once. But the Sovereign, though expressing kindly sympathy, was obliged, in view of the rigid rules of the service, to refuse her petition, and the Princess had to bear as best she could this addition to her burden.

At this time the Crown Princess's relations with Bismarck had undergone some improvement. On February 23, 1879, Bismarck gave to Busch a most unflattering picture of the old Emperor, but he described the Crown Princess as unaffected and sincere, like her husband, " which her mother-in-law is not." He observed that it was only family considerations (the Coburger and the Augusten-burger more than the uncle in Hanover) that made the Crown Princess troublesome, formerly more so than at present. " But she is honourable and has no pretensions."

It was thought that the Crown Princess was sadly in need of mental change and refreshment after the two terrible blows which had deprived her of her child and of her sister. She, therefore, went to stay in Rome *incognito* during the April of 1880, being only attended by a lady-in-waiting and her " chambellan." To those of her English friends whom she happened to meet she spoke constantly of her dead son, saying that he had been the most promising of her children, and that she felt as if she could never be resigned to her loss. In answer to a kindly suggestion that she had so many duties to perform that she would soon be taken out of herself, she said: " Ah, yes, there is much to do and one cannot sit down with one's sorrow, but the mother who has lost her child carries a heavy heart all her life."

During this stay in Rome, the Princess spent almost the whole of each day in the picture galleries, and in the evening she generally dined with some of her English friends and members of the diplomatic corps. As was always her wont, she managed to see all the more interesting strangers who were just then in Rome, many being asked to meet her at the British Embassy. One night, when Lady Paget asked her whom she would like to meet, she answered instantly : "Cardinal Howard and Mr. Story" (the American sculptor). The Princess, however, could not stay as long in Rome as she would have liked, for she had to hurry back to be present at the Emperor's golden wedding festivities.

Fortunately for the Crown Princess, there came other thoughts to distract her from her grief. She welcomed her first grandchild, the Hereditary Princess of Saxe-Meiningen giving birth to a daughter, and in April, 1880, her eldest son Prince William was betrothed to Princess Victoria of the House of Schleswig-Holstein-Augustenburg, an alliance entirely approved by his parents. The Crown Prince, in a letter to Prince Charles of Roumania, said that it was really a love-match, and that the young Princess possessed remarkable gifts of heart, mind, and character, as well as a certain gracious dignity. It was also felt that the marriage would be a sort of compensation to the Augustenburg family for the loss of the Elbe Duchies.

In September, 1880, the Crown Princess had the joy of welcoming back Prince Henry from his voyage round the world, and the marriage of Prince William took place in February, 1881, amid universal rejoicings.

The Crown Princess's influence on the artistic life of Germany was shown by a little incident connected with her eldest son's marriage.   On the occasion of the wedding the town of Berlin decorated the streets in a particularly original and beautiful way, and other Prussian towns gave the young people as a wedding present a really artistic table service.   The Crown Prince exclaimed : " And whom have we to thank that such things can be done by us in Germany to-day ?   Not least my wife ! "

In the following March, when the Crown Prince was in Russia attending the funeral of Alexander II, who had been assassinated by Nihilists, the Princess received an anonymous threatening letter, informing her that her husband would also fall a victim to the Nihilists in the next few hours. She was in a dreadful state of agitation until reassuring telegrams arrived.

A son was born to Prince and Princess William on May 6, 1882, and the old Emperor William telegraphed to the Crown Prince : " Praise and thanks to God !   Four generations of Kings living ! What a rare event !   May God shield the mother and child ! "

In November of the same year, the Crown Princess had a curious conversation with Prince Hohenlohe, who thus records it :

" It may be that Christian consolation does not suffice one, but it is better to keep this to oneself and think it over. Plato's dialogues and the ancient tragedies she finds very consolatory. Much that she said was true. But she is too incautious and hasty in her verdicts upon things which are, after all, worthy of reverence."

CHAPTER XVI

SILVER WEDDING: THE CROWN PRINCE'S ILLNESS

THE Crown Prince and Princess now looked forward to celebrating their silver wedding on January 25, 1883.

The festivities were rather dashed by the sudden death, only four days before, of Prince Charles of Prussia, the Emperor's brother. The old Prince had never liked his English niece, and it was whispered in the diplomatic world that he had much preferred to die before rather than after the celebrations in which she was to be so conspicuous a figure!

Preparations for commemorating the anniversary with due honour had been made for fully a year before, and money was being collected for various presentations, when it was intimated that the Crown Prince and Princess wished the subscriptions to be devoted to public and philanthropic objects. This made a great impression, and the central committee raised the large sum of £42,000, mostly in quite small contributions. It was presented to the Prince and Princess on February 16, with the request that it should be used for charitable purposes chosen by their Imperial Highnesses.

The money was accordingly distributed among the various charities with which the Crown Prince and Princess were connected, and some of which they had themselves founded—such as the workmen's colonies for reclaiming the unemployed and finding temporary occupation for them; institutions for the technical and practical education of working men in their leisure hours; the promotion of health in the home; the Victoria School for the training of nurses; and the Victoria Foundation for the training of young girls in domestic and industrial work. The city of Berlin had a separate fund, which reached the round sum of £10,000, and of this £5900 was spent on building a nursing institute.

The death of Prince Charles caused the postponement of the festivities to the end of February, when they were held in what we should call "full State." The Prince of Wales represented Queen Victoria, and the Emperor Francis Joseph also sent his heir-apparent.

The principal ceremony was both impressive and artistic, and there we can trace the influence of the Crown Princess. It consisted in a representation of the Court of Queen Elizabeth, arranged by the artists of Berlin. The Crown Prince, in the uniform of the Queen's Cuirassiers, and the Crown Princess in white satin and silver lace, led the magnificent procession, in which all the Royal personages took part. After the Crown Prince and Princess had taken their seats between the Emperor and Empress, a dramatic representation of the Court of Charles the Bold, of Burgundy, with its picturesque troubadours, was given, followed by the Elizabethan Pageant. Then came what was perhaps the most interesting scene of all—a large assemblage dressed to represent the great painters of the Renaissance in Italy, Germany, and the Netherlands, who advanced, one by one, and did obeisance to the Crown Prince and Princess as patrons of the arts.

In May, 1883, the Princess paid a private visit to Paris. She only stayed three days, but during those three days undertook more intelligent sight-seeing than most women of her then age would have found possible. She was entertained at luncheon by Lord Lyons, and at dinner at Saint Germain by Prince Hohenlohe, who in his diary rather ungraciously observes: "Rural excursions with Royal personages are not exactly among the pleasant things of life."

During this visit the Princess said to a French friend that one of the lives she would have liked to lead would have been that of a little bourgeoise of the Rue Saint Denis, going on high-days and holidays to the Théâtre Français.

The Crown Princess was now able to carry out her cherished project of building an English church dedicated to St. George in Berlin, largely with the £5700 which was contributed in England for the silver wedding celebrations. The wisdom of this employment of the money subscribed may perhaps be doubted, for it can only have confirmed the idea prevailing in some quarters that the Princess remained, and would always remain, an English-woman in all her feelings and sympathies. However, the laying of the foundation-stone, which the Crown Princess performed herself in the spring of 1884, was carried out with considerable ceremony.

The Crown Prince made a speech on the occasion, in which he recalled that King Frederick William IV had assigned one of the rooms in the palace of Monbijou to the use of the English congregation, and that the King's brother, the then Emperor, actuated by the same feelings, had granted the land on which the church was to be built. The Crown Princess took the keenest interest in the building, and followed the carrying out of the architect's plans in every detail.

After the death of Field-Marshal Baron von Mantueffel, Stadthalter of Alsace-Lorraine, it was suggested that the Crown Prince might be his successor, but the old Emperor refused to consider the notion, while being willing to consider the appointment of the young Prince William. It is said that the Crown Princess herself went to her father-in-law and begged him not to put so great an affront on her husband. The post was, there-fore, conferred on Prince Hohenlohe.

In the November of 1885, Matthew Arnold

paid a visit to Germany in order to obtain information as to the German system of education. The
Crown Princess was keenly interested in the inquiries he was making. With her usual energy,
she went to considerable personal trouble in order
to help him, and she arranged, among other things,
that Mr. Arnold should make a short stay on Count
Redern's property, in the Mark of Brandenburg.

In one of his letters Arnold gives a charming
account of a soirée at the New Palace: "The
Crown Princess came round the circle, and I kissed
her hand, as everyone here does when she holds it
out. She talked to me a long time, and said I
must come and see her quietly, comfortably." A
few days later he dined at the palace, the only
other guest being Hoffmann, the great chemist.
Arnold sat next the Crown Princess, who "talked
I may say all dinner. She is very able and well-
informed."

A day or two later came a message asking him
to tea with the Crown Princess: " She was full of
the Eastern question, as all of them here are ; it
is of so much importance to them. She talked,
too, about Bismarck, Lord Ampthill, the Emperor,
the Empress, the Queen, the Church, English
politics, the German nation, everything and everybody indeed, except the Crown Prince and herself."

Mr. Arnold was very anxious to meet "the
great Reichs-Kanzler" himself, but this was not
easy, as the great man was reputed to be almost

inaccessible : but the Crown Princess herself wrote and asked Bismarck to receive her compatriot.

Matthew Arnold was struck by the lack in Berlin of what certainly exists in London and Paris, namely, an agreeable, cultivated society consisting mainly of upper middle-class elements. He observed that in Berlin there was, in addition to the Court, only groups of functionaries, of soldiers, and of professors.

As may be gathered from much that has already appeared in this volume, the Crown Princess was ever pathetically anxious that England and Germany should be on the most friendly terms of confidence and affection. Consequently she went through some days of considerable anxiety, in the spring and early summer of 1884, over the "incident" of Angra Pequena. When Lord Granville decided to recognise German sovereignty in this territory, the Crown Princess was quite as pleased in her way as Bismarck was. Lord Ampthill, in a letter to Lord Granville, observes : " The Crown Princess, who dined with us last night, was beyond measure happy at the general contentment and altered tone of the Press."

This Lord Ampthill, the Lord Odo Russell of former days, was a valued friend of the Crown Princess. She was always, naturally, on terms of friendship with her mother's representative in Berlin, but Lord Ampthill's appointment had given her special satisfaction. The Ambassador's

T

premature death in 1884 was a great grief to the Princess, and the day after his death the Crown Prince himself came to the villa, where Lord and Lady Ampthill had lived near Sans Souci, to lay a wreath on the coffin.

The health of the old Emperor now began to give occasion for anxiety. He had been born on March 22, 1797, and when he reached his eighty-seventh birthday in 1884 it seemed as if his course was almost run. In the circumstances the Crown Prince and Princess could scarcely help anticipating the time when, as it then seemed, the great powers and responsibilities of the throne would be theirs. But it is certainly true to say that the feeling of duty was paramount in their minds, and that nothing was further from their thoughts than to covet the Imperial purple for its own sake. They regarded it as the symbol of all that they were determined to do for the welfare and happiness of the people.

Even if they had been blind to the apparently immediate consequences of the old Emperor's failing health, they would have been enlightened by the altered demeanour of Prince Bismarck. He showed clear signs of a desire to cultivate better relations with the Heir Apparent and his family, and he even attended an evening party given by the Crown Princess on the occasion of her birthday.

Not long afterwards, early in 1885, the Crown

Prince sounded Bismarck as to whether, in the event of the Emperor's death, he would remain in office. The astute Chancellor said that he would, subject to two conditions, namely, that there should be no foreign influences in State policy, and that there should be no Parliamentary government; it is said that the Crown Prince assented with an eloquent gesture.

The real tragedy of the Crown Princess's life surely lies in these years of waiting. She could not—assuredly she did not—for a moment wish that the old Emperor should die. She had nursed him devotedly during the long illness caused by Nobeling's attempted assassination, and it is a significant fact that she alone had been able to persuade the stern old soldier to leave his hard camp bed for a soft invalid couch. She knew as well as anyone the Emperor's noble qualities, and she cherished for him a warm and filial affection.

Yet it was patent, especially to all those who shared the strong political and constitutional opinions of the Crown Princess, that the aged Sovereign had outlived his usefulness to his country. She could not help being conscious that in her husband, and in herself, too, there lay capacities of national service of which William I and his consort had never dreamed.

If the word "disappointment" is used of the Crown Princess's long-deferred hopes, it was in no sense the baulking of any commonplace ambition.

The tragedy lay in the failure of the pure and single-hearted dedication of her husband and herself to bettering the lot of those vast, silent millions on whose pains and toil the pomp of thrones and empires, the exquisite refinements of civilisation, the discoveries of science, and the delights of art and literature, seemed to her to be all ultimately based.

The sympathies of one of the most warmhearted women who ever lived were thus continually torn and divided, for while it seemed to her loyal nature an act of treachery to look forward to the old Emperor's death, she was continually being reminded, by the demeanour of those about her, that that event, which would so entirely alter her position, was expected almost daily.

In the midst of this subtle mental and spiritual conflict, the Crown Princess was struck by yet another arrow from the quiver of fate, inflicting an anguish of anxiety which even her bitterest enemies would surely have wished her to be spared.

In April, 1886, the Crown Prince suffered from a severe attack of measles, which probably left him in a weakened state, as this disease is apt to do when it attacks a man of over fifty. However, he was thought to have recovered sufficiently to visit the King and Queen of Italy on the Riviera in the autumn, and it was there, while out driving, that the Prince caught a severe cold, which brought on an affection of the throat.

The Princess herself undertook, with great efficiency, the chief responsibilities of nursing the patient. But the throat affection did not yield to treatment, and the terrible suspicion that it might never so yield must often have assailed the Princess, even in these early months of her husband's illness. But she did not betray the anxiety gnawing at her heart; on the contrary, she showed throughout a gallant optimism which, as we now look back on it, seems intensely pathetic.

It was the more necessary that the Princess should never for a moment relax her cheerfulness, because the patient himself soon began to suffer from periods of deep depression. To one friend he even said that his time had already passed away, and the future belonged to his son; to another he declared that he had become an old man and stood with one foot in the grave.

On the Emperor William's ninetieth birthday, March 22, 1887, the sailor son of the Crown Princess, Prince Henry of Prussia, was formally betrothed to his cousin, his mother's favourite niece, Princess Irene of Hesse.

During the festivities given in honour of the event, it began to be whispered among the guests that the Crown Prince's throat affection was more serious than had as yet been acknowledged. But it is said that the word " cancer " was only first mentioned in connection with the case when, in deference to the highest medical advice of Berlin, he was sent to Ems to be treated for " a bad cold with bronchial complications following on measles."

The Crown Prince and Princess, with their family, went to Ems in the middle of April and spent a month there. Not only did this bring no improvement, but the patient became perceptibly worse. He was brought back to Berlin, and a consultation of the most eminent medical experts, including Bergmann, Gerhardt, and Wagener, was held, as the result of which a growth in the throat of a malignant character was diagnosed.

Bismarck in his *Reminiscences* contradicts two curious stories which are worth notice, if only for the reason that they have obtained a certain amount of currency, and one of them is even to be found in an English work on the Emperor William II.

The first of these stories is that, after his return from Ems, the Crown Prince signed a document in which, in the event of his surviving his father, he renounced his succession to the throne in favour of his eldest son. There is not, says Bismarck, a shadow of truth in this story.

The other statement is that any heir to the Prussian throne who suffers from an incurable physical complaint is, by the Hohenzollern family law, excluded from the succession. The importance of this provision, if it really existed, is obvious; and, at the period we have now reached, when the physical state of the Crown Prince became a subject of intense public interest, it obtained wide currency and no small amount of credit. If, on a strict interpretation of such a rule, the Crown Prince was excluded from the succession, it might have been argued that his eldest son was also incapable of succeeding, owing to the weakened state of his arm. But Bismarck declares categorically that the Hohenzollern family law contains no provision on the matter at all, any more than does the text of the Prussian constitution.

Bismarck goes on to say that the doctors who were treating the Crown Prince resolved at the end of May to carry out the removal of the larynx under an anæsthetic without having informed the Prince of their intention. The Chancellor, however, immediately raised objections; required that they should not proceed without the consent of the Prince; and, further, that as they were dealing with the successor to the throne, the consent of the head of the dynasty should also be obtained. The old Emperor, therefore, after being informed of the circumstances by Bismarck, forbade the doctors to carry out the operation without the consent of the Crown Prince.

It must be remembered, in considering the diagnosis of the German experts, that laryngology was at that time almost in its infancy, and it was natural that the Crown Princess should have clung desperately to the belief that a mistake had been made. Indeed, it is said that Professor Bergmann himself advised that the opinion of some other eminent throat specialist should be obtained before it was decided to have recourse to surgical interference.

This was the position when the eminent English throat specialist, Dr. (afterwards Sir) Morell Mackenzie was summoned. There is no need here to go over in detail the painful controversy which was engendered by this step, and which was embittered, not only by thorny questions of professional etiquette, but also by irrelevant political passions. Our purpose is rather to state the principal facts, and leave the reader to form his own conclusions.

The Crown Princess was widely believed to have insisted that the English specialist should be called in simply because of her English prejudices, and this was considered an affront to the medical profession in Germany. As a matter of fact a list of the most eminent throat specialists in Europe was drawn up. One was a Frenchman, another a Viennese, and the third was Morell Mackenzie. The Frenchman was discarded for political reasons, the Viennese for other reasons, and it was a consensus of political and medical opinion which led to the choice of the English specialist.

On May 20, 1887, Dr. Morell Mackenzie arrived in Berlin. The German physicians informed him that they believed they had to deal with a cancer, but they desired his diagnosis. Mackenzie performed more than one small operation to serve as a basis for a microscopic examination, which was entrusted to Professor Virchow, probably the greatest physiologist then living. It was Virchow who reported, to the exultant relief and joy of the Crown Princess, that, while he found a certain thickening of the membrane, he had "discovered nothing to excite suspicions of a wider and graver disease."

Henceforth there was a party in Berlin who were convinced that the growth, if growth it was, in the Crown Prince's throat was benign. But it may serve as an illustration of the passions which the whole affair aroused when it is stated that there were many who asserted that Virchow had been deliberately deceived, and that the English specialist had refrained from submitting to him those portions of the membrane which would have clearly shown the presence of malignant disease. It was this monstrous accusation which chiefly served to inflame the controversy on both sides.

Virchow's report greatly relieved the anxieties of the Crown Prince and Princess at the time, and, relying on it implicitly, they went to England with their daughters in the middle of

June for three months. They stayed at first on the healthy heights of Norwood, in the south of London, going later to Scotland and the Isle of Wight.

While at Norwood they saw many distinguished English people, though even then the Prince was prohibited from uttering a word above his breath. Those who met the Prince at this time were painfully struck by his appearance. He was much thinner, and he spoke only in a whisper, but the Princess, who, being always with him, did not notice the gradual change which had come over him, was full of hope. Indeed, she found time to continue her interest in social work. She was present at a gathering held in Drapers' Hall to promote the training of women teachers, and her old friend Lord Granville made a charming little speech about her youth.

The Crown Prince was present with his wife at Queen Victoria's Golden Jubilee, and it is still remembered how great an impression was made on the London populace by his knightly figure in his white Cuirassier uniform. His was the central and by far the most magnificent presence, like some paladin of mediæval chivalry, in the mounted escort of princes which surrounded the venerable Sovereign on her way to and from Westminster Abbey.

During their stay in Scotland, the Crown Prince was asked by a gentleman to name his steam launch. He chose the name *The White Heather*, showing how his thoughts travelled back to the day, nearly thirty years before, when he had gathered on a Scotch mountain the symbolic sprig of white heather to give to the Princess Royal.

The Crown Prince and Princess returned to Germany in the middle of September, and proceeded to Toblach, in the Tyrol. But the climate there was considered too chilly, and the patient was moved to Venice at the end of the month. It was from Venice that the Prince wrote to an old friend a pathetic letter full of hope, in which he said that the real trouble was now overcome, and that it was only necessary to avoid speaking and catching cold. Early in October the Prince was again moved to Baveno, on Lake Maggiore, and at the beginning of November to the Villa Zirio, at San Remo. From San Remo the Princess telegraphed for Dr. Morell Mackenzie, who arrived on November 5.

The Villa Zirio was a comfortable house standing in its own grounds. The first floor, which consisted of two suites of large rooms, was occupied by the Crown Prince and Princess. On this floor were also the rooms of the Princess's lady-in-waiting, Countess von Bruschl. The second floor was assigned to the three young princesses and the rest of the suite.

Unfortunately, owing to the great curiosity

and anxiety felt all over Europe as to the progress of the Crown Prince's illness, the little Italian town was filled with newspaper representatives, their headquarters being a large hotel opposite the Villa Zirio.   In fact, during the winter of 1887–8, all the world was watching the race between the two lives—that of the ninety-year-old Emperor, and that of his son, already stricken with a mortal disease, on whom so many fair hopes rested.

The Crown Prince and Princess owed a great deal, at this troubled period of their lives, to the devotion and vigilant loyalty of their friend and servant, Count Theodor Seckendorff, whose official position in the Crown Princess's Household was that of " chambellan."

Seckendorff was once well described by an English friend as " the Baldassare Castiglione of the present day."   He was, indeed, " the perfect courtier."   His father, a distinguished diplomatist, had been attached to the Prussian Legation in London, and so the Count knew England and the English intimately.   Indeed, he had obtained leave to accompany Lord Napier of Magdala on the Abyssinian campaign, and he was also with that distinguished commander on the North-West frontier of India.   Afterwards he was on the staff of the Crown Prince in the Franco-German War, and was chosen by the latter to be one of the officers to escort Napoleon III to Wilhelmshöhe.

Thereafter the Count's relationship with the Crown Prince and Princess became even closer.

A man of fine literary and artistic taste, and a really good artist, Count Seckendorff spoke English, Italian, and French with ease and distinction, and he retained—what few men and women seem able to retain in the world of Courts—a great simplicity of manner and an absolute sincerity of nature. While patriotically devoted to his own country, he was also a true lover of England, and he always did everything that lay in his power to ease the often strained relations between the two nations. After the death of the Empress Frederick, Count Seckendorff continued in faithful and kindly touch with her native country. He organised the Loan Exhibition of British Art in Berlin as late as 1908, and his premature death, two years later, caused much sorrow to a large circle of attached friends in both London and Berlin.

To return to the life at San Remo; in a letter written about this time the Crown Princess says:

" We are passing through a time of heavy trial, but the knowledge that the nation has not forgotten us, and that it hopes and sympathises with us, is a perpetual source of comfort. If it be God's will, this confidence will remain the Crown Prince's most valued future possession, and be the greatest help to him in achieving his noble ideals. Who can tell how many days may yet be granted to him ? But when we see him so virile and fresh,

we can only trust to the strength of his constitution and believe that his health will not fail
him in carrying out his duties, though even in
the happiest circumstances he will have to econo-
mise his strength and use his voice as little as
possible."

From San Remo, too, the Crown Prince wrote
to his beloved French tutor a touching letter, in
which occurs the following passage :

" As to the life we are leading here, it could
not be more intimate and more *gemütlich*.   First
of all, my wife nurses me as might a true Sister
of Charity, with a calm and knowledge truly
admirable.   Our daughters surround us with their
loving tenderness, and the Riviera is a delightful
climate and does us much good."

Even then, the Crown Princess had not given
up hope.   Her husband still looked in good health ;
he slept well, and his appetite was excellent.

On December 1, the Princess herself wrote
to M. Godet :

" We are profoundly touched by the many
proofs of sympathy which reach us from all sides.
I cannot help feeling that it must make you very
happy to know that all the care you took, in old
days, in developing that pure and noble soul, has
now brought to him these universal tributes of
respect and confidence."

Alas, even then the Prince had heard from the
physicians his sentence of death, which he received

with the same stoicism he had shown on the field of battle.

Christmas came, and was celebrated with characteristic kindliness by the Prince, who arranged magnificent gifts for his wife and the little circle of intimate friends at San Remo. But his health steadily declined, and a sudden operation had to be performed early in January.

Meanwhile the aged Emperor had caught a chill in the severe Berlin winter. His magnificent constitution was already enfeebled by age, and to his physical weakness were now added the distress and anxiety caused by the news from San Remo, which became continually more and more disquieting. The end soon came, and the stout old soldier sank and died on March 9, 1888, less than a fortnight before his ninety-second birthday.

CHAPTER XVII

THE HUNDRED DAYS' REIGN

ON the morning of March 9, 1888, the Crown Prince was walking in the gardens of the Villa Zirio, when a telegram was brought to him. He took it up with languid interest, but when he read the address, " To His Imperial Majesty the Emperor Frederick William," there was no need to open the envelope, and it is said that his habitual self-control deserted him, and he burst into tears.

A pathetic, and yet in its way a magnificent, scene followed in the great drawing-room on the ground floor of the villa. The Households of the new Emperor and Empress had assembled there and stood in a circle waiting. . . .

Suddenly the Emperor appeared, and we have the following striking description from one who claims to have been a witness of what occurred :

" He had become handsome again, as in the radiant days of his youth. His beard, with a few silver streaks, glowed in the brilliant light cast by the chandelier. Tall and well built, he dominated the entire company. His blue eyes were slightly misty. His delicate complexion, now heightened with a little colour, seemed to show the real tranquillity which had taken possession of his soul; and his mouth with the red lips had now that fascinating smile which characterised him. With a firm step he walked straight to a small table in the middle of the drawing-room and wrote—for the tube in his throat prevented him from speaking— a few lines, which he signed. An officer read out the paper aloud—it was the announcement of the death of the Emperor William I and of his own accession as Frederick III. The Emperor then walked towards the Empress, made a long and reverent bow, paying full homage to his wife's devotion, and with a grave and tender gesture passed round her neck the Ribbon of the Black Eagle."

It is also recorded that the Emperor walked up to Dr. Morell Mackenzie and, after shaking him warmly by the hand, wrote for him the following words: "I thank you for having made me live long enough to recompense the valiant courage of my wife."

The Emperor Frederick, with the Empress and their daughters, set out for Berlin on March 10, making what was then the swiftest journey in the records of Continental travel. The only interruption, and that was very short, was to enable the Emperor to receive the greetings of his old friend, King Humbert of Italy, who had himself travelled by forced marches for the purpose.

Amid a terrible storm of sleet and snow, on

U

the night of March 11, the Imperial party entered
Berlin.

Those who then saw the Emperor, whatever
their political predilections, were amazed at his
look of health and strength. For months past a
thick veil of secrecy had been drawn over the life
at the Villa Zirio. Naturally, therefore, rumour
had had it all her own way, and in Germany
the general pessimism was undoubtedly fostered
by the medical profession. They had persuaded
themselves that the Emperor was already *in
articulo mortis,* and ₁the Empress was openly cen-
sured for bringing him back at all. It was even
believed by many that he might very well die on
the journey owing to the sudden transition from
the warm, equable climate of San Remo to the
biting cold of Berlin.

The one certain fact which had been published
was that he had undergone the operation of trache-
otomy, and that he could not speak owing to the
tube in his throat. But, apart from that, to the
general astonishment, the Emperor was, or seemed
to be, not very different from his normal condition.
At once he took up the reins of power, granting
audiences, and dealing for many hours every day
with State affairs.

Though the joy with which the friends of the
new Emperor and Empress hailed their accession
was dashed by the thought of how brief must be
the new reign, yet it is abundantly evident that

no such idea occurred to the Empress herself, and that very fact seems to enhance the poignancy of the whole tragedy.

At the beginning of the Emperor Frederick's reign, a distinguished German wrote to a friend: "The Empress, as you have rightly judged, is making her way among the people. However brief her tenure of power will be, the more will the public at large perceive the truly astounding richness and resource, the practised leadership, and the affectionate disposition of that rare creature. She is indefatigable, and gives a fresh indication of the grand aims she has in view each day."

It is significant to note how all those who knew the Empress even slightly welcomed the fact of the Emperor's accession. Thus Mrs. Augustus Craven: "Somehow I hope the present Emperor will live. Anyhow I am thankful that he is still alive, and that *she* is Empress of Germany, also that perhaps after all the very great deal there is in her is not to be lost for Germany and for Europe."

The feeling in the Court and political world is clearly shown in the memoirs of Prince Hohenlohe. He was received by the Empress a week after her return to Berlin, and he says that he found her unchanged: "her frank and cheerful manner filled me with astonishment."

Three days later Prince Hohenlohe noted in his diary that already officials were complaining of the interference of the Empress in public business. Bötticher told him that she had induced the Emperor to refuse his signature to the Anti-Socialist Bill, and that he had only given way after Bismarck had explained the matter to the Empress. The Minister added that the Emperor had little power of resistance to the influence of the Empress, and that she, again, was under the influence of "certain advanced ladies." If the Emperor's illness, he went on, was of long duration, all kinds of things might happen, but if the Emperor were well, or should become so, the influence of the Empress would diminish.

A few days later Prince Hohenlohe was himself able to judge how far this was true about the Empress, for he went out to call on his Sovereign at Charlottenburg, and found him with his wife. The Empress excused her presence by pleading the necessity of supporting the Emperor during the audience. The whole of the conversation had to be carried on, so far as the Emperor was concerned, by means of writing-tablets. Hohenlohe observed that the Emperor would benefit by the amount of work he had to do, at which the Sovereign nodded approvingly. At the end of the interview :

" The Emperor placed his hand on my shoulder and smiled sadly, so that I could hardly restrain my tears. He gave me the impression of a martyr ; and, indeed, no martyrdom in the world is comparable with this slow death. Everyone who comes near him is full of admiration for his courageous and quiet resignation to a fate which is inevitable, and which he fully realises."

But it is plain that the Empress had not yet resigned herself to consider his death as in any way imminent. Later in the same month, Hohenlohe had an audience of the Empress, and during their conversation she said something which made it clear to her old friend that she still entertained illusions as to her husband's real condition—indeed, he was himself so shaken by what she said that he wrote in his diary: " It is perhaps possible that the illness will be of long duration. The expectation of a speedy end has not yet been confirmed."

There can be no doubt that the accession of the Emperor Frederick was expected in not a few quarters to mean the almost immediate fall of Bismarck, but this expectation left out of account various important factors of the situation. Both the new Emperor and his Empress, though, as we have seen, they profoundly disapproved of Bismarck's policy as a whole, nevertheless fully realised the Chancellor's patriotism and the unparalleled services which he had been able to render to the German people. Bismarck, in his own account of his relations with the Emperor, recalls that they began as far back as 1848, when Prince Frederick William was only seventeen, and he had since received from him various proofs of personal confidence, notably on the occasion of the Dantzig episode in 1863. This confidence was, Bismarck declares, quite independent of political principles and differences of opinion, and though many attempts to shake it were made from interested quarters, they had no permanent success.

Later Bismarck also asserted roundly that the Emperor Frederick made it easy for him, by his amiability and confidence, to transfer to him the affection he had cherished for his father. He was both more open than his father had been to the constitutional idea of Ministerial responsibility, and also less hampered by family traditions in adjusting himself to political necessities. And Bismarck goes on to state that "all assertions of lasting discord in our relations are unfounded."

On the subject of the Crown Princess's influence Bismarck said :

" I could not assume that his wife had the same kindly feeling for me ; her natural innate sympathy for her home had, from the beginning, shown itself in the attempt to turn the weight of Prusso-German influence in the groupings of European power into the scale of her native land ; and she never ceased to regard England as her country. In the differences of interest between the two Asiatic Powers, England and Russia, she wished to see the German power applied in the interests of England if it came to a breach. This difference of opinion, which rested on the difference of nationality, caused many a discussion between her Royal Highness and me on the Eastern question, including the Battenberg question. Her influence on her husband was at all times great, and it increased with years, to culminate at the time when he was Emperor. She also, however, shared with him the conviction that in the interests of the dynasty it was necessary that I should be maintained in office at the change of reign."

It is interesting here to recall that on August 31, 1870, after the battle of Beaumont, Busch obtained from Bismarck the following opinion of the then Crown Prince:

"He will be reasonable later on, and allow his Ministers to govern more, and not put himself too much forward, and in general he will get rid of many bad habits that render old gentlemen of his trade sometimes rather troublesome. [It is to be feared that this uncomplimentary allusion is to the old Emperor.] For the rest, he is unaffected and straightforward; but he does not care to work much, and is quite happy if he has plenty of money and amusements, and if the newspapers praise him."

A very superficial judgment of the Emperor Frederick, and the suggestion that he was too fond of money is particularly gratuitous. As a matter of fact, only the year before his accession, in 1887, a certain Frenchman, Ballardin by name, died, leaving the whole of his fortune, valued at several million francs, to the then Crown Prince. M. Ballardin appeared to have been so embittered by disputes with the French authorities that he determined to show his hatred and contempt for his native country by the novel method of bequeathing his property to the German Crown Prince, who, however, absolutely refused to accept even the smallest portion of the legacy. That is certainly not the action of a man who could be accused of a love of money.

It may here be stated, on this subject of money, that when the Emperor Frederick succeeded to the throne, there was in the hands of Baron Kohn, the private banker of the old Emperor William, a sum of fifty-four million marks (£2,700,000), which was bequeathed ,to the Emperor Frederick as a kind of family treasure, to be controlled by the head of the House of Hohenzollern for the time being. When the Emperor Frederick died, however, it was found that the great bulk of this money had been invested abroad by his orders in the name of his widow; her uncle, the Duke of Saxe-Coburg-Gotha, and her cousin, King Leopold of Belgium, being the trustees. It is even asserted that the late Prince Stolberg resigned at the time his office of Minister of the Imperial Household in consequence of what he considered the diversion of this sum of money from the Hohenzollern family. According to another version, however, only a portion of this money became the absolute property of the Empress, the remainder being hers for life, with power of appointment among her younger children.

To return to Busch; he also obtained from Bismarck a curious anecdote of the Empress:

"I took the liberty to ask further what sort of woman the Crown Princess was, and whether she had much influence over her husband. 'I think not,' the Count said; 'and as to her intelligence, she is a clever woman; clever in a womanly way. She is not able to disguise her feelings, or at least not always. I have cost her many tears, and she could not conceal how angry she was with me after the annexations (that is to say of Schleswig and Hanover). She could hardly bear the sight of me, but that feeling has now somewhat subsided. She once asked me to bring her a glass of water, and as I handed it to her she said to a lady-in-waiting who sat near and whose name I forget, 'He has cost me as many tears as there is water in this glass.' But that is all over now."

This incident about the glass of water evidently much impressed Bismarck, for he told it to Busch again some months later, when he said of the Crown Princess, "She is in general a very clever person, and really agreeable in her way, but she should not interfere in politics."

The Empress's relations with Bismarck after her husband's accession were more pleasant than they had ever been before. The Emperor naturally leaned upon his wife, and her influence perhaps appeared greater than it was. But, whatever its precise extent, Bismarck, with his intensely practical mind, saw that it was at any rate a factor in the situation, and he made use of it accordingly. It was, indeed, as natural for him to cultivate her good will now, as it was for him a little later to heap contumely and insult on her head. Such conduct was utterly incomprehensible to the Empress, with her upright, loyal nature; she would have suffered less from the Chancellor had she been able to find the key to both his greatness and his littleness.

But, even at this time, when Bismarck had the strongest reasons for conciliating the Empress, there was one question, that of the Battenberg marriage, on which he felt compelled to do battle with her, and in which he vanquished her in fair fight.

The Empress, different as she was in many respects from her mother, was absolutely at one with Queen Victoria in her views of everything which should regulate family life. Thus, she was as firm a believer in the importance of securing happy marriages for her sons and daughters as the Queen had proved herself to be. That the union of two human beings should be guided by

State considerations was to her abhorrent. She had welcomed with eager delight her niece, Princess Irene of Hesse, as a daughter-in-law; she knew that the latter's sister, Princess Victoria, had formed a happy marriage with Prince Louis of Battenberg. Now it was Prince Louis's brother, Alexander of Bulgaria, who had been from boyhood a favourite with her sister, Princess Alice, whom the Empress desired to see married to her second daughter, Princess Victoria. The alliance had been mooted some four years before, but was then considered, by Bismarck especially, as quite out of the question, if only because the hero of Slivnitza had earned the intense hostility of the Tsar Alexander.

In July, 1885, Bismarck told Hohenlohe that, whereas the Emperor and the Crown Prince were in favour of the marriage of Princess Victoria with the King of Portugal, the Crown Princess and the young Princess herself preferred the Prince of Bulgaria, and that there was "great skirmishing" going on over the business.

More than a year later, in October, 1886, the old Emperor himself spoke to Hohenlohe of the matter, and with some bitterness, declaring that the Crown Princess and Princess Victoria still entertained the idea of this alliance. He said he had questioned the Crown Prince, who had denied it, and he further observed that in politics his son was ruled by his wife.

In 1888 the Empress still desired the marriage because she believed that the affections of her daughter were seriously engaged.   But, changed as were all the conditions of her own and the new Emperor's life, she at once found arrayed against her the same powerful influences as before, with the addition of that of her eldest son, the new Crown Prince.   The difference of opinion in the Imperial family became known to the whole of Europe, and was very frankly discussed in the English and Continental Press.   Matters seemed at a deadlock. On the one side were ranged the Empress and all those Royal personages who by kinship or marriage were connected with the Battenberg family ; on the other were the Crown Prince, Bismarck, and, it was whispered, the Emperor Frederick himself, who had a great dislike to any marriage that savoured of a *mésalliance*.

This was the position when Queen Victoria arrived at Charlottenburg to visit her stricken son-in-law.   Bismarck, with his usual unerring eye for the potentialities of a situation, seized the opportunity.   He sought an audience of the Queen, and succeeded in convincing her by his arguments that the Battenberg alliance was really extremely inadvisable.   Not until she found her mother ranged among the opponents of the marriage did the Empress yield, and consent, to use her own phrase, "to sacrifice her daughter's happiness on the altar of the Fatherland."

We have a slightly different, and probably less accurate, account of the termination of the affair in Hohenlohe's journal of May 17, 1888:

"The Empress had said that in the end it would be no misfortune if Bismarck did retire. This was at once retailed to him, whereupon the newspaper war. Malet reported to Queen Victoria at Florence that it was very disadvantageous for English interests that the Queen should appear to interest herself in the Battenberg match. It would be well, more particularly in view of her impending visit to Berlin, to prevent people from thinking she favoured the marriage. The English Ministry also concurred in this. Thereupon Queen Victoria wrote a severe letter to her daughter, the Empress; and during her stay also she expounded her views in an energetic fashion, which produced unhappy and tearful scenes. The relations between Queen Victoria and the Imperial Chancellor have shaped very well. They were enchanted with each other."

The Empress's belief that she had been fighting for her daughter's happiness added a special bitterness to her defeat at the hands of Bismarck. It may, however, be stated that the day came when the Empress Frederick acknowledged that she had been mistaken, at least to some extent, in the qualities which she had attributed to Alexander of Battenberg, and she lived to see her daughter make a happier marriage than the Battenberg alliance would probably have ever been.

Not the least pathetic feature of the Hundred Days' reign was the gallant persistence of the Empress in fulfilling the duties of her new station. She only held one Court, and one who was present has left a vivid description of the strange scene:

" The Empress was dressed in the deepest mourning, indeed wrapped in black from head to foot, her face hidden by a crape veil, while a long procession of women likewise veiled in crape filed past the throne, their black gowns high in the neck and skirts banded with crape a quarter of a yard wide, while long folds of double crape fell upon the floor in guise of Court trains."

On May 24, the marriage of Prince Henry, the second son of the Emperor and Empress, to his cousin, Princess Irene of Hesse, was celebrated at Charlottenburg. It was a bright and happy day in the midst of sadness, and everything was done to surround the ceremony with brilliance.

Death was now drawing very near to the doomed Emperor. On June 1 he was conveyed by boat from Charlottenburg to the New Palace, where he had been born, where he had spent the happiest days of his married life, and the name of which he now changed to " Friedrichskron." But he was not allowed to die in peace; his last days were disturbed by what is known as the Puttkamer incident.

Puttkamer, a typical Bismarckian, had been Minister of the Interior for seven years. In his official announcement of the old Emperor's death, he had actually made no allusion to the new Emperor; the latter in consequence insisted on the Minister's retirement as the condition of his signing the Bill prolonging the life of the Reichstag to five years. Puttkamer's resignation was gazetted on June 11, and on the same evening Prince Bismarck gave a dinner at which the fallen Minister was the guest of honour.

The Emperor Frederick died at Friedrichskron on June 15. The first message written by the widowed Empress was to the aged Empress Augusta :

"She whose one pride and happiness it was to be the wife of your son grieves with you, afflicted mother. No mother ever had so good a son. Be proud and strong in your sorrow."

CHAPTER XVIII

EARLY WIDOWHOOD : THE FALL OF BISMARCK

IT is said that one [of the last acts of the dying
Emperor was to place Bismarck's hand in that of
the Empress as a token of reconciliation. But
there was no reconciliation. On the contrary, the
Emperor Frederick was no sooner dead than
Bismarck once more became all-powerful, and
ruthlessly he used his power.

The accession of the young Emperor William
was followed by an astounding outburst of violence
against the Empress Frederick on the part of
Bismarck's tools, his agents in the Press and elsewhere—indeed, the Empress once told an intimate friend that no humiliation and pain which
could be inflicted on her had been spared her.

The first humiliation took a strange and terrible
form ; a cordon of soldiers was drawn round the
New Palace, when the Emperor Frederick was
known to be dying, in order that no secret documents might be removed without the knowledge
of the new Emperor.

The Empress, aware that this was the work of
Bismarck, requested an interview with him, but
Bismarck replied that he had no time, as he was

so fully occupied with his master, the new Emperor. As a matter of fact, everything at the New Palace which the late Emperor or the Empress Frederick considered to be important had been placed out of Bismarck's reach. For a considerable time these private papers were entrusted to the care of a person in the Empress's confidence, who resided outside the country, but ultimately they were sent back to Germany.

Unfortunately not all the late Emperor's papers had been so carefully guarded, and, to the anguish of his widow, his memory became involved in acute, and it may even be said degrading, controversy.

In the well-known review, the *Deutsche Rundschau*, Dr. Geffcken, a Liberal publicist who had been honoured by the Emperor Frederick's friendship, published extracts from the diary of the late Sovereign. They were designed to defend his memory against his traducers, and in particular to prove that it was he who suggested the united German Empire. It seems that the diaries were found locked up at the Villa Zirio, and it was stated that they were given, or at least shown, by the Emperor Frederick to Baron von Roggenbach, the Baden statesman.

Bismarck at first affected to believe, and apparently he succeeded in persuading the Emperor William, that the published extracts were forgeries. The offending number of the review

X

was accordingly suppressed, and Geffcken was arrested on September 29 on a charge of high treason. He was acquitted of criminal intention in the following January, and in the interval the *Cologne Gazette* charged Sir Robert Morier, then British Ambassador in St. Petersburg, with having given information to Marshal Bazaine of the movements of the Prussian forces in 1870. Fortunately Morier was able to produce convincing documentary evidence of his innocence, but it was generally felt that this monstrous attack on the Empress Frederick's old friend was really directed against the Empress herself.

The Empress behaved with the greatest dignity and self-restraint during this time of bitter persecution, and in the many diaries and memoirs of the period we can find but one reference which reveals how she really felt. This reference is in Sir Horace Rumbold's *Recollections*. He tells of the deep feeling with which the Empress spoke of the suffering she had passed through and the wrongs she had endured. " She spoke of them with an exceeding bitterness, emphasising what she said with clenched hands and betraying an emotion which suddenly gained me, and more than explained the Queen's well-known reference to her as her ' dear persecuted daughter.' "

It may be asked why the young Emperor William did not intervene to protect his mother from the hostility of his Chancellor. Unfortunately there is no doubt that at this time there was an estrangement between mother and son. Years before, Bismarck had taken precautions to prevent the heir presumptive from imbibing the liberal principles of both his parents, and had caused him to spend the impressionable years of early manhood entirely under the influence of his grand-father, the old Emperor, and the military glories of the new Empire. Bismarck no doubt thought that he had obtained a complete ascendancy over his new master. It was significant that, whereas on his accession the Emperor Frederick had ad-dressed his first message to the nation at large through the Chancellor, the Emperor William addressed his first messages to the Army and Navy, the civilians having to wait a day or two for their recognition. Another indication of the character of the new régime was afforded by the Emperor William's reversal of his father's decision to name the New Palace, Friedrichskron.

These and other incidents show how the Emperor began his reign under the domination of Bismarck, but it is pleasant to record that the estrangement from his mother, which the old Chancellor un-doubtedly fostered, was not of long duration.

It is curious how seldom, among the many studies, criticisms, and estimates of the Emperor William II, we find his extraordinary versatility attributed to the influence of heredity; and yet it is easy to see now that the Empress Frederick ought to have enjoyed much greater popularity in Germany than she did as a matter of fact enjoy at any time, if only because she was the mother of such a son.

We can best perhaps realise the remarkable qualities which the Empress brought into the House of Hohenzollern by comparing her eldest son with his predecessors on the throne. King Frederick William IV had a mind which appeared incapable of appreciating matters of greater importance than the etiquette of Courts and the prescriptions of mediæval heraldry. As we know, during the last years of his life his intellect was clouded much in the same way as was that of King George III of England. King Frederick's brother and successor, the old Emperor William, possessed remarkable strength of character combined with little capacity or intellect, as Bismarck very frankly explained, both to his creature, Busch, and in other recorded expressions of opinion. As for the Emperor William's father, the ill-fated Frederick, it was no doubt from him that the son derived that dash of romantic idealism characteristic of both monarchs.

But undoubtedly William II was always much more the son of his mother than of his father, which seems, indeed, to be the rule in families of less exalted rank. We have seen how the Empress really received from her father the training of a man, and, it may be added, of an extremely versa-

tile man. If fate had compelled her eldest son
to earn his own living in a private station, it is
extraordinary to think of the number of professions
in any one of which he could have attained a
competence, if not indeed high distinction. From
his mother, rather than from his father, he inherited a great appetite for work and an extraordinary aptitude for detail; and he showed himself
at different times to have had in him the making,
not only of a soldier and a sailor, but of a musician,
a poet, an artist, a preacher, and an orator.

Compare this with his grandfather, the old
Emperor, who, if he had not been born in the
purple, could only have been a soldier, and not,
it must be added, one who could have held very
high commands. Compare him again with his
father; the Emperor Frederick, if he had not been
born in the purple, though he certainly showed
greater military capacity than the old Emperor,
nevertheless would probably not have been happy
or successful in any private station other than that
of a great moral teacher.

The Emperor William's affinity to his mother
in character, temperament, and accomplishments
becomes the more striking the more it is investi-
gated. He shared with her a certain impulsiveness, a deficiency in what is ordinarily called tact,
which really amounts to a constitutional inability
to appreciate the effect which a particular word or
action will necessarily have on other people. This,

which seems a negative quality, is really a positive one, interwoven with a high courage, and a contempt for the mean little dictates of conventional prudence, which have always commanded the admiration of generous minds. This remarkable similarity between mother and son assuredly furnishes the key to the somewhat complex question of their relationships at different periods. They were in fact too much alike for their relations to be always harmonious.

The widowed Empress did not owe all her unhappiness to Bismarck alone. In 1889 Gustav Freytag published a volume of Reminiscences of the Emperor Frederick which attracted a great amount of attention, more perhaps than they intrinsically deserved. But Freytag's position among German writers as novelist, poet, dramatist, and historian, was so great that everything he wrote had its importance, and in addition to that it was known that he had at one time been admitted to the confidence of the then Crown Prince, whose political Liberalism he appeared to share.

Freytag was a Silesian by birth, and this no doubt did him no harm with the Emperor Frederick, who was warmly attached to Silesia, and delighted in the graphic pictures of life in that province which Freytag drew in his novels. The Empress made Freytag's acquaintance in the early years of her married life—indeed, the first German novel which she read with her husband was Freytag's *Soll und Haben*. The novelist had been presented to the Prince Consort by his patron, Duke Ernest of Saxe-Coburg-Gotha, and it was natural in all the circumstances that the Crown Princess and her husband should have shown the great writer marked signs of favour.

It is all the more extraordinary, therefore, that in his Reminiscences Freytag should have drawn such a picture of the Emperor Frederick as must have deeply distressed his then newly-made widow. It was a picture which she herself knew to be inaccurate, and which indeed could only gratify the personal hostility of Bismarck and his adherents. There is no need to linger long over this picture, but it demands some notice because it, so to speak, gathers together in a convenient form the principal features of what may be called the Bismarckian view of both the Empress and her husband.

It has been said that Freytag apparently shared the Crown Prince's Liberalism, but he was also steeped in Prussian particularism, and it was this that brought him to his almost blind admiration of Bismarck, and rendered him incapable of appreciating the political conceptions of the Emperor Frederick. Freytag, indeed, was a bad judge of character, the presentation of which was his weak point as a novelist.

Allusion has already been made to the fact that the Crown Prince invited Freytag to accompany him with the Third Army in the Franco-

German War, and the Reminiscences terminate soon after the battle of Sedan. After 1870 the Crown Prince hardly ever saw Freytag, and never with any real intimacy ; yet on this slender foundation of knowledge the novelist revived, under the specious cloak of affection, some of the worst charges of the Reptile Press, and of the insulting commentary which Bismarck published on the late Emperor's diary.

The principal charge for our purposes here is that the Crown Prince was subjected to foreign influence, and was entirely dominated by his wife. In effect Freytag suggests that through the Crown Princess, Princess Alice, and other members of the English Royal family, important secrets of German military movements reached the French commanders. " Both the Empress Frederick and Princess Alice," he says, " wrote to their august mother and the family in London, and what crossed the North Sea could be sent to France again in letters a few hours later. It is therefore not unnatural that the French learned by way of England a variety of news about our army which with greater propriety would have remained concealed."

Such a charge is incapable of complete disproof, but at any rate it is obvious that Freytag could know nothing of the contents, either of the Crown Prince's letters to his wife, who was at that time working day and night in the German hospitals, or of the letters of the Crown Princess and her sister to their relations in England. Yet he describes Princess Alice as " at heart during the whole of the war a brave German woman," which is a plain insinuation that the Crown Princess had not her whole heart in the success of the German arms. The whole plan of *dénigrement* is the more subtle, for Freytag professes the most ardent admiration for the ability of the Crown Princess, her rich natural gifts, and her keen soaring intellect. At the same time he says :

" The Crown Prince's love for her was the highest and holiest passion of his life, and filled his whole existence ; she was the lady of his youth, the *confidante* of all his thoughts, his trusted counsellor whenever she was so inclined. Arrangements of the garden, decorations of the house, education of the children, judgments of men and things, were in every respect regulated by him in accordance with her thoughts and wishes. It is perfectly intelligible that so complete an ascendancy of the wife over the husband, who was destined to be the future ruler of Prussia, threatened to occasion difficulties and conflicts, which, perhaps, would be greater for the woman than the man—greater for the wife who led and inspired the husband whose guidance she ought to have accepted."

Here again we see the limitations of Freytag's undoubtedly great intellect, as well as his instinctive German middle-class conception of woman's sphere. To the North-German the idea of woman as a comrade, as being even approximately on a level with her husband, was then, and is still to a great extent, inconceivable. In that view of matrimony the wife is really a chattel, or at best a respected housekeeper.

It may be asked, how could Freytag have supposed that the Emperor Frederick would have submitted to such domination on the part of his wife ? The answer is that Freytag's conception of the Emperor's character was hopelessly erroneous. He is obliged to confirm his title to be considered the originator of the idea of a German Empire, but he attributes it to a mere love of pomp and ceremony, a passion for Court millinery. The plain truth is that few monarchs have been simpler in their personal tastes than the Emperor Frederick ; the etiquette, the monotony, and the restraint of Court life bored him, and he was never so happy as when he could escape to the congenial society of savants, artists, and writers. It is certainly true that his imaginative and poetic gifts induced him to try to infuse some elements of dignity and meaning into the routine of Court ceremonial, but that he cared for such ceremonial in itself, or attached to it any greater value than that of symbolism, is frankly absurd.

Freytag even accuses the Crown Prince of having been ready to risk civil war in order that he might secure the creation of the Imperial dignity after the Franco-German War. This is based on a misapprehension of the Prince's discussions with Bismarck at Versailles. The Crown Prince believed that force would be unnecessary, and that the South German States would accept the Constitution proclaimed by the majority of the Princes assembled at Versailles. It is possible that he would have advocated compulsion if Bavaria and Würtemberg had thrown themselves into the arms of Austria, but he well knew that that contingency was in the last degree improbable.

Early in 1889 the Empress Frederick suffered another bereavement which, though not of course to be compared with many which she had endured, nevertheless added perceptibly to her state of melancholy and depression. This was the death of the venerable Empress Augusta, which broke a much valued link with the happy past. From those days in the early 'fifties when that highly-bred and highly-cultivated Princess had become " Aunt Prussia " to the Royal children at Windsor, and even more after the marriage of the Princess Royal, she had remained a loyal and most kindly and affectionate friend to her daughter-in-law. The two Royal ladies looked upon life from widely different angles, and the elder must often have disapproved of the way in which the younger interpreted her duty. But the Empress Augusta never faltered in her admiration and affection for one who was so entirely unlike herself, and in these latter days the death of the Emperor Frederick had brought them, if possible, even more closely together.

The dramatic fall of Bismarck—the " Dropping the Pilot " of Sir John Tenniel's memorable cartoon in *Punch*—occurred in March, 1890. It could hardly have been regretted by the Empress Frederick, but she was far too magnanimous, and we may add too well aware of Bismarck's incomparable services to the Empire, to regard the event as in any sense a personal triumph for herself.

What is truly astonishing, in view of all that had passed, is that the fallen Minister should have turned to her for sympathy, and should even, according to some authorities, have begged her to exert on his behalf her now growing influence with her son. It is said that she then reminded him that his past treatment of her had deprived her of any power of helping him now, but such an answer does not accord with what we know of the Empress's whole character. She was surely incapable at such a moment of adding anything to the humiliation of her old enemy. Besides, Professor Nippold speaks of Bismarck's having himself written : " Her influence over her husband was very great at any time, and became greater with the years, to culminate at the time when he was Emperor. But also in her was the conviction that my position close to the throne was in the interest of the dynasty."

There are, indeed, different versions of what took place in the now famous interview between Bismarck and the Empress Frederick. It is quite possible that she regarded the Minister's dismissal from office as an imprudent and even dangerous step. However that may be, Prince Hohenlohe declares that Bismarck did not entreat the Empress to intercede for him with the Emperor; he merely said, when the Empress asked if she could do anything for him, " I ask only for sympathy." But he certainly did ask to be received by her in audience, although he must have vividly remembered the insolent message which he had sent her immediately after the Emperor Frederick's death, when she had requested him to come to her.

A year later, at Homburg, Prince Hohenlohe and the Empress Frederick had a long conversation over the Bismarck affair. She said she was not at all surprised at his dismissal, that " Bismarck was of a combative nature and would never cease to fight. He could do nothing else." She talked of previous incidents, of Bismarck's groundless distrust of her, and of the Empress Augusta, and expressed the opinion " that we had only to thank the old Emperor's quiet gentleness for any success of Bismarck's. He was a very dangerous opponent, but not a Republican. He was too Prussian for that. But the Brandenburg-Prussian noble was determined to rule, though it were with the King."

CHAPTER XIX

THE PLANNING OF FRIEDRICHSHOF:
VISIT TO PARIS

THE Empress's relations with her son improved after the fall of Bismarck. She was particularly touched by the many tributes which he paid to his father's memory, and she now felt encouraged to try and build up again the fragments of her tragically broken life.

The Emperor William had placed at his mother's disposal the palace in Unter den Linden in Berlin where the Emperor and Empress Frederick lived while they were Crown Prince and Princess, as well as the Charlottenhof at Potsdam, and the Schloss at Homburg.

Charlottenhof is in the Royal grounds at Potsdam, at some distance from the New Palace. It was built by Frederick William IV in 1826, in imitation of a Pompeian villa, and in the grounds are fountains, statues, and bronzes which were brought from Herculaneum and Pompeii.

As to Homburg, the Empress had always been very fond of the place; she had often spent part of the summer at the old Schloss, and she valued its associations with the daughter of another British Sovereign, for the delightful gardens to which Thackeray refers in *The Four Georges* were laid out by the Landgravine Elizabeth, daughter of George III.

When the Empress Frederick decided to build a house after her own heart, it was to the neighbourhood of Homburg that her thoughts naturally turned. Perhaps another reason which governed the choice of that neighbourhood was the fact that the widowed Empress's beloved brother, King Edward, was so fond of the place, and for many years went there each year.

Some account of Friedrichshof will be not only interesting but really necessary for our purpose, for this noble castle and estate at Cronberg in the Taunus mountains were so entirely the creation of the Empress's own mind and taste that they throw a strong light on her personality and character.

Her Majesty was able to build Friedrichshof out of the large sum, estimated at nearly a quarter of a million, which she had inherited from an intimate friend, the Duchess of Galliera, within a few months of the Emperor's death.

In the days when as Crown Princess she was living at the old castle at Homburg, the Empress had once visited Cronberg.

After the tragic events of 1888 her Majesty longed to have a place of her own where she could occupy her mind in building and improving. The Empress remembered the visit to Cronberg, and as the inquiries she caused to be made about its climate, soil, and so on, proved satisfactory, she decided on the purchase without delay. The owner was one Dr. Steibel, son-in-law of Mr. Reiss, a Manchester manufacturer who built the short line of railway connecting Frankfort with Cronberg. The property consisted of a villa and a few acres, but, as some neighbouring properties were bought up, the estate was enlarged to some 250 acres. Fortunately the pine forests surrounding the estate were communal property.

The Empress resolved that Friedrichshof should be primarily a memorial to her husband, a sort of model *domus regalis*, as was shown by the pathetic inscription on the porch, " Friderici Memoriæ."

The first thing to do was to make roads, and this, with draining, building, and planting, occupied fully four years, from 1889 to 1893.

The villa of Dr. Steibel was practically demolished, and in its place rose a stately mansion in the style of the early sixteenth century. There are many examples of this style, which marks the period of transition from Gothic to Renaissance, to be found along the Rhine and throughout Hesse and Nassau. The schloss itself and the stables, which are in the style of a Rhenish or Hessian farmhouse, as well as the out-buildings, were all designed by Herr Ihne, a famous Berlin architect; but the Empress herself personally superintended the carrying out of all his plans.

The Empress's first idea was to call the place Friedrichsruh, but it was pointed out that name might cause confusion with Prince Bismarck's estate in the north of Prussia. The name Friedrichshof was then suggested by Princess Victoria, and finally adopted.

The improved relations between the Emperor William and his mother were exhibited early in 1891. He was desirous of testing the real feeling of the Paris populace towards Germany, and so with his sanction, possibly even at his direct request, the Empress Frederick went to Paris. If her visit had been a success, there is no doubt that the Emperor would have next proposed to visit Paris himself, as he had long been keenly desirous of doing. But the memories of the Franco-Prussian War were more lasting than the Emperor imagined, and his mother's mission, so far as it was intended to improve Franco-German relations, was a failure.

It was on February 19, 1891, that the Empress Frederick arrived in Paris. Her visit, though not technically of an official character, could not be called *incognito*, as she and her daughter, Princess Margaret, attended by a considerable suite, stayed at the German Embassy.

The general surprise in Paris was so marked that a *communiqué* was issued to the French Press. In this it was pointed out that the Empress, having consented to accept the position of patron

Y

of an art exhibition about to be opened in
Berlin, had asked some notable French artists to
contribute paintings. A number of these, notably
M. Bouguereau and M. Detaille, had accepted,
and she had felt bound to come to Paris and
thank them personally.

It was erroneously said, not only in the French
but also in the German papers, that this was the
first visit the Empress had paid to Paris since the
Franco-Prussian War. This was not the case. She
had been there three times, but on the previous
occasions she had stayed at the Hotel Bristol, and
had travelled in real *incognito.*

The first three or four days of her stay, whatever the public thought of the reason assigned for
it, passed off well. The Empress visited a considerable number of studios and picture galleries,
and she also made large purchases in some of
the curiosity-shops for which Paris has always
been famous. The German Ambassador gave a
dinner party each evening in honour of his august
guest, and many members of the Diplomatic Corps,
notably Lord and Lady Lytton, were asked to
meet her.

Meanwhile, the German Press, which had been
kept beforehand completely in the dark as to the
visit, was now devoting to it a great deal of not
very kindly attention. It was hinted that the
young Emperor wished to effect a thorough reconciliation with France, and with this idea in view

had asked his mother to *tâter le terrain*. These hints aroused the susceptibilities of the Boulangist party. Much ill-feeling had been awakened by the arbitrary suppression of the Ligue des Patriotes, and long before the Empress's visit a huge protest meeting had been arranged. The meeting was held, and inflammatory speeches were delivered in favour of "la Revanche," but no insult of any sort was levelled at the Imperial visitor. In fact the Empress later testified to the perfect courtesy which she had received from every class of Frenchman and Frenchwoman.

It suddenly became known that twice—once alone with the German Ambassador, and then, on another day, attended by a large suite—the Empress had driven out from Paris to view the ruins of the Palace of Saint Cloud, believed by the French to have been wantonly destroyed by the Prussians in 1870. The Empress also visited Versailles and the neighbouring battlefields.

The news of these excursions aroused very bitter feelings among many otherwise sober and sensible Parisians, to whom the memories of l'Année Terrible, and especially of the Prussian occupation of Versailles, were still painfully vivid. Their indignation was intensified when it became known that some ill-advised Government official had directed that a laurel wreath placed at the foot of the monument to Henri Regnault, the greatest French painter of his generation, who was killed at Buzenval, in the last desperate sortie from Paris, should be removed on the occasion of the visit of the Empress to the Ministry of Fine Arts.

This was indeed pouring oil on the fire! It was rumoured that this special act of tactless stupidity would be the subject of an interpellation in the Chamber. The depth of feeling aroused is illustrated by one fact, which did not, however, find its way into the Press. All those painters who had accepted the Empress's invitation to exhibit at Berlin received each morning, till their acceptances were withdrawn, the following *macabre* visiting-card:

> " HENRI REGNAULT,
>
> " 69ᵉ battalion de marche, 4ᵉ compagnie,
>
> " BUZENVAL."

Meanwhile, the less responsible section of the Paris Press had also added fuel to the flame by such headings as " Insultes aux Français "— " Visites Impériales à Saint Cloud et à Versailles."

The French Government reluctantly informed the German Ambassador that it would be advisable that the Empress, who had already prolonged her visit for several days longer than had at first been arranged, should leave Paris. On February 26 the following note was sent to the Press: " The Empress Frederick will leave Paris to-morrow morning for London at 11.30 *via* Calais." As a matter of fact, the Imperial party left for London the next day by the ten o'clock express *via* Boulogne.

But the "incident" was by no means over. The French artists who had accepted the invitation to exhibit their works at Berlin all withdrew their acceptances, and as a result the German Press burst forth into most violent and coarse abuse of France and of the French. Indeed, it looked at one moment as if nothing could prevent the two nations from rushing at each other's throats.

The Empress was greatly distressed, and it is on record that she wrote to her son a long private letter, pointing out that she had been personally very well received, and indeed most courteously treated, during her stay in Paris.

It is clear that in France all parties, and even those members of the Diplomatic Corps who were personally attached to the Empress, regretted, if they did not blame, her imprudence, for what had finally lighted the tinder was the expedition to Versailles. With all her love of French art and her sympathy with the French "intellectuals"— her great admiration for Renan was well known— the Empress Frederick had always taken on the whole what may be called the German view of the French character—that is, she regarded the French as gay, frivolous, and lacking in ballast and in the deeper qualities of humanity. If they had been what their Imperial guest believed them to be, the nation as a whole would have shrugged its shoulders and diplomatically remained silent, however *froissée* it might have been at such lack of tact on the part of a great personage.

Some months later the Empress spoke of the matter to English friends with deep regret, but still with a curious lack of understanding. She even mentioned the subject to the then French Ambassador in London, M. Waddington, eagerly telling him that she had experienced nothing but respect and even sympathy during the first part of her visit, and expressing her astonishment and distress at the feeling her visit to Versailles and the battlefields round Paris had provoked. She had brought herself by then to share Queen Victoria's view, namely, that the whole thing had been a more or less histrionic demonstration against the French Government.

It showed, however, the Empress's largeness of mind that during this same visit to England which followed her hasty departure from France she spoke with the warmest admiration of the verse of Paul Déroulède, the great chauvinist leader of the Revanche party.

This was the last intervention of the Empress Frederick in public affairs.

In the following year the Empress had the grief of losing a very old friend in the person of Lord Arthur Russell. Of these three, gifted brothers, who were at once so alike and so different, she said pathetically : " The chief charm of

the two others to me used to be that they were
Lord Odo's brothers, until I came to know
them well and to appreciate each one for his
own sake."

There burst forth, late in the year 1892, a
most extraordinary scandal, in which the Empress
Frederick, although the affair was almost ostentatiously unconnected with her, could not but be
deeply interested.

Various members of the Imperial family, as
well as members of their Households, began to be
assailed with scurrilous anonymous letters, which
not only contained shrewd and well-aimed abuse
of each individual, but which also revealed all
sorts of shameful secrets to those from whom they
had been sedulously hidden. Long-buried family
skeletons were dragged out into the light of day
and no one was spared. Indeed, the greatest
sufferers were those most closely clustered round
about the throne. There was, however, one
exception. The widowed Empress was neither
attacked nor even mentioned, and the attempt was
evidently made, by the writer or writers of these
extraordinary communications, to respect, as far as
was possible, the feelings and prejudices of the
Emperor's mother.

Nothing was left undone to discover the per-
petrators of this most evil and incomprehensible
practical joke, if practical joke it was. At first it
was supposed that the letters emanated from two

people, presumed to be husband and wife, but soon it became clear to thoughtful investigators, and these comprised all the more intelligent members of the Berlin Court world, that many more than two or even three persons must be implicated in the conspiracy.   Indeed, the Empress Frederick is said to have observed to a friend that she felt sure that many of those who had at first been victims had now become aggressors, and that practically everybody was taking the opportunity of slinging mud by way of revenge for real or fancied injuries.

This is not the place to deal with the long and complicated story of what came to be known as the anonymous letter scandal.   No really satisfactory conclusion was ever attained.   Even now German opinion, notably among those most chiefly concerned with the exhaustive investigation which took place by the Emperor's command, is hopelessly divided.   The affair ended in the imprisonment— unjust as it turned out—of a high Court official, in a fatal duel, and in many tragi-comedies.

CHAPTER XX

LIFE AT FRIEDRICHSHOF

IT was not in the Empress Frederick's nature ever to be idle, and she was particularly fond of planning and arranging palaces and gardens.

For a long time the building of Friedrichshof kept her happy and contented. She took up her residence at Homburg and drove over every day, being on the friendliest terms, not only with the architect and builder, but also with the masons and the other workmen. One might say that she watched the laying of nearly every stone, and she must have felt sorry when the work was done. Still, there was plenty of occupation left for her, when the building was finished, in superintending the furnishing and other arrangements. At this time she showed not the least sign of failing health or strength—indeed, for her age she was remarkably strong and even robust.

There is no need to enlarge upon the details of the drawing-rooms and other apartments of the castle, but some of the pictures and sculpture were of particular interest. For instance, there were many curious portraits of members of the House of Hanover; a sketch, by Titian, of

the Emperor Charles V of Germany; a fine portrait of Frederick the Great; and many busts and
statues of the Empress's relatives, including a
beautiful marble bust of her son, little Prince
Waldemar.

The fireplace in the library deserves mention,
being of Istrian stone in the Venetian style—
indeed, all through the castle the fireplaces were
of remarkable artistic beauty. Thus, that in
the great dining-room was of marble supported
on columns, and surmounted by a bust of the
Emperor Frederick.

In the library was placed a replica of the altar-
piece in Cologne Cathedral, representing the Adoration of the Magi. The bookcases, running nearly
all round the room, contained the Empress's collection of some thirty years. One case was devoted
entirely to books dedicated to her, and the
authors of many of them had been admitted
to her personal friendship. Another section contained all the books written on the subject of the
English Royal family, and many of these were
gifts with inscriptions in Queen Victoria's large,
clear handwriting.

Every book in the library had been examined
by the Empress, and many of them had been
read and re-read. This was notably the case in
the section devoted to political economy, a subject in which she was intensely interested.
Here were to be seen all the works of Jeremy

Bentham, a gift from Dean Stanley; here, too, were kept the Empress's marvellous collection of autographs, begun when she was twelve years old, and containing the handwriting, not only of practically all the Royal personages of Europe, but also of statesmen, artists, and literary and scientific men, who had all made their mark in their several callings.

The Empress was indeed a collector. Her possessions afforded her intense pleasure; to use her own expressive phrase : " One loves one's own things so much; one strokes them with one's eyes."

There was arranged in glass cases her collection of coins and medals, which contained some particularly fine and rare examples from the Brandenburg-Prussian, English, French, and Vatican mints. One case was devoted to a numismatic portrait-gallery of her own relations.

Her collection of photographs, each properly titled, took up 300 portfolios. When going over these the Empress would wax enthusiastic over the views of the places where she had herself stayed, particularly those in Italy, such as Rapallo, S. Margherita, Baveno, and Portofino. A very favourite city of hers was Triest, of which she seemed to know every stock and stone.

In the library, too, there was much to recall the Emperor Frederick. Every word that her husband had ever written, however trivial, the

Empress carefully preserved. All his marginal notes were treated with fixative, and one of her chief cares when sending any books to institutions was to make sure that there was nothing written in her husband's own hand in them.

The Empress was fond of collecting curiosities, —bits of old oak, old sculpture, and silver—and she amused herself from time to time in bargaining for these things in cottages and dealers' shops. Nor was she superior to the familiar pride of the collector in displaying her treasures afterwards and explaining what bargains she had secured.

The Empress, especially as a young woman, did not care very much for reading, though she was fond of being read aloud to, as are most Royal personages. She was, however, passionately interested in books, and it is recorded that in her tenth year she spent all her pocket-money on them. As she grew older, she read more, but she read in order to instruct herself rather than for pleasure. As a matter of course she always read all those books published in her native country which made any stir, whether they were memoirs, books of exploration, essays, or novels.

At half-past ten every morning (Sundays excepted) the Empress went into her library to work. She was an extremely rapid reader, and if her intellectual interests—science, theology, philosophy, history, literature, archæology, art, economics, hygiene—may have seemed too discursive, there is abundant evidence to acquit her of dilettanteism. She possessed in all these different branches a solid foundation of knowledge, which enabled her to understand and appreciate the discussions of experts.   Like her brother, King Edward, she possessed in a high degree the truly Royal gift of assimilating knowledge from conversation, and she had been so well " grounded," so to speak, that whenever she talked with a specialist in any subject she knew just what questions to ask.

When reading a book, the Empress almost always made notes in the margin. This is interesting as showing how restlessly alive, and in a sense over-stimulated, her brain must always have been.   It was perhaps a fortunate thing during her long illness, for even then she never felt any wish to be idle, or to sit alone and think of herself.

In the grounds of Friedrichshof her Majesty was able to indulge to the full her love of gardening.   Not only did she know the Latin names of every plant and flower, but she was a really practical gardener, able to design landscape schemes.

The rosery, for instance, was her creation. About half an acre in extent, it resembled the rosery at Birkhall, on the Balmoral estate.   It sloped gently upwards, divided into numerous little terraces, bearing double rows of half-standard roses, and it was bounded partly by a creeper-clad wall, and partly by trellis-work over which roses were trained.   In the flower-beds of the ordinary garden her Majesty showed her strong preference for old-fashioned English flowers— indeed, throughout she evidently aimed at re- producing the mingled beauty and repose so char- acteristic of English gardens.   All kinds of trees, too, she planted, and many have the added interest of an iron tablet recording that it was planted by some Royal or distinguished visitor.

The Empress certainly had no lack of occupa- tion and interest at Cronberg.   She had always been fascinated by restoration and excavation work, and fortunately Cronberg possessed both an old castle and an old church, which she eagerly set herself to preserve for future generations.   At the old Burg she found many ancient remains, such as arrowheads, keys, &c., and, most impor- tant of all, several Gothic iron " Ofenplatten." She was interested in every detail.   Once she spent a long time hunting for a passage-way which she knew must be there because of the " pechnaze," or slit in the wall through which boiling lead used to be poured in mediæval sieges. When out riding she always kept a keen look-out for survivals of the past.   Thus she was much interested in the iron crosses to be found in the Taunus, and she proposed to draw all the different kinds and publish a book about them.

To the restoration of Cronberg Church the

Empress devoted an immense amount of personal trouble. Two Ministers and some important officials had to be approached before the order from the Cabinet was obtained granting the necessary financial help. When it was at last issued, the Empress herself brought it to Cronberg, and, arriving there in the evening, carried it the first thing in the morning to the pastor. Hardly a nail was put in the church without her knowledge. She studied and re-studied for months the details of windows, doors, hinges, &c. Her delight was great when under the whitewash she discovered some frescoes of the fifteenth century.

A tablet was put up in the choir setting forth what the Empress had done for the restoration of the church, but here the truly modest nature of the woman showed itself. She had the tablet removed from the choir, and refixed in a place high up where it is practically unseen.

It is pleasant to look back on these comparatively happy years at Friedrichshof. The Empress as a rule dressed very simply in black. Her only jewellery were two gold rings, one with a sapphire and two diamonds, and the other a smooth ruby, while a miniature of the Emperor Frederick hung round her neck. She was up early every morning. She liked to see everything bright and gleaming in the Castle, and not a speck of dust was allowed. At eight o'clock it was her habit to go out riding for two hours. She was an excellent horsewoman and full of daring; even when nearing sixty she still jumped difficult ditches and obstacles, and she always rode young and spirited animals. Once she was pushed against a wall by a frisky horse, and later she had the more serious accident which some think brought about her final illness. But even in the worst weather she never gave up her morning ride.

During her widowhood the Empress had at last the joy of knowing that she was really loved and understood by her neighbours, both gentle and simple. She was regarded at Cronberg much as Queen Victoria was regarded in the neighbourhood of Balmoral. She made herself acquainted with practically the whole population, not only with the poor, on whom she was able to shower intelligent gifts and much practical good advice, but also with that difficult intermediate class who, all the world over, generally remain out of touch with the great house of the village.

People of this class dwelt in little châlets which began to spring up over that healthy and beautiful neighbourhood, but even their thorny pride was not proof against the Empress's friendliness, in which there was never any touch of condescension or patronage. There were not a few artists living in the neighbourhood, and with some of these the Empress was on specially intimate terms. She was fond of dropping in and finding them at work. The Empress was full of quaint conceits and ideas; thus, when she was going to see an artist or anyone in whom she took a special interest, she liked to choose his birthday for the visit. Her energy was extraordinary. One observer who saw a great deal of her in her widowhood declares that she used to go up-stairs and down-stairs like a young girl, and when she greeted the company assembled at table every compulsion of etiquette seemed to be instantly removed.

Naturally Cronberg benefited by her great knowledge of hygiene. To the elaborately equipped hospital which she founded there, she gave the most punctilious care. She often cut her roses herself and took them to the sick. The Empress also built a poorhouse, a Victoria school, and a library for the people, and she arranged the Victoria and Kaiser Friedrich public park. She hated leaving Cronberg every autumn: "The departure is dreadful to me," she said on one occasion: "when I am travelling I feel like a mussel without its shell."

Professor Nippold, in his book on the first two German Emperors, has drawn a very sympathetic and understanding picture of the Empress Frederick.

She had, he says, a most cheerful temperament, and a rapid eye for the humorous, in spite of so many terrible blows of fate. She always saw everything from the good side and quickly forgave people their faults; no one was allowed to speak

z

ill of anyone in her presence. She was often misunderstood and unjustly accused, and when she saw things written against her in the papers she was terribly wounded. For instance, it was said that she had prevented the building of a tower on the " Altkönig" for the public to enjoy the view, but the fact was that she had never heard anything about the proposal. Sometimes she could hardly be restrained from answering some of these base accusations. She was also accused of parsimony, and her income was enormously exaggerated. The claims on her purse were innumerable. She had forty-two philanthropic institutions which she had to help, and in one year there were thirty-seven bazaars, to each of which she had to send gifts. Altogether her expenses were enormously heavy.

When the Empress is blamed for being a thorough Englishwoman, let. it be said at once, exclaims Professor Nippold, that everything good and praiseworthy in England she tried to introduce into her own adopted country. She was always vexed and pained when things were said against England, more especially in the case of England's colonies. " The English," she would say, " arrange everything in the Colonies most beautifully,— roads, railways, post, telegraphs, hospitals, schools, and police, and then everyone, to whichever nation he belongs, can trade undisturbed. And I cannot think that for that England should be thanked

in such an evil way!" Many people regarded it
as an injustice to Germany that she should have
had such warm sympathies with England. She
was through and through an Englishwoman, if
not by descent, yet by every impression received
in childhood and by education.

The professor goes on to express the opinion
that no Englishman or Englishwoman, of whatever age, ever gives up his or her nationality and
love of country, in whatever circumstances they
may find themselves, "a contrast to so many
Germans, who are far less faithful to their nationality. The Empress Frederick, as eldest child
of Queen Victoria of England, had the title of
Princess Royal, and she could not help feeling herself the first princess of a wonderful Empire of very
old culture, and this proud feeling never left her."

This estimate and defence of the Empress is
particularly valuable as coming from a man of
shrewd intelligence and observation, who was himself a German.

On another occasion Nippold wrote of the
Empress with clear insight: "One thing this distinguished woman never understood—to hide her
feelings. She never posed; everything was sincere
in her in the true sense of the word."

In her will the Empress left Professor Nippold
a letter-weight, which she had used every day,
as a souvenir of a conversation they had had one
evening in her study. This letter-weight, which

always lay on her table, was composed of an old Roman bronze—a broken Sphinx figure—on a marble slab. A ring bound this figure to the slab, and the inscription engraved was: "This stone was picked up by H.R.H. Princess Elizabeth on the walk of Frogmore, 1808."

Professor Nippold goes on to say that while the Empress was talking to him one evening a telegram arrived which obviously had to do with the crisis which led to the Greco-Turkish War. As Nippold saw that she was much preoccupied with the telegram and had to think of the answer, and yet did not want to send him away, he delicately asked to be allowed to wait and look at the pictures. When the Empress resumed the conversation, the professor asked about a picture which hung in the study. She named the different figures in the group, among them being that young Princess Elizabeth who had found the stone.

That she should have left Nippold the letter-weight showed, as he truly says, the wonderful memory and kindly attention in which consists *la politesse des princes.*

This Princess Elizabeth married one of the last Counts of Hesse-Homburg. Since then a monument to that Royal house has been erected in Homburg, and in the Emperor's speech at the unveiling on August 17, 1906, occurred these words: " I commemorate the Landgräfin Elizabeth, a daughter of George III of England. She

was a real mother to this country and worked and
cared for her adopted fatherland. The Hom-
burgers to this day think of her with real thankfulness and reverence."

Professor Nippold gives a characteristic letter
which he received from the Empress, evidently
on the subject of those historical studies of the
House of Hohenzollern to which, as we have
already mentioned, the Emperor Frederick at one
time devoted himself with ardour. The letter is
so interesting, especially in the views which it
expresses on the subject of royal biography, that
to quote it in full needs no apology:

"DEAR PROFESSOR,—Many thanks for sending
the separate pages from the *Deutsche Revue* of
February, and for your excellent report, which has
so much in it that does my heart good. You
mean well and truly, not only as regards history,
but also with the noble men who now lie in their
graves, and whose deeds and influence should be
properly appreciated in wide circles and through
the proper medium.

"The work grows, however, even as you work
upon it; the subject becomes more and more important, and one should ask oneself whether the
time has come thus to lift the veil. Would it not
be wiser and more cautious to close these papers
for the *Revue*, and then to continue your labours,
so that later a book could appear for which we

could utilise this material, but not lightly or too soon? The letter of which you send me a copy —from our Kaiser Friedrich Wilhelm IV—should not, for instance, appear without the letter from my father, but that would arouse a fearful storm of discussion. In the political world there is so much tinder ready that one must do all one can to avoid bringing in anything exciting.

"As long as Bismarck is alive, it is very difficult! Also these things affect my mother, so that I should like very much to have a serious talk with you before the publication continues in the *Deutsche Revue*. Professor Ranke has handled the life of Friedrich Wilhelm IV as the Court here wished it to be treated. Similar books have now appeared, with authorisation, with regard to the Kaiser Wilhelm, and in Weimar, I believe, someone is writing a book on the Kaiserin Augusta. All these writers, however, are strictly conservative and orthodox in religion (therefore one-sided), and of all those currents which flowed into the lives of the dead, no word is spoken, in the sense that I mean. It is impossible thus to omit and yet give the public a true picture of the persons, of their time, and of the parts they played. You will see for yourself the consequences of such publication. You have more experience than I, and perhaps you can reassure me."

CHAPTER XXI

LAST YEARS

DURING the last years of her life, the Empress Frederick paid repeated visits to England, where she had many attached friends.

She much enjoyed a visit to the Bishop of Ripon in 1895, when she was able to study the wood-carving in the cathedral, as well as Fountains Abbey and other places of historical interest. It was characteristic of her that only a few moments before she left Ripon, while she was actually waiting for the carriage to take her to the station, she exclaimed, "How much I should like to paint this view!" Drawing materials and a paint-box were brought her; she sat down, and in a few minutes produced a charming sketch of the cathedral amid fields and trees.

As an artist the Empress was undoubtedly far more than a mere amateur, especially in sculpture. It is said that on one occasion, having given a commission to the famous German sculptor, Uphues, for a colossal statue of the Emperor Frederick, she visited his studio one day when he was at work on the clay model. This did not seem to her to promise a good likeness, and she thereupon set to work on the clay herself, and in about half an hour she quite transformed the model, so that when it was carried out in marble it became universally recognised as the best presentment in existence of the Emperor's features. Uphues also made a bust of the Empress herself, which was set up in 1902 on the Kaiser Friedrich Promenade at Homburg.

The Empress had first met the Boyd Carpenters in 1866, soon after the death of Prince Sigismund. She happened to hear a sermon from the then Canon Boyd Carpenter which brought her much comfort, and the acquaintance then begun developed into warm friendship.

The Bishop had a great admiration for the Empress's sympathetic alacrity of mind. " She had wide range," he writes, " and quick intellectual sympathies ; she understood a passing allusion ; she followed the track of thought ; there were no irritating delays ; there were no vacant incoherences in an observation, which show that the thread has been lost. She had read ; she had thought ; she had travelled ; she had observed ; she had mixed with many of the foremost minds of the time ; she had taken practical part in many great and humane enterprises. Consequently her range was large, and her mental equipment was well furnished and ready for use. Conversation with her could never become insipid."

The Empress always did everything she could

to improve Anglo-German relations, and the feeling aroused by the famous telegram which her son sent to President Kruger in January, 1896, keenly distressed her. She wrote to her old friend Sir Mountstuart Grant Duff:

"But even this most sad episode between our two countries has not shaken my faith in our old opinions that there are many, many higher interests in common, why we should get on together and be of use to each other in helping on civilisation and progress. I trust that a good understanding will outlive hatred and jealousy."

And again: "When I think of my father and of all his friends and of our friends, it appears to me almost ludicrous that Germany and England should be enemies."

In 1897 the Empress Frederick took part in the Diamond Jubilee, driving in the procession with Princess Henry of Battenberg. The sight of the two widowed sisters, who had put aside their grief to join in that great day of national rejoicing, deeply touched many of the spectators. The Empress herself wrote of this occasion in which she "gladly and thankfully joined with proud heart":

"The weight of lonely, hidden grief often feels heaviest when all surroundings are in such contrast. And yet the heart of man is so made that many feelings find room in it together; so gratitude and thankfulness mingle with memories so sad that they can never lose their bitterness."

Madame Waddington, the wife of that old Rugby and Cambridge man who filled with such distinction the post of French Ambassador in London, has left a record of a conversation she had with the Empress in August, 1897. Madame Waddington, who was an American by birth, was struck by a question the Empress asked her, namely, whether she did not find it difficult to settle down in France after having lived ten years in London—"the great centre of the world." Madame Waddington replied that she was not at all to be pitied for living in Paris, that her son was a Frenchman, and all his interests were in France; and she adds: "Au fond, notwithstanding all the years she has lived in Germany, the Empress is absolutely English still in her heart."

They had some talk about Wagner, and Madame Waddington informed the Empress that there was a difficulty as to the performance of *Die Meistersingers* at the Grand Opera owing to the fact that Frau Wagner considered the choruses too difficult to translate or to sing with the true spirit in any language but German. The Empress replied:

"She is quite right; it is one of the most difficult of Wagner's operas, and essentially German in plot and structure. It scarcely bears translation in English, and in French would be impossible; neither is the music in my mind at all suited to the French character. The mythical legends of the Cycle would appeal more to the French, I think, than the ordinary German life."

The Empress was a real connoisseur in music, of which she had a wide knowledge, though her skill as a performer was considered to be inferior to that of Queen Victoria.

Like her mother, the Empress Frederick was a great letter-writer. She wrote in a mixture of German and English, choosing the most telling expressions, and she was in constant communication with various distinguished Englishmen for years. To them she sent long and very frank letters about everything that interested her, especially foreign politics.

As has been already indicated in this book, the Empress was in the habit of showing, far more clearly than most Royal personages allow themselves to do, exactly what she felt about those whom she met even for the first or the second time. This found either an answering antagonism or a reciprocal liking in those with whom she was brought in contact. Many of the distinguished men whom she heartily admired speak of her, and that in their most secret letters and diaries, with an admiration approaching enthusiasm. But now and again comes a discordant note. Such may be found in Mr. G. W. Smalley's *Anglo-American Memories*.

The old journalist describes her in a way which gives a far from pleasant impression of the Empress towards the end of her life. He was presented to her by the then Prince of Wales at Homburg, and the first thing he noticed was that, though she was very like Queen Victoria, her manner was less simple and therefore had less authority. He also criticises her dress, and observes that both the late Queen and her eldest daughter " showed an indifference to the art of personal adornment."

Mr. Smalley admits that the Empress has a much greater vivacity than the Qeeen, but he thinks that this vivacity becomes restless, and that her mind can never be in repose. He says drily that, from her marriage and down to the day of the Emperor Frederick's death, she had lived in a dream-world of her own creation, her belief being so strong, her conviction that she knew what was best for those about her so complete, that the facts had to adjust themselves as best they could to that belief and that conviction.

As was the Empress's way when a stranger, and especially a foreigner, was presented to her, she at once began to talk of Mr. Smalley's country and of what she supposed would interest him. Instead of allowing him to say what he thought, she plunged directly into American topics, especially commenting on what she supposed to be the position of women in the United States. It soon became clear, or so he thought, that she had a correspondent in Chicago from whom she had derived her impressions. " She talked with clearness, with energy and almost apostolic fervour, the voice penetrating rather than melodious."

Mr. Smalley said to himself that all that she asserted might be true of Chicago, but of what else was it true? And he was evidently much nettled that she generalised from the " Windy City " to the rest of the United States.

Instead of seeing, as probably most women would have seen, that she was speaking to an auditor who was fast becoming prejudiced, the Empress continued to unburden herself in the frankest, freest way to this journalist whom she had never met before. She even seems to have touched on politics, on Anglo-German relations, on the internal affairs of Germany :

" Never for a moment did this dreamer's talk stop or grow sluggish. Carlyle summed up Macaulay in the phrase 'Flow on, thou shining river'; he might in a sardonic mood have done the same to this Princess."

It was an illuminating interview, declares Mr. Smalley, throwing light on events to come as well as on those of the past, and he goes on to explain that multitudes of Germans shared Bismarck's distrust of the Crown Princess, and believed that she wanted to Anglicise Germany. He reiterates what has so often been said—that she told all-comers that what Germany needed was Parliamentary government as it was understood and practised in England. In little things as in great

she made no secret for her preference for what was
English over what was German :

" Judgment was not her strong point, nor was
tact ; if I am to say what was her strong point, I
suppose it would be sincerity.   Her gifts of mind
were dazzling rather than sound ; impulse was not
always under control.   Her animosities, once roused,
never slept, as Prince Bismarck well knew."

Seldom has a more prejudiced view of the
Empress been given to the world, but it is interesting as showing how she sometimes impressed
those who had been fascinated by the Bismarck
legend when they were brought into passing
contact with her eager, enthusiastic mind.

To a fall from her horse at Cronberg in the
autumn of 1898 may be traced the beginning of
that merciless disease which ultimately killed her.

It was a bad accident.   The horse reared and
the Empress fell on the wrong side on her head with
her feet under the horse and her habit still clinging
to the saddle.   Her head was much bruised, and
her right hand was injured and trodden on by the
horse.   She was not at all frightened, indeed she
took it very calmly, observing :

" I have ridden for fifty years, and it is natural
that an accident must come sooner or later.
But I shall ride to-morrow.   I'm going to try
and paint and write some letters, in spite of my
hand."

But her injuries did not yield to treatment,

and very soon began the long martyrdom of pain which she bore for more than two years with the same stoic fortitude which the Emperor Frederick had shown. The disease was undoubtedly cancer, and it is suggested that it had been gathering force for quite a number of years. However that may be, it was certainly known in 1900 that a cure was impossible.

The most terrible feature of these last months was the severe pain which seized the Empress at intervals. It was characteristic, both of her courage and of her kindly nature, that during these attacks she would not see even the members of her family, to whom the sight of her sufferings would have been so distressing. But in the intervals she occupied herself with conversation, or one of her ladies would read aloud to her, and she even painted a little. Her son, the Emperor, was constant in his attentions, coming over almost daily from Homburg, but even he was only allowed to remain with her a few minutes at a time.

Physically the patient had suffered a great change. Her cheeks, which had been round and apparently in the bloom of health, gradually became thin and sunken, and her face assumed that curious transparent paleness which is an unmistakable sign of approaching death.

It is said that when the Empress received the news of Queen Victoria's death, in January, 1901, she said to those about her: " I wish I were dead too." But for more than six months longer she bore with extraordinary fortitude the chronic suffering which the most able physicians were unable to relieve. Her consideration for those around her was constant. On one occasion, in a spasm of agony, she cried out loudly and seized the nurse's hand; then at once apologised: " I am so sorry, I am afraid I hurt you." The nurse said afterwards, " I have only been with the Empress for a week, but already she has filled me with higher ideals, and I am going back resolved to be a better nurse than ever."

As long as it was possible, the Empress continued her painting and drawing; and to the very end she was especially happy when she was able to work with some practical object in view, such as the laying out of a new rose-garden or suggesting alterations in architectural plans. Her greatest pleasure—and she was intensely susceptible to happiness even during the last six sad months—was a visit from her eldest brother. When she was expecting King Edward, she supervised closely every little arrangement made for his comfort and convenience, and while doing so she would be wheeled in her bath-chair about the rooms he was to occupy.

She felt most deeply the attacks which were then being made in Germany on England, and even on King Edward, at the time of the Boer

War. An article in the *Vossische Zeitung*, which observed that such attacks on a constitutional Sovereign were unworthy of a great nation, gave her much satisfaction.

King Edward paid his last visit to his sister at Cronberg in February, 1901. A contemporary chronicler notes that everything was arranged to show that the visit was meant for the Empress Frederick and not for her son. This was doubtless by the wish of the Emperor himself, for though he did all due honour to his uncle, meeting him at Frankfort and conducting him across the lovely Taunus Valley to the very door of Friedrichshof, he took leave of King Edward at the threshold, so that the brother and sister might be alone at their first meeting.

Among the last English visitors received by the Empress at Friedrichshof were her old friends, the Boyd Carpenters. This was in May, 1901.

They found her on their arrival lying on a couch in her beautiful garden, and the Bishop was struck by her likeness to Queen Victoria—a likeness enhanced by the black dress and by the form of hat which she wore. The Empress rejoiced in the spring and in the colour which was spreading everywhere through her garden. She still took a practical interest in everything concerning the beautiful home she had created. The Bishop gives one instance : the great blue face of the clock, the tower of which dominated Fried-

2 A

richshof, needed re-painting. Before she decided what exact tint should be used, she caused slips of paper giving different shades of blue to be held up against the face of the clock. Then she made up her mind.

Once, as they passed through the flower garden together, she quoted to the Bishop the words, " The effectual prayer of a righteous man availeth much." Another time, looking round at the beauty of the trees she had planted, she said, " I feel like Moses on Pisgah, looking at the land of promise which I must not enter."

When parting from Mrs. Boyd Carpenter, for whom she had a great regard, the Empress gave her a bracelet of her own, one she had often worn and with which she had affectionate associations.

To the Bishop she gave a seal which had belonged to Queen Victoria, and which had been in the room when the Queen died. It commemorated a picnic in Scotland, in which the Queen, the Prince Consort, and Princess Alice had shared. The seal, mounted in silver and set in Aberdeen granite, was a cairngorm found by Prince Albert and Princess Alice on that day.

The Bishop remained with her a moment at the very last, and she said to him, " When I am gone I want you to read the English Burial Service over me." And then she characteristically explained to him exactly what would have to be done to make this possible. When the end came three months later, thanks to the prompt acquiescence of the Emperor, his mother's wishes were carried out.

The Empress became much worse at the beginning of August, and, by the wish of her son, Canon Teignmouth-Shore was telegraphed for. He arrived at Friedrichshof on August 5, and in the presence of the Emperor and the Empress's daughters the Canon knelt down and offered some prayers from the Office for the Visitation of the Sick. The whole sad scene, he says, was quite overpowering and far too sacred for him to describe. "The dying Empress was at first slightly conscious, and I could see a gentle movement of her lips as we said the Lord's Prayer."

Towards six o'clock in the evening the Canon was again summoned to the sick-room. "The sweet noble soul was just passing away. I said a few prayers at the bedside, concluding with the first two verses of that exquisite poem, 'Now the labourer's task is o'er.'"

A butterfly flew into the room and hovered for a while over the dying Empress, and when she had breathed her last it spread its wings and flew out into the free air again.

The Emperor desired Canon Teignmouth-Shore to arrange with Dr. Boyd Carpenter for a private funeral service to be held at Friedrichshof.

On the following Sunday the Canon preached

a funeral sermon in the English church at Homburg. In it he made a statement with regard to her Majesty's religious views which deserves quotation:

" 'The religious conceptions which inspired and guided this life, alike in its humblest and in its loftiest spheres of action, were, as I believe, neither crude nor complex nor dogmatic; they were clear and simple and broad — an absolute faith in the Fatherhood of God, and in the Brotherhood and redeeming love of Him who died that we might live."

The Lutheran funeral service, which was held in the parish church of Cronberg, was most impressive in its simplicity. At one point of the service the Crown Prince and three of his young brothers rose from their seats, and, having put on their helmets, drew their swords and took their places at each corner of the coffin of their grandmother, where they remained until the end of the service.

This old church, which, as we have said, the Empress had herself restored, dates back to the middle of the fifteenth century. On the organ, which is of exquisite tone, Mendelssohn often played when he visited the Taunus.

Perhaps the most touching of all the hundreds of wreaths sent for the funeral was one of simple heather which had been made by the Emperor's younger children. Attached to it was a sheet of black-edged paper on which they had all written their names in large childish characters.

The Empress was buried beside her husband and her son Waldemar in the Friedenskirche at Potsdam, and the sarcophagus over her tomb is by her artist friend, Begas.

Of memorials to her, there is the bust at Homburg already mentioned. In the English church at Homburg, where she attended divine service for the first time after the death of her husband, is a memorial consisting of four reliefs, placed in the spandrels of the arches in the aisle, representing the four Evangelists. A striking statue of the Empress in coronation robes by Gerth was unveiled by the Emperor William in October 1903. It is opposite the statue of her husband in the open space outside the Brandenburg gate at Berlin.

So lived, and so died, this most gifted and generous lady, who was rendered illustrious, not by the symbols of her Imperial station, but by her many winning qualities of heart and intellect.

We cannot do better than quote in conclusion from the remarkable tributes which were paid to her memory by the late Lord Salisbury and the late Lord Spencer.

Lord Salisbury, who was then Prime Minister, in moving an address of condolence with King Edward in the House of Lords, summed up in

masterly fashion both the beauty and the tragedy
of the Empress's life :

" When the then Princess Royal left these
shores, there was no person, either of contemporary
experience or in history, before whom a brighter
prospect extended itself in life, and all that
could make it desirable spread itself before her.
She had a devoted husband, himself one of the
noblest characters of his generation, who probably
centred in himself more admiration than any man
in his rank or in any rank. She had every prospect
of becoming the Consort of the Emperor—an
absolute emperor—of the greatest of the Continental Powers. She had every hope that she
would share fully in his illustrious position, and in
no small degree in the powers that he wielded.
This was before her for nearly thirty years, and in
that time she had all the enjoyments which were
derived from her own great abilities, her own
splendid artistic talents, and from the powers
which she exercised over the artistic, æsthetic, and
intellectual life of Germany. She occupied an
unexampled position. Then suddenly came the
blow, first on her husband and then on herself.
By that fell disease—which probably is the most
formidable of all to which flesh is heir—her dream
of happiness, of usefulness, and glory was suddenly
cut short. The blow, in striking her husband,
struck herself in even greater degree ; and she felt
—she could not but feel—how deeply she shared

in all the disappointments, all the sufferings, that attached themselves to his history. When he had been Emperor only a few weeks, he died, and then she spent her life in retirement. Her health failed, and she, too, fell under the same blow, passing through years of suffering, with the sympathy of all connected with her and all those who knew her. She was deeply valued in this country by those who knew her, and they were very many. She had an artistic and intellectual charm of no common order; she spread her power over all who came within her reach; and her gradual disappearance from the scene was watched with the deepest sorrow and sympathy by numbers in her own country and in this."

The motion was seconded on behalf of the Opposition by Lord Spencer, who, it will be remembered, was a near kinsman of that Lady Lyttelton to whom was entrusted the charge of the Empress's early childhood:

" Her Imperial Majesty had no ordinary character. Brought up with the greatest care and solicitude by her Royal and devoted parents, she early and ever afterwards showed the highest accomplishments, not only in art but in literature. She was herself an artist of no small merit, and her power of criticism and influence in art was even of a higher order. In this age, which had been so remarkable for the enormous number of persons who have joined in endeavours to alleviate

the sufferings of the human race, whether in peace
or in war, I venture to think that no one stands in
a higher position than the Empress Frederick of
Germany.   During those wars, in which her illustrious husband played such a splendid part, she
exerted herself to do all she could to alleviate the
sufferings of the wounded, and she had ever in
peace used her endeavours to promote the same
objects among the suffering poor of her country.
No one, I am sure, will be remembered in the
future with more affection and devotion on this
account than her Majesty.   She was always sympathetic and energetic with regard to other matters.
There was nothing which stirred her sympathies or
energies more than the education and improvement
of her own sex.   She did much in this respect in
her adopted country ; but we cannot consider her
life without remembering the beautiful simplicity
and earnestness of it.   She was devoted to duty,
and although she suffered intensely during her life
when her noble husband was afflicted with the
terrible disease which took him off, and during the
sad years in which the same malady afflicted her,
she always showed a patient endurance which will
remain an example for all mankind.   I cannot but
refer to her great charm in private as well as in
public life.   It so happened that very early in
my life, before she was married, she honoured
me with her acquaintance.   It was only on rare
occasions I had the privilege of continuing that

acquaintance, but I have from time to time within the last few years seen her Majesty, and I shall always recall, as one of the most delightful recollections of my life, the charm and influence of her conversation."

INDEX

ABEKEN, Herr, 246, 247
Aberdeen, Lord, 49
Adelaide, Queen Dowager, 3, 28
Albert, Prince, 1, 2, 4, 5, 7, 8, 9;
his children's affection, 11, 12,
212; Exhibition of 1851, 17, 18;
view of German politics, 27, 28,
38, 39, 47, 48, 54, 114, 125, 126–
133, 139, 140, 163, 166, 167; training of the Princess Royal, 34–36;
her betrothal, 37–39, 42, 47–52;
and marriage, 61–70; letters to
his daughter, 72, 73, 76, 77, 81,
82, 88–91, 105, 106–108, 114, 115,
116, 118, 119, 125, 126, 128–133,
136, 139, 140, 149, 150; visits
to his daughter, 120–124; acquaintance with Morier, 157;
first meeting with Bismarck, 163;
theory of monarchy, 128–132;
narrow escape, 122; death, 150–
153, 155
Alcott, Miss, 15
Alexander of Bulgaria, Prince, 315–
318
Alexander I, the Tsar, 23; Alexander II, 267, 273, 282
Alexandra, Queen, 109, 110, 179, 197,
267
Alice, Princess (Grand Duchess of
Hesse), 4, 6, 11, 12, 49, 61, 64, 107,
118, 132; wedding, 155, 199,
208, 215–217, 225, 228, 236, 240,
241; death, 278, 328, 329
Althorp, Lord, 6, 9
Ampthill, Lord and Lady, 257, 289,
290, 343
Anderson, Mrs., 51
Angeli, Von, 255, 260, 268, 269
Arnold, Matthew, 287–289
Augusta, German Empress, 17, 19,
26, 28, 40, 61, 65, 66, 78, 79, 156,
157, 158, 187, 217, 231, 233, 236,
250, 272, 319; death, 331, 332,
333; 358
Augustenburg, Duke Christian of
Sonderburg-, 182

Augustenburg, Hereditary Prince
Frederick of Sonderburg-, 182–
185, 213, 214, 280
Austria, Emperor Francis Joseph,
175, 199, 214, 285

BABELSBERG, 91, 92, 94, 98, 110, 111
Bacourt, Monsieur de, 79
Baden, Prince Regent of, 39
Ballardin, M., 312
Barclay & Perkins's draymen, 70
Battenberg marriage, the, 311, 314–
318
Bavaria, King of, 231, 245
Bazaine, Marshal, 231, 244, 322
Beatrice, Princess (Princess Henry
of Battenberg), 119, 361
Begas, 255
Benedek, 221
Benedetti, 233
Bergmann, Prof., 294
Bernhard of Saxe-Meiningen, Prince,
270, 271
Bernhardi, Theodor von, 159, 190
Bismarck, Prince, opinion of the
English marriage, 41; relations
with Crown Princess, 153, 154,
163–166, 261–263, 279, 280, 290,
291; relations with Morier, 158,
210; accession to office, 160,
167; Dantzig incident, 169,
170; relations with Crown Prince,
176, 177, 290, 291; policy on
Schleswig-Holstein question, 184,
185, 188, 213–214; attitude to
royal personages, 213; Austrian
war, 213–215, 220–224; visit to
Paris, 226; at a royal christening,
231; Franco-German war, 232–
234, 241–244, 249, 252; the Imperial Dignity, 245, 246, 260;
"British petticoats," 261–263;
and Hinzpeter, 265, 266, 271;
and the Regency of the Crown
Prince, 272–275, 288, 289; and
the Crown Prince's illness, 294,
295; relations with the Emperor

and Empress Frederick, 308–312, 313–317, 319–324, 326–331, 358, 365, 366 ; fall, 332, 333
Bleibtreu, 256
Bloomfield, Lady, 40, and Lord, 76, 137
Blumenthal, Field-Marshal, 220
Bornstedt, country life at, 112, 113
Bötticher, 308
Bouguereau, M., 338
Boyd Carpenter, Bishop, 67, 359, 360, 369–371
Brühl, Countess Hedwig, 191
Brunnemann, Privy Councillor, 99
Brunnow, 88
Buccleuch, Duke of, 67
Buchanan, Mr., 46
Bucher, 241, 270
Bunsen, Baron, 28, 154
Bunsen, Mme., 26
Busch, 241, 270, 279, 311, 313, 324

Canning, Lord, 49
Carlyle, 112, 162, 365
Charles Anthony of Hohenzollern, Prince, 98
Charles of Prussia, Prince, 284, 285
Charles of Prussia, Princess, 80
Charles of Roumania, Prince and Princess, 219, 269, 281
Charlier, Mme., 10
Charlotte, Princess, 1
Charlotte, Princess (daughter of the Empress), 118, 269–271, 281
Christian IX of Denmark, King, 183, 190
Churchill, Lord Randolph, 276
Clarendon, Lord, 31, 36, 43, 95, 126, 145, 146, 149, 157, 257
Cobden, 46, 70
Coburgers, the, 175, 187
Colenso, Bishop, 203
Connaught, Duke of, 107, 271
Consort, Prince. See Albert, Prince
" Court Circular," official, 8
Craven, Mrs. Augustus, 307
Craven, Mrs. Dacre, 253

Dantzig incident, the, 168–170
Darwin, Charles, 202, 203
Delane, John, 148
Delbrück, Prof., 278
De Ros, Captain, 104–106
Déroulède, Paul, 342
Detaille, M., 338
Deutsche Revue, 357
Deutsche Rundschau, 321
Devonshire, Louise Duchess of, 97

Dino, Duchesse de, 79
Droysen, J. G., 35, 36
Duff, Sir M. E. Grant, 361
Duncker, Frau, 159
Duncker, Herr Max, 137, 138, 154, 159, 160, 184, 186, 188

Edinburgh, Duke of, 64, 65, 70, 267
Edward VII, King, 6, 13, 14, 20, 21, 64, 65, 70, 107, 110, 114, 151, 161, 179, 264, 267, 285, 335, 349, 364, 368, 369
Eliot, George, 277
Elizabeth, Landgravine, the, 335, 356, 357
Elizabeth of Prussia, Queen, 135, 136
Ernest of Hanover, King, 74
Ernest of Saxe-Coburg and Gotha, Duke, 3, 39, 42, 86, 176, 186, 312, 327
Eugénie, Empress, 20, 21, 44, 45, 195, 225
Exhibition, of 1851, 16, 17, 18 ; of 1862, 155 ; of 1867 (Paris), 225

Faraday, 93
Faucit, Helen, 62
Fitzmayer, Colonel, 46
Frankfort Congress, 175
Frederick Charles of Hesse, Prince, 251
Frederick Charles of Prussia, Prince, 188, 220
Frederick, Grand Duke of Baden, 183
Frederick, Prince of Netherlands, 270
Frederick, the Emperor—
As Prince Frederick William of Prussia—First visit to England, 15–19, 26 ; betrothal, 30–33, 40, 44 ; visits England again, 52 ; marriage, 62–71 ; admiration of England, 86 ; pride in his eldest son, 103, 104, 108, 109 ; New Palace at Potsdam, 110–112 ; country life at Bornstedt, 112, 113 ; military promotions, 113, 114, 117, 167 ; hope of the Junkers, 117
As Crown Prince—Death of King Frederick William IV, 134–136 ; his father's coronation, 140–148 ; death of his father-in-law, 150–153 ; visits to England, 155, 176, 297–299 ; to Italy, 161, 227, 292 ; to the East, 228 ; to

Paris, 228, 229; the Dantzig incident, 168–170; relations with Bismarck, 168–174, 176, 184, 214, 215, 222–224, 242, 252, 272–276, 290, 291; admiration of England, 172; Schleswig-Holstein question, 183–185; in the Danish War, 186–190; hatred of war, 188, 225, 239; work for soldiers and their families, 189, 225, 238, 243, 244; family life, 191–200, 210–212, 260; the Austrian War, 216–218, 220–224; freemasonry, 107, 108, 270; the Franco-German War, 231, 239, 240, 242–244; the Imperial Dignity, 245–247; regency, 272–276; illnesses, 259, 260, 292–303; silver wedding, 284–287

As Emperor—Accession, 304, 305; journey to Berlin, 305; State business, 306–308; relations with Bismarck, 308–311, 314–319; monetary position, 311–313; death, 319; Freytag's reminiscences, 326–331

Frederick, the Empress, physical descriptions of, 59, 60, 162, 367

As Princess Royal—Birth, 1, 2; christening, 3, 4; education and childhood, 6–21; first meeting with her husband, 15–19; visit to Paris, 20, 21; betrothal, 30–33; training by her father, 34–36; confirmation, 48–50; an accident, 51; marriage, 59–71; arrival in Berlin, 75; reception, 76–84; the Old Schloss, 84, 85; influence of and on her husband, 86; conditions at the Prussian Court, 87; Babelsberg, 91; social preferences, 92, 93; visits of her parents, 93–98; new residence in Berlin, 99, 100; birth of Prince William, 101–115; New Palace at Potsdam, 110–112; country life at Bornstedt, 112, 113; birth of Princess Charlotte, 117, 118; interest in politics, 87, 88, 99; paper on ministerial responsibility, 127, 128; nursery management, 124

As Crown Princess—Description of death of King of Prussia, 134–136; anniversary of marriage, 137; coronation of her father-in-law, description, 140–149; colonel of Hussar Regiment, 147, 148, 201, 269; political views, 149, 159, 160, 176, 177, 187, 226, 240, 289; death of her father, 150–155; relations with Bismarck, 153, 163–166, 168, 170–173, 187, 188, 214, 215, 241, 242, 243, 270, 271, 279, 280, 290, 291; love of England, 190; visits to England, 155, 156, 159, 176, 271, 276, 277, 297–299; love of France, 249, 250; birth of Prince Henry, 156; position in Prussia, 156, 157; relations with her husband, 158–160, 169, 170–173, 198–200, 262, 274, 275; visits to Italy, 161, 280, 281; favourite newspapers, 174, 175; patriotism, 166, 176, 186, 187, 241, 243, 247, 271; popularity, 174, 201, 251; Schleswig-Holstein question, 180–184; work for army and other nursing, 189, 190, 236–238, 253, 254; family life, 191–200, 210–212, 228, 260; artistic tastes, 191, 192, 194, 195, 255, 256, 260, 268, 269, 282, 285, 286; musical tastes, 191, 192, 194, 198, 201; literary tastes, 191, 192, 194, 198, 202; as botanist, 192; interest in science, 255; pistol-shooting, 192; education of children, 197, 211, 212, 263–266; social preferences, 201, 202, 255, 256, 277; religious position, 202–207, 257, 283; art and industry, 208, 209, 226; bereavements, 217, 219, 278, 279; work for soldiers and their families, 225, 234–236, 238; visits to Paris, 229, 286; work for education, 257–259, 285, 288, 298; visit to Russia, 267; affection for the old Emperor, 291; her husband's last illness, 292–303

As Empress, 304–319; relations with Bismarck, 308–311; influence over her husband, 308, 310, 311, 314–318; the Battenberg marriage, 314–318; her first and last Court, 318; death of the Emperor, 319

As Dowager Empress—Relations with Bismarck, 320–323, 327, 328, 358, 366; relations with her son, the Emperor William II, 320–323, 334, 337; comparison with him, 323–326; planning of Friederickshof, 334–337; life

there, 345–371; patriotism, 329,
361, 362; visit to Paris, 337–342;
death of Empress Augusta, 331,
332; the anonymous letter
scandal, 343, 344; collections,
346–348; reading, 348, 349;
gardening, 349, 350; restoration
work, 350, 351; personal tastes,
351–353; philanthropy, 353;
character sketches, 353–355, 360,
363–366; views on royal biography, 357, 358; visits to England, 359; artistic tastes, 359,
360; musical tastes, 362, 363;
religious position, 357, 358, 372;
last illness, 366–370; death and
funeral, 371–373; tributes in the
House of Lords, 373–377
Frederick the Great, King of
Prussia, 80, 110, 112, 194, 231,
266, 346
Frederick VII of Denmark, King,
178, 181, 182
Frederick William III, King of
Prussia, 58, 85, 100, 167, 194
Frederick William IV, King of
Prussia, 19, 28, 29, 30, 32, 37, 39,
56, 75, 84, 94, 98, 100; death,
134–136; political testament,
142–144, 158, 194, 287, 324, 334,
358
Freemasonry, 107, 108, 270
Freytag, 122, 167, 239, 326–330
Friedberg, Dr., 275, 276
Froude, 162, 277

Galliera, Duchess of, 335
Garter, Order of the, 68
Geffcken, Dr., 172, 321, 322
Geibel, 194
George of Hanover, King, 224
Gerhardt, 294
Gerlach, General, 29, 30, 41
Germany in 1858, 54–58
Gerth, sculptor, 373
Gloucester, Duchess of, 3, 111
Godet, Pastor, 52, 153, 302
Goethe, 79, 191, 194
Gontaut Biron, M. de, 249, 250
Gontaut, Duchesse de, 250
Goschen, Mr. (afterwards Lord),
276
Gotha, Dowager Duchess of Saxe-
Coburg and, 4, 53, 115
Gower, Lord Ronald, 195, 196, 231
Granville, Lord, 22, 23, 49, 95, 145,
175, 230, 233, 261, 289, 298
Grenzboten, 192

Hardenburg, 57
Hagen, Prof., 255
Heine, 194
Henry of Prussia, Prince, 156, 212
264, 265, 270, 279, 281, 293, 318
Hertel, painter, 269
Hildyard, Miss, 51
Hintze, Prof., 142, 143
Hinzpeter, Dr., 124, 210, 265, 266
Hobbs, Mrs., nurse, 123, 124
Hodel, 271, 274, 275
Hoffmann, 93, 255, 288
Hohenlohe, Prince, 240, 257, 258,
272, 282, 286, 287, 307, 309, 315,
317, 333
Hohenlohe-Langenburg, Princess of,
61, 76
Howard, Cardinal, 281
Humbert, Prince (afterwards King
of Italy), 227, 292, 305
Huxley, 202

Ihne, Herr, 336
Irene of Hesse, Princess, 293, 315, 318

Keeley, Mr. and Mrs., 62
Kent, Duchess of, 4, 21, 53, 64, 124;
death of, 138
Kinglake, 277
Kohn, Baron, 312
Kreuz Zeitung, 131
Kruger, President, 361

Lees, Miss, 253
Leiningen, Prince, 53
Leo XIII, Pope, 275
Leopold I, King of the Belgians, 3,
31, 45, 48, 49, 51, 61, 64, 65,
103, 104, 150, 312
Leopold, Prince of Hohenzollern-
Sigmaringen, 230
Letze, Fraulein, 258
Loftus, Lord Augustus, 232, 233
Louis, Prince (Grand Duke of
Hesse), 118, 132, 156, 216, 225,
228, 241
Louis of Battenberg, Prince, 315
Louise, Queen of Prussia, 40, 64, 75
100, 143, 194
Louise of Prussia, Princess (Grand
Duchess of Baden, 16, 17, 39, 40,
123
Lutteroth, painter, 269
Lyell, Sir Charles, 202, 203
Lyons, Lord, 286
Lyttelton, Sarah Lady, 6–14, 17,
66, 115, 375
Lytton, Lord and Lady, 338

MACAULAY, 365
Macdonald incident, the, 120–122, 125, 126, 138, 139
Macdonell, Lady, 218
Mackenzie, Sir Morell, 296, 297, 299, 305
Magdeburg Cathedral, 74
Malakoff, Duke of, 88
Malet, Sir Edward, 317
Malmesbury, Lord, 95
Manchester, Duchess of (Louise), 97
Manteuffel, Baron, 56, 57, 95, 96, 98, 287
Margaret, Princess (daughter of the Empress), 251, 337
Margherita, Queen of Italy, 251, 292
Marie of Roumania, Princess, 219
Martin, Dr., 102
Martin, Sir Theodore, 27, 48, 96, 127
Mary of Cambridge, Princess (Duchess of Teck), 50, 69, 155
Mecklenburg, Grand Duchess of, 110
Melbourne, Lord, 3, 4, 7, 24
Millet, J. F., 14
Moltke, 44, 52, 242, 261
Monarchy in England, 2
Morier, Sir Robert, 157–159, 168, 170, 173, 174, 209, 210, 322
Motley, J. L., 161, 162
Moustier, 88

NAPIER of Magdala, Lord, 300
Napoleon, Emperor of the French, 20, 21, 32, 43, 44, 167, 225, 229, 233, 234, 253, 300
National-zeitung, 174
Neale, Countess Pauline, 80
Nightingale, Florence, 19, 189
Nippold, Prof., 332, 353–358
Nobeling, 271, 275, 276

" OLD " Royal Family, the, 1, 24, 64
Ollivier, M., 229
Oscar, painter, 255

PAGET, Sir Augustus, 59, 109
Paget, Walpurga Lady, 59, 109, 281
Palmerston, Lord, 31, 49, 64, 121, 139, 148, 179, 187
Perry, Mr., 18, 33
Phelps, the actor, 62
Playfair, Dr. Lyon, 277
Ponsonby, Mrs., 277
Poschinger, Margaretha von, 259
Putbus, Prince, 242
Putlitz, Frau, 210–212

Putlitz, Gustav, 103, 191, 192–200
Puttkamer incident, the, 318, 319

RADZIWILL, Princess Elise, 17
Raglan, Lord, 104–106
Ranke, Prof., 358
Redern, Count, 288
Regnault, Henri, 339, 340
Reinhold, sculptor, 255
Reiss, Mr., 336
Renan, 203, 341
Ripon, Lord and Lady, 277
Roggenbach, Baron, 321
Roon, Von, 244
Rumbold, Sir Horace, 322
Russell, Lord Arthur, 342
Russell, Lord John, 3, 121, 122
Russell, Lord Odo. See Ampthill
Russell, Sir W. H., 231

SALISBURY, Lord and Lady, 271, 274, 373
Saturday Review, 125
Saxe-Meiningen, Hereditary Princess of, 118
Saxony, King of, 245
Schellbach, Prof., 93
Schleinitz, Baron, 125, 139
Schleswig-Holstein Duchies, 138 ; history of, 179–183 ; the war, 185–190
Seckendorff, Count, 300, 301
Sigismund, Prince (son of the Empress), 199, 208, 212, 217–219, 227, 228, 360
Smalley, G. W., journalist, 363–366
Sophia, Princess (afterwards Queen of the Hellenes), 230, 231, 249
Spencer, Lord, 375
Stanley, Dean, 347
Stanley of Alderley, Lord, 175
Steibel, Dr., 336
Stein, 57, 58
Stockmar, Baron, 2, 10, 31, 33, 34, 73, 82–84, 90, 95, 96, 99, 103, 109, 114, 123, 128, 136, 138, 154, 157
Stockmar, Baron Ernest, 73, 157, 160, 170, 171
Stolberg, Prince, 312
Story, Mr., 281
Strauss, 203, 204
Sumner, Archbishop, 49
Sussex, Duke of, 4

TEIGNMOUTH-SHORE, Canon, 371, 372
Tenniel, Sir John, 332
Times, The, 37, 70, 71, 125, 139, 148, 170, 171, 172, 175, 233

Titian, 268
Thiers, 250
Thomas, G. H., 144
Türr, General, 234

UPHUES, sculptor, 359, 360

VICTORIA of Hesse, Princess, 315
Victoria, Princess, daughter of Empress Frederick, 216, 217, 220, 311, 314–318, 337
Victoria, Princess of Schleswig-Holstein-Augustenburg, 281
Victoria, Queen, 1, 2, 3; education of her children, 4–6, 8, 10; Exhibition of 1851, 17, 18; marriages of her children, 25, 26; Princess Royal's betrothal, 30–32, 37, 38, 40, 43–45, 47–50; a caricature, 29; birth of first grandchild, 102–104; sees him for first time, 122–124; description of the New Palace, 111; birth of Princess Charlotte, 118; death of Prince Consort, 150–152; relations with Morier, 173, 174, 210; relations with Bismarck, 187, 188, 316, 317; attitude in Danish War, 179, 186, 187, 188; Austrian War, 216; Franco-German War, 233, 234; intervention on behalf of France, 261, 262; visit to the Emperor Frederick, 316, 317; the Battenberg marriage, 316, 317; death, 367
Virchow, Prof., 297
Volkszeitung, 175
Vossische Zeitung, 368

WACE, poet, 12
Waddington, M., 342, 362

Waddington, Mme., 362
Wagener, 294
Wagner, 362, 363
Waldemar, Prince (son of Empress Frederick), 227, 278, 346
Walewski, 88
Wangenheim, von, 89
Wellington, Duke of, 3
Werner, Anton von, painter, 256, 268
Westmorland, Priscilla Lady, 108, 109
Wilberforce, Bishop, 49
Wilberg, painter, 269
William I, German Emperor; as Prince of Prussia, 17, 26, 28, 38, 40, 61, 66, 94; regency, 98, 99, 103, 117, 204; succession as King William I, 134, 135, 138; coronation, 140–142, 144–149, 158, 166, 168–170, 172, 173, 185, 214, 221–223, 226; Emperor, 230, 231, 233, 238, 244–247, 261; attempted assassinations, 271–276, 280, 287; failing health, 290–293, 300, 295; death, 303, 311, 312; character, 324, 325, 358
William II, German Emperor, birth and christening, 101–109, and Queen Victoria, 122–124; 142, 143, 197, 210, 211, 212; education, 263–266, 269, 270; betrothal and marriage, 281, 282, 287; accession, 320–323; comparison with his mother, 323–326; relations with his mother, 334, 337, 361, 369, 371
Wittenberg, 74
Wodehouse, Lady, 23
Wrangel, Field-Marshal von, 74, 80, 95, 98, 101, 185, 186, 188, 231
Würtemberg, King of, 231

Printed by BALLANTYNE, HANSON & Co.
at Paul's Work, Edinburgh

ImTheStory.com

Personalized Classic Books in many genre's

Unique gift for kids, partners, friends, colleagues

Customize:

- Character Names
- Upload your own front/back cover images (optional)
- Inscribe a personal message/dedication on the
  inside page (optional)

Customize many titles Including
- Alice in Wonderland
- Romeo and Juliet
- The Wizard of Oz
- A Christmas Carol
- Dracula
- Dr. Jekyll & Mr. Hyde
- And more...

CPSIA information can be obtained at www.ICGtesting.com
Printed in the USA
BVOW010934191212

308678BV00027B/1599/P